Vision 2020

Vision 2020

The Housewright Symposium on the Future of Music Education

Edited by
Clifford Madsen

ROWMAN & LITTLEFIELD
Lanham • Boulder • New York • London

Published by Rowman & Littlefield
An imprint of The Rowman & Littlefield Publishing Group, Inc.
4501 Forbes Boulevard, Suite 200, Lanham, Maryland 20706
www.rowman.com

6 Tinworth Street, London SE11 5AL, United Kingdom

British Library Cataloguing in Publication Information Available

Library of Congress Control Number: 2020941919
ISBN 978-1-4758-5900-3 (pbk. : alk. paper)
ISBN 978-1-4758-5901-0 (electronic)

∞ ™ The paper used in this publication meets the minimum requirements of American National Standard for Information Sciences Permanence of Paper for Printed Library Materials, ANSI/NISO Z39.48-1992.

Contents

WHERE WE STAND

Looking back over the past twenty years, we have many reasons to celebrate. The passage of the Every Student Succeeds Act by the United States Congress in 2015 marked the recognition of music study as important in the education of the whole child. In that law, Congress described music as part of a well-rounded education for all students. And we've made progress: Many communities support sequential music education in their schools and beyond.

Advocacy continues to be integral to our work. State music education associations (MEAs) have organized advocacy days with state legislatures to support music and the other arts in schools. Our association's divisions have fostered greater inclusion, access, diversity, and equity in music programs. The National Association for Music Education (NAfME) has channeled the energy of thousands of stakeholders. These strong alliances continue to be powerful agents of change.

But the journey is not over. This moment is pivotal to our association, and it is both exciting and sobering. We have a unique opportunity to revisit the words, thoughts, and vision of those who came before us and to discover opportunities to grow.

CRITICAL QUESTIONS

We are faced with a plethora of questions. Where are we compared with twenty years ago? How have the social, cultural, and political discourses shaped our concerns and efforts? If we could hit a "reset" button, what would we do differently, and why? What is our vision for NAfME, the state MEAs, students from prekindergarten through college, school administrators, music educators, general educators, researchers, Collegiate members, partners, and stakeholders?

These are important questions that only we can answer. It's our time to make the difference that will affect both the present and the future. It's our time to speak out and act in response to our vision. Greatness lies before us. Millions of students in the United States and other countries stand to benefit from the work that we do in the coming months and years.

THE PATH AHEAD

What is your own vision of music education in the future? What steps do you believe you should take toward greatness? How are you preparing to make your vision a reality?

Read this reprint edition for ideas and inspiration, and share your thoughts with others in the field and in your community. You are the future of music

Looking to a Musical Future

Introduction to the Reprint Edition of Vision 2020

We have arrived as music teachers and as a profession at the year 2020—the one envisioned by those who launched the Housewright Symposium on the Future of Music Education. Held at Florida State University in Tallahassee September 23–26, 1999, this gathering was named after Wiley Housewright, a former president of Music Educators National Conference (MENC). The symposium took place under the guidance of June M. Hinckley, then-president of MENC (now the National Association for Music Education). Hinckley's vision for this meeting came to fruition when 175 music educators, industry representatives, community arts representatives, and students gathered to speculate about what music education might look like in 2020 and the directions the field might take. The presentations of participants in this symposium were published in 2000 as *Vision 2020,* and the reprint you are now reading shares the ideas of the likes of Wiley Housewright, Clifford Madsen, Judith Jellison, and many others.

The contributors to this book asked leading questions about the value of music education, its place in the curriculum, and its future in the United States and beyond. Preservice music teachers in the intervening twenty years may have been asked to read chapters like "Why Study Music?" or "How Can All People Continue to Be Involved in Music Education?"—questions whose answers are as relevant today as they were at the end of the last century.

to be the very best for music education. Recognizing him near the end of a magnificently productive career demonstrates the deep appreciation that countless colleagues and friends wish to accord him as we further some of his goals for excellence in teaching music. I would also like to recognize other people at The Florida State University for their participation in bringing this project to fruition: Jon Piersol, John Deal, Steve Kelly, and, especially, the students of CMENC. And while I take full responsibility for all of the errors contained in this document, I give my deepest appreciation to Teresa Miller for her tireless and detailed work on the manuscript. From the vision of a single person, June Hinckley, to a collective vision representing the most thoughtful and diligent thinking of some of our most outstanding music educators, this document is advanced in an attempt to help chart our course into the next millennium.

CKM

Clifford K. Madsen is coordinator of music education at the School of Music, The Florida State University, in Tallahassee.

Preface

Rarely have I been involved in a project that has generated as much genuine excitement as that evident throughout the procedures and activities culminating in this document. As I went through these manuscripts, I experienced several consequential insights having to do with how fortunate we are in music education. The first of these concerned an ongoing realization that we all need to be continuously involved in our professional organizations and support them in every way possible. No organization is stronger than its leadership, and over the years we have been fortunate, indeed, to have outstanding leaders: The leadership of MENC has sustained and supported our activities beginning many, many years before the Tanglewood Symposium and continuing to this day with the present Housewright Symposium. The second realization was that society, technology, and music will always be in constant flux, necessitating continuous attention from concerned professionals; lack of personal involvement will surely erode the hard-fought accomplishments of the past. Finally, I realized how special it is to be involved in a project that brings together such remarkable people across the broad spectrum of music education in a concerted effort to plan for our future. While working on these papers, I attempted to maintain this diversity and preserve the individual style and "flavor" of each paper. No attempt was made to make a uniform document, and the reader will note differences across the presentations.

This has also been a special activity for me because of the long association that I have had with Wiley Housewright. For more than forty years I have been the recipient of his intellectual and musical prowess. I will never forget sitting in his Introduction to Graduate Studies in Music Education class many years ago where one of his constant themes was the responsibility of each individual to advance "all things good," including our responsibility

education in your community, your school, and in NAfME, your association. Be the change.

Kathleen D. Sanz, President, National Association for Music Education (2018–2020)

Mackie V. Spradley, President, National Association for Music Education (2020–2022)

Chapter One

MENC

From Tanglewood to the Present

Michael L. Mark

Michael L. Mark is professor emeritus in the music department at Towson University in Towson, Maryland.

This paper will set the stage for Vision 2020: The Housewright Symposium on the Future of Music Education by describing the events that were critical to MENC and to music education from the time leading up to the Tanglewood Symposium in 1967 to the present. The reason for reviewing past events, for studying history, is to understand why things are as they are now and to help approach the future in as educated a manner as possible. The distinguished historian and former Librarian of Congress Daniel Boorstin analyzes the relationship between past and future by differentiating the seers and the prophets of ancient ages. He writes that seers "forecast how events turn out," while "the prophet prescribed what men should believe, and how they should behave."[1] This distinction also holds for the Tanglewood Symposium, when MENC emulated the prophet, not the seer.

The last thirty years have seen more change, and faster change, than any other three decades in history. Now, only thirty-two years after that symposium, the United States has become a different society in many ways. American's think differently, live differently, behave differently, and have different expectations of the future. This raises critically important questions: How have these differences affected music education, and how have they affected MENC? What if the Tanglewood Symposium hadn't occurred? What course would MENC have taken from then to now? Before we tackle these questions, let us examine some of the facts of the Tanglewood Symposium.

MENC began expanding its functions dramatically in the second half of the twentieth century, and especially since the Tanglewood Symposium, to fulfill its ongoing mission of advancing music education and the professional growth of its members.[2] Its role has been critical because with its membership, committees, publications, workshops, conferences, and symposia, MENC alone has the organizational structure and credibility to guide the profession through an era of accelerated, profound change. This paper traced the activities that MENC has undertaken as the umbrella organization for the music education profession. It describes a variety of roles assumed by the organization in intellectual leadership, curriculum, professional development, advocacy, and professional standards.

Trends in music education and in every other discipline generally occur in response to a particular societal need. That need is usually expressed first in some sort of large, clearly defined social movement, and later is often confirmed in the form of legislation or judicial decisions. The Tanglewood Symposium is a good case in point. It did not take place in a vacuum. It was a commanding response to what was happening in, and to, American society at that time. And so before looking at the symposium, let us examine its societal backdrop to see why the Tanglewood Symposium occurred. There were several reasons for the symposium. One of them was plain and simple anger. Our professional leaders were angered by the Yale Seminar on Music Education of 1963. That seminar was supported by a large government grant to analyze school music and to propose improvements. But the analysis and proposing were done by musicologists, composers, and performers who knew little or nothing about music education, and who did this without the participation of music educators. Professional music education leaders were exasperated by the Yale Seminar. In fact, Tanglewood might have been called a seminar too, but its leaders chose to call it a symposium to distance it as far as possible from the Yale Seminar.[3] The Tanglewood Symposium allowed professionals to analyze their own venue.

Now, let's look at the larger societal reason for the Tanglewood Symposium. There were three momentous catalysts of the 1960s that changed the way that Americans viewed their society—school reform, civil rights, and technology. Together, these three characteristics of the 1960s profoundly influenced the United States, and in doing so, they also influenced MENC.

The first catalyst: school reform. School reform began with the creation of the Department of Health, Education, and Welfare (HEW) in 1953. The Bureau of Education of HEW was the first attempt of the federal government to influence the school curriculum, which until that time had been considered the province only of state and local governments. Earlier, the few education issues of interest to the federal government were handled by the Federal Security Agency. We might measure the progress of school reform by the problem areas identified by the United States Bureau of Education in 1954:

illiteracy, the relationship between school dropouts and juvenile delinquency, special instruction for exceptional children, the education of children of migratory workers, and the education of teachers. These issues are still with us, and our continual efforts toward reform since the 1950s have not produced satisfactory results. Reform efforts intensified when the Soviet Union advanced beyond us in the space race by launching Sputnik in 1957. This was a rude awakening for Americans because we had thought that we were the most technologically advanced country in the world. We suddenly realized that technologically, the Soviet military was capable of threatening our security. Then, the American public learned that our schools were failing to prepare students well enough to meet the military technological needs of the Cold War. The federal government responded by gradually extending its powers to areas that had previously been the domain of state and local governments. When the federal government took an active role in school curriculum for the first time, we entered what would be a continuous, ongoing, and never-ending era of school reform. This was in the early 1960s, before MENC had firmly established itself in the government relations arena. That function was to evolve in response to a particularly misguided education objective that has colored virtually every reform effort to the present. Many reformers lost sight of the fact that the basic skills—reading, writing, and mathematics—are simply the tools that open the gate to education but are not an education in themselves. These skills have been spotlighted extensively now for four decades. They have been a major focus of education policy development, assessment, and funding. The emphasis on skills, rather than education, has posed a threat both to music education and to society in general, and since the late 1960s, MENC has dedicated much time, energy, and money to persuading the public, policymakers, and its own practitioners that music has a legitimate place in the education of all children.

School reform continues to this day, but "reform" is no longer the correct term. The work implies that after something is reformed we go about our business in a new, enlightened manner. It would be better just to call it "change" because it echoes the ongoing change in society. Whatever the correct formula might be to fix our schools, we have not found it yet. Nor do we always take a carefully reasoned approach to reform. Allen Britton wrote in 1958:

> American music educators have demonstrated what may be considered an easy readiness to climb aboard any intellectual bandwagon which happened to be nearby, and to trust it to arrive at destinations appropriate for music educators, or worse, to adopt its destinations as their own without careful enough scrutiny of the intellectual properties involved.[4]

Now, forty years later, change has become the way of life for educators and for all Americans. In 1967, music educators had to look to a future that was radically different from their realities of the 1960s, especially in the relationship between their profession and the public. Somebody had to lead the way, and that, of course, was the Music Educators National Conference.

The second catalyst: Civil rights. Civil rights defined the era in which American belatedly decided to honor the constitutional principle of equality of all Americans. The civil rights movement of the 1960s was fueled both by idealism and the demand for fairness on the part of many Americans. Congress had passed civil rights legislation much earlier that the 1960s. In fact, the first civil rights law was passed in 1866, and the second in 1875. Those laws were generally ignored, and they were pushed aside in the 1880s and 1890s by other statutes that we call Jim Crow laws, which led to the doctrine of "separate but equal." The principle of separate but equal legally segregated white and black Americans from each other in most areas of daily living. But the doctrine did not provide equality to black Americans in any aspect of life. In 1954, the *Brown v. Topeka* Supreme Court decision desegregated the schools, and we saw the first truly significant step toward equal civil rights. The decision did not integrate the schools; it just made segregation illegal. New housing patterns, permissive welfare laws, ineffective drug enforcement laws, and policies that concentrated the poorest citizens in urban ghettos worked together to prevent widespread desegregation. Finally, Congress passed a strong Civil Rights Law in 1966, this one with teeth, and in 1968, the Supreme Courts affirmed the 1866 Civil Rights Bill, 102 years after its original passage.

Civil rights, along with the war in Vietnam, was the backdrop of societal change, and it set the stage for the introduction of multicultural studies in schools. There were other large social issues during the 1960s as well, especially the war in Vietnam. The decade of the 1960s was turbulent. Demonstrations and marches were common throughout the country, in the streets and schools and on campuses, and they were often violent. This was how many Americans demonstrated to their leaders that they wanted change, and the leaders responded positively with judicial decisions and powerful legislation to empower not only black Americans, but also women, young people, and others.

The third catalyst: technology. Americans were very familiar with technology by 1967, but had not yet learned to use it to their greatest advantage. Its applications for individuals were years in the future, but most people were aware that their lives would be more and more affected by technology. They just did not know in what ways.

THE TANGLEWOOD SYMPOSIUM

MENC began to prepare the music education profession for the future during a time of change, progress, and turmoil. It was against the backdrop of the change, progress, and turmoil of the 1960s that the leadership of MENC began to prepare the music education profession for the future. The leadership recognized that a shallow attempt to cure symptoms would not serve the organization for the long term. The first step had to be nothing less than visionary, and it was. It was the Tanglewood Symposium, held during two weeks in the summer of 1967 at Tanglewood, Massachusetts, the summer home of the Boston Symphony Orchestra. MENC cosponsored the symposium with the Berkshire Music Center, the Theodore Presser Foundation, and the School of Fine and Applied Arts of Boston University. Its purpose was to plan MENC's future directions by defining the role of music education in an evolving American society that was dealing with the new realities of rapid social, economic, and cultural change. The symposium brought together music educators and representatives of business, industry, and government, and it produced the Tanglewood Declaration, clearly the profession's most important vision statement of recent times. The declaration made clear the imperative for the music education profession to address itself to the musical needs of every constituency in a nation that had only recently reached a fair degree of consensus on civil rights, that was beginning to realize that it would be more and more affected by rapidly developing technology, and that had become painfully aware of the inadequacy of its schools (see appendix A, p. 13).

The Goals and Objectives Project. After the Tanglewood Symposium presented its vision for the future, MENC had to find a way to realize the vision. It did that with the Goals and Objectives (GO) Project in 1969. The GO Project, led by Paul Lehman, identified two critical responsibilities pertaining to future professional needs: Those of MENC, and those of the profession in general. The broad goal of MENC was to conduct programs and activities to build a vital musical culture and an enlightened musical public. The goals of the profession were to carry out comprehensive music programs in all schools, to involve persons of all ages in learning music, to support the quality preparation of teachers, and to use the most effective music education techniques and resources.

The GO Project identified thirty-five objectives (see appendix B, p. 14), from which the MENC National Executive Board selected eight to receive priority treatment. These eight goals were to:

1. Lead in efforts to develop programs of music instruction challenging to all students, whatever their sociocultural condition, and directed toward the needs of citizens in a pluralistic society;

2. Lead in the development of programs of study that correlate performing, creating, and listening to music and encompass a diversity of
   musical behavior;[5]
3. Assist teachers in the identification of musical behaviors relevant to
   the needs of their students;
4. Advance the teaching of music of all periods, styles, forms, and cultures through grade 6 and for a minimum for two years beyond that
   level;
5. Develop standards to ensure that all music instruction is provided by
   teachers well prepared in music;
6. Expand its programs to secure greater involvement and commitment
   of student members;
7. Assume leadership in the application of significant new developments
   in curriculum, teaching-learning patterns, evaluation, and related topics, to every area and level of music teaching; and
8. Lead in efforts to ensure that every school system allocates sufficient
   staff, time, and funds to support a comprehensive and excellent music
   program.[6]

The eight priority goals, along with other of the thirty-five, were addressed
by means of publications, conference sessions, new committees and commissions, and administrative actions, and by expanding MENC's sphere of influence to make it the umbrella organization for American music education.
MENC has seriously undertaken each of them. Some, however, are not attainable because many factors are beyond the control of MENC. When a
solution to a problem looks promising, some condition changes and the solution no longer fits the problem. This is one of the difficulties of a dynamic
organization as it plans for the future.[7] Nevertheless, the ability of MENC to
move forward dynamically and aggressively at that particular time is remarkable.

Mary Hoffman pointed out in the *Music Educators Journal* in 1980,
during her MENC presidency, the particular difficulties the organization had
to deal with: several changes in MENC's administrative leadership; an ambitious, successful building fund drive; the move to a new building in Reston,
Virginia; and of particular significance, the depressed world economy of the
early 1970s that resulted from the international oil crisis. The economy had a
profound effect on school music programs throughout the country. Many
were reduced and others completely discontinued. The MENC leadership,
undeterred by these roadblocks, forged ahead with its ambitious and visionary plans.[8]

After the GO Project, MENC appointed two commissions to begin implementing the recommendations. It created the National Commission on Organizational Development to recommend changes in the organization, struc-

ture, and function of MENC, including all of its federated and affiliated units. The second commission, the National Commission on Instruction, was to plan, manage, and coordinate a wide variety of activities. It published *The School Music Program: Description and Standards*,[9] whose roots were in the earlier MENC source books of 1947 and 1955.[10] The other objectives of the GO Project were to be the responsibility of the Music Education Research Council, the Publications Planning Committee, the public relations program, and the *Music Educators Journal (MEJ)*.[11] In fact, entire issues of *MEJ* were devoted to single topics that originated in the Tanglewood Symposium and the GO Project. They included youth music, electronic music, world musics, music in urban education, and music in special education. National, regional, and state conferences have offered numerous sessions to suggest ideas and methods for practical approaches to fulfilling the Tanglewood recommendations. The publications program expanded significantly and offered many books and pamphlets in support of the goals.

INTELLECTUAL LEADERSHIP

Research. MENC has been deeply involved in research for some time by 1967 through its publications and a variety of research projects and events. The Music Education Research Council (MERC) established the Society for Research in Music Education (SRME) in 1960 to encourage and advance research in music education. MERC eventually oversaw the *Journal of Research in Music Education*, which had been founded in 1953, and later it assumed responsibility for *Update: Applications of Research in Music Education*. MERC found a way to involve many more music educators in its research program with the creation of the Special Research Interest Groups (SRIGs) at the 1978 MENC national convention. Now there are thirteen SRIG's.[12] Each publishes a newsletter and meets at MENC national conventions.

MENC and Schirmer Books cosponsored the publication of the *Handbook of Research on Music Teaching and Learning*,[13] edited by Richard Colwell, in 1992. The *Handbook* is a definitive guide, a *vade mecum*, to the music education research resources, methodologies, issues, and controversies, and is one of the most significant events in the history of music education research. It contains original essays by fifty-five American, Australian, British, and Canadian scholars.

Research findings have also been disseminated at a variety of MENC-related symposia since the late 1970s. MENC cosponsored the three-part Ann Arbor Symposium from 1978 to 1980 to explore the relationship between research in behavioral psychology and in music education psychology. That symposium appears to have been a model for numerous future symposia sponsored by MENC and its SRIGs, and by universities. Their subjects have included the relationship between music education and social anthropology, philosophy of music education, general research, general music, early childhood education, conducting, history, social psychology, and others.

Philosophy. One of the most critical needs of the music education profession at mid-century was for a central unifying philosophy. MENC had played a key role in 1954 when it began the process of professional philosophical introspection by appointing its Commission on Basic Concepts, which represented music education, psychology, sociology, and philosophy. The commission's report was published as the 1958 yearbook of the National Society for the Study of Education, entitled *Basic Concepts in Music Education.*[14] This landmark work, along with another book, *Foundations and Principles of Music Education* (1959) by Charles Leonhard and Robert House,[15] provided the framework for the development of an aesthetic philosophy of music education. The two books and other writings of the 1950s and 1960s encouraged music educators to teach music for its own value, rather than for its extramusical, or ancillary, benefits.

The movement leading to the philosophy of aesthetic education reached maturity with the publication of Bennett Reimer's book, *A Philosophy of Music Education.*[16] This book immediately became the primary work of the music education philosophical literature. The first of the eight points of the Tanglewood Declaration was consonant with this philosophical position. It stated: "Music serves best when its integrity as an art is maintained." MENC expanded its involvement in music education philosophy when it approved a new SRIG in Philosophy in 1992. Since then, philosophy has received a good deal of attention at MENC professional meetings.

Psychology. The profession has also seen major developments in psychology since the Tanglewood Symposium. Since the 1970s, many psychologists and music education researchers have focused their efforts on musical perception, cognition, and other specialized interests. More recently, researchers have concentrated on the theories of multiple intelligences of such psychologists as Howard Gardner, Philip Phoenix, Elliot Eisner, and Paul Hirst. Howard Gardner points out the "one evident factor in the rethinking of intelligence is the perspective introduced by scholars who are not psychologists."[17] That statement is clearly true in music education, where scholars have complemented the work of psychologists by examining the relationship between theories of intelligence and music education. MENC has supported these interests in its publications and through several of its SRIGs, including those that focus on affective response to music, creativity, learning and development, philosophy, measurement and evaluation, and perception.

CURRICULAR DEVELOPMENTS

New trends in general music. During the 1950s and 1960s, two European music curricula spread rapidly throughout the United States. The Orff and Kodály methods were welcomed in American schools partly because they incorporated techniques that were consonant with conceptual learning principles, which was a central part of school reform at that time. MENC had helped disseminate conceptual education in music with its 1967 publication of *The Study of Music in the Elementary School: A Conceptual Approach*, edited by Charles Gary. Both the Kodály and Orff approaches developed in the United States independently of MENC, but MENC was partly responsible for their success because their practitioners presented them frequently at its conferences and in its publications. Later, both the Orff and Kodály organizations became MENC allied organizations.

The most ambitious MENC program to address curricular issues during the 1960s was the Contemporary Music Project (CMP), which was funded by the Ford Foundation and MENC. CMP's innovative curriculum developments were presented in many seminars, workshops, and published materials. A critically important aspect of the program's success was that it demonstrated MENC's ability to organize, implement, and complete a nationwide high-budget curriculum development program. This might well have given the organization the experience and confidence to undertake new large-scale programs in the future.

ADVOCACY

Advocacy has become one of MENC's most critical functions. MENC positioned itself for advocacy at the national level when it relocated its headquarters from Chicago to Washington in 1956, but its advocacy activities began in earnest in 1966 with the appointment of Joan Gaines as director of its new public relations program. As MENC began planning for the Tanglewood Symposium, it also prepared the way to make the public more aware of the role of music education in American society. One of the early actions occurred in 1968, when the Ford Foundation extended its funding of the Contemporary Music Project for an additional five years. One of the CMP programs, the Young Composers Project, shifted its focus, and was renamed the Composers-in- Residence to Communities Program. For five years, communities, and not just schools, benefited from the presence of professional composers. Could there be a more effective public relations plan? The need for public relations increased in the early 1970s when the declining global economy directly threatened school music programs with severe budget restrictions. MENC recognized that it would need to commit more resources to promoting music education to policymakers. It refocused its efforts from public relations to government relations, although it has continuously maintained a strong public relations program as well. MENC began its government relations efforts by working with federal legislators and presenting workshops for state and divisional MENC units. These workshops became a routine feature of national, regional, and state conferences and have been ever since. As MENC became more deeply involved in this activity, it replaced the designation "government relations" with the term "advocacy," which described its activities more accurately. Since then, MENC has participated proactively in federal legislative agendas by providing expert witness in many diverse federal issues,[18] and MENC presidents and executives have testified on Capitol Hill on behalf of music education. By the 1980s, MENC had acquired considerable expertise in advocacy.

Coalitions. MENC has been a leader in building coalitions of arts education organizations. Coalitions are necessary because they represent greater numbers of people and wider interests than are possible in any one organization, and they multiply political influence. For years before the Tanglewood Symposium, MENC had worked closely with such organizations as the National Association of Secondary School Principals, the National Association of Elementary School Principals, the Association for Supervision and Curriculum Development, the American Association of School Administrators, and others.

Within the arts education fields, MENC recognized that public policies that affect any area of arts education usually affect all of the arts education disciplines. Samuel Hope wrote in 1989: "Unity has been the rallying cry of the American arts advocacy movement for nearly thirty years. A fundamental principle of arts advocacy remains that unity is essential for effectiveness."[19] MENC had cooperated with the professional associations in dance, art, and theatre since the 1960s in an organization known as DAMT (dance, art, music, theatre). DAMT was recognized officially by the United Stated Office of Education and the John F. Kennedy Center for the Performing Arts in joint projects that set the stage for later cooperative efforts.

In 1986, MENC and the American Council for the Arts (ACA) called together thirty-one leaders of arts and arts education organizations at the Pew Memorial Trust in Philadelphia, were they formed the Ad Hoc National Arts Education Working Group.

The meeting produced "The Philadelphia Resolution," which stated the basic principles agreed upon by all the organizations in regard to the value of arts education and the need to strengthen it in American education.[20] The resolution was a strong advocacy tool for dealing with policy-making bodies.

That coalition became the National Coalition for Education in the Arts (NCEA) in 1988. Its mission was to develop and monitor policy affecting education in the arts.[21] This alliance was the one that successfully advocated the inclusion of arts education in the *Goal 2000: Educate America Act* (Public Law 103-227) of 1994, which was probably MENC's most significant advocacy triumph. Also, in 1994, the National Coalition for Music Education sponsored a summit meeting in Washington, DC. The meeting brought together forty-nine organizations dedicated to many specialized facets and interests in the music education profession. They met to discuss the most effective ways in which their organizations could cooperate in a wide range of music education issues.[22] In 1998, MENC sponsored the third Music Education Summit, this one attended by representatives of more than eighty-five organizations, and again resulting in a strong instrument of advocacy.

THE DEVELOPMENT OF PROFESSIONAL STANDARDS

In 1974, the National Commission on Instruction published *The School Music Program: Description and Standards*,[23] which came from the Tanglewood Symposium recommendation that MENC provide leadership in developing high-quality music programs in all schools. This book presented standards in curriculum, staffing, facilities, equipment, and levels of other kinds of support, and it described the ideal school music program as a benchmark against which lay people and educators could compare the programs in their own schools. Paul Lehman wrote in the second edition in 1986 that the book "has been used extensively by superintendents and principals, state departments of education and state supervisors of music, music educators, and laymen. It has been referred to and quoted by various groups concerned with accreditation or certification, and it has been cited in innumerable curriculum guides. It has been the most popular publication in the history of MENC."[24]

The two editions of *The School Music Program* were written in response to the national demand for higher education quality and accountability. By setting standards and achievement levels, MENC demonstrated to the public and to policymakers that the music education profession considered its work to be substantive and consequential, and that it continually sought to improve itself.

National Standards for Arts Education. The standards published in the two editions of The School Music Program were valuable in their own right, but they were actually a prelude to a new set of standards written in response to the *Goals 2000 Act* of 1994. The earlier standards were established for a profession that was still trying very hard to convince the American people that music should be a curricular subject. Now, with the passage of the *Goals 2000 Act*, national goals were written to satisfy a congressional mandate. This mandate assured wide recognition for the new standards, and since then, many state departments of education have adopted identical or similar arts education standards for their own reform efforts.

By advocating, creating, and then promoting the National Standards, MENC extended a framework for curriculum development to the entire profession.

SUMMARY

What if the Tanglewood Symposium had not taken place? If the Tanglewood Symposium had not taken place, it is likely that MENC would nevertheless have addressed itself to many of the issues that it has undertaken in the last thirty years. It is unlikely, however, that it would have been able to do so in such a disciplined and sequential manner that used the organization's strengths to the greatest advantage. It is difficult to imagine how different the music education profession would be today if no entity existed to encourage, nourish, and sustain it as MENC has. MENC has given structure and direction to the profession, helping focus it on critical issues and taking leadership in working through them. In doing so, MENC has enabled the music education profession to maintain its ability to help fulfill the musical needs of individuals, communities, and the nation. It has empowered the profession to remain a diverse and dynamic component of American education. Judging from all it has done for the music education profession, it appears justified in having changed its name in 1998 from the Music Educators National Conference to MENC—The National Association for Music Education. It clearly has established itself as the leadership organization for the entire profession.

It would be irresponsible to draw the simplistic conclusion that all of the progress that MENC has made since 1967 is the direct result of the Tanglewood Symposium and the GO Project. No strategic plan can guide an organization for over thirty years without constant renewal. There have been some strategic plans for MENC, but none of the magnitude and scope of the symposium and the GO Project. Mary Hoffman articulated a fundamental truth of long-range planning when she wrote in 1980: "In an organization such as MENC, long-range planning is, in essence, long-range hoping. Too many deviations can arise on what would seem a straight path toward any single goal or objective . . . Perhaps it is time to undertake a reevaluation of the GO Project as it applies to a new decade."[25] She was referring to the decade of the 1980s.

This leaves us with the question of who plans for MENC and how. There is no way to know when the goals and objectives of the GO Project no longer resided in the memory of MENC officers and administrators. MENC President June Hinckley concludes that the influence of the Tanglewood Symposium has become "a way of thinking" for the MENC leadership.[26] This way of thinking has continued to guide the organization along the zigzag path of general school reform.

CONCLUSION

Now, in 1999, almost two decades after Hoffman's suggestion, MENC and The Florida State University cosponsor the Housewright Symposium to help guide MENC through the next twenty years. One might ask whether another symposium is necessary when the basic principles derived from Tanglewood are still relevant. Symbolically, the new millennium would seem an appropriate time for professional introspection and planning, but it, in itself, does not sufficiently justify a second major event of this type. The new societal order, however, does. The civil rights revolution of the 1960s is no longer revolutionary. Its music education derivative, the study of multicultural music, has become a curricular norm. The school reform movement that swept the country in the 1960s still continues. Reform is ubiquitous now, and June Hinckley refers to it as "reform du jour." It's a familiar part of the life of every educator. Technology refuses to stand still, but even so, music educators feel secure with it. Almost everything that music educators do has a new face since the 1960s. We have come to accept that what is effective and appropriate now probably will be outdated in a very short time. The need for MENC to undertake the Housewright Symposium is exactly the same as the need for the Tanglewood Symposium. But the times are different. Again, MENC must play the role of prophet, rather than seer.

APPENDIX A: THE TANGLEWOOD DECLARATION

By Allen Britton, Arnold Broido, and Charles Gary

The intensive evaluation of the role of music in American society and education provided by the Tanglewood Symposium of philosophers, educators, scientists, labor leaders, philanthropists, social scientists, theologians, industrialists, representatives of government and foundations, music educators and other musicians led to this declaration:

We believe that education must have as major goals the art of living, the building of personal identity, and nurturing creativity. Since the study of music can contribute much to these ends, *we now call for music to be placed in the core of the school curriculum.*

The arts afford a continuity with the aesthetic tradition in man's history. Music and other fine arts, largely non-verbal in nature, reach close to the social, psychological, and physiological roots of man in his search for identity and self-realization.

Educators must accept the responsibility for developing opportunities which meet man's individual needs and the needs of a society plagued by the consequences of changing values, alienation, hostility between generations, racial and international tensions, and the challenges of a new leisure.

Music educators at Tanglewood agreed on the following:

1. Music serves best when its integrity as an art is maintained.
2. Music of all periods, styles, forms, and cultures belongs in the curriculum. The musical repertory should be expanded to involve music of our time in its rich variety, including currently popular teenage music and avant-garde music, American folk music, and the music of other cultures.
3. Schools and colleges should provide adequate time for music in programs ranging from preschool through adult or continuing education.
4. Instruction in the arts should be a general and important part of education in the senior high school.
5. Developments in educational technology, educational television, programmed instruction, and computer-assisted instruction should be applied to music study and research.
6. Greater emphasis should be placed on helping the individual student to fulfill his needs, goals and potentials.
7. The music education profession must contribute its skills, proficiencies, and insights toward assisting in the solution of urgent social problems as in the "inner city" or other areas with culturally deprived individuals.
8. Programs of teacher education must be expanded and improved to provide music teachers who are specially equipped to teach high school courses in the history and literature of music, courses in the humanities and related arts, as well as teachers equipped to work with the very young, with adults, with the disadvantaged, and with the emotionally disturbed.

——From Documentary Report of the Tanglewood Symposium (Washington, DC: Music Educators National Conference, 1968), p. 139.

APPENDIX B: THE GOALS AND OBJECTIVE PROJECT

The purpose of the Goals and Objectives Project was to identify the responsibilities of MENC as they pertained to future needs. The project, directed by Paul Lehman, began in 1969 with a steering committee and the following eighteen subcommittees, each of which related in some way to the Tanglewood Declaration.

1. Preparation for Music Educators

2. Musical Behaviors—Identification and Evaluation
3. Comprehensive Musicianship—Music Study in the Senior High School
4. Music for All Youth
5. Music Education in the Inner City
6. Research in Music Education
7. Logistics of Music Education
8. Fact Finding
9. Aesthetic Education
10. Information Science
11. Music for Early Childhood
12. Impact of Technology
13. Music in Higher Education
14. Learning Processes
15. Musical Enrichment of National Life
16. MENC Professional Activities
17. Professional Organization Relationships
18. Music of Non-Western Cultures

After the committee reports were condensed, Paul Lehman drafted the proposed MENC goals and objectives. This statement was submitted to the federated and associated organizations, and by the chairpersons of the national committees. In October 1970, the MENC Executive Board adopted the following two goals for MENC, four for the profession in general, and thirty-five objectives.

The goals of MENC shall be to conduct programs and activities to build:

A vital music culture
An enlightened musical public

The goals of the profession are:

Comprehensive music programs in all schools
Involvement of people of all ages in learning music
Quality preparation of teachers
Use of the most effective techniques and resources in music instruction.

The objectives:

1. *Lead in efforts to develop programs of music instruction challenging to all students, whatever their sociocultural condition, and directed toward the needs of citizens in a pluralist society

2. *Lead in the development of programs of study that correlate perform-
    ing, creating, and listening to music and encompass a diversity of
    musical behaviors
3. *Assist teachers in the identification of musical behaviors relevant to
    the needs of their students
4. *Advance the teaching of music of all periods, styles, forms and cul-
    tures
5. Promote the development of instructional programs in aesthetic educa-
    tion
6. Advocate the expansion of music education to include preschool chil-
    dren
7. Lead in efforts to ensure that every school system requires music from
    kindergarten through grade six and for a minimum of two years be-
    yond that level
8. Lead in efforts to ensure that every secondary school offers an array of
    music courses to meet of all youth
9. Promote challenging courses in music for the general college student
10. Advocate the expansion of music education for adults both in and out
    of school
11. *Develop standards to ensure that all music instruction is provided by
    teachers well prepared in music
12. Encourage the improvement and continuous updating of preservice
    and inservice education program for all persons who teach music pro-
    grams and in the certification of music teachers
13. *Expand its programs to secure greater involvement and commitment
    of student members
14. Assist graduate schools in developing curricula especially designed
    for the preparation of teachers
15. Develop and recommend accreditation criteria for the use of recog-
    nized agencies in the approval of school and college music
16. Support the expansion of teach education programs to include special-
    izations designed to meet current needs
17. *Assume leadership in the application of significant new develop-
    ments in curriculum, teaching-learning techniques and technology, in-
    structional and staffing patters, evaluation, and related topics to every
    area and level of music teaching
18. Assume leadership in the development of resources for music teach-
    ing and learning
19. Cooperate in the development of exemplary models of desirable pro-
    grams and practices in the teaching of music
20. Encourage maximum use of community music resources to enhance
    educational programs

21. *Lead in efforts to ensure that every school system allocates sufficient staff, time, and funds to support a comprehensive and excellent music program
22. Provide advisory assistance where music programs are threatened by legislative, administrative, or other action
23. Conduct public relations programs to build community support for music education
24. Promote the conduct of research and research-related activities in music education
25. Disseminate news of research in order that research findings may be applied promptly and effectively
26. Determine the most urgent needs for information in music education
27. Gather and disseminate information about music and education
28. Encourage other organization, agencies, and communications media to gather and disseminate information about music and education
29. Initiate efforts to establish information retrieval systems in music and education, and to develop data bases for subsequent incorporation into such systems
30. Pursue effective working relationships with organizations and groups having mutual interests
31. Strengthen the relationships between the conference and its federated, associated, and auxiliary organizations
32. Establish procedures for its organizational program planning and policy
33. Seek to expand its membership to include all persons who, in any capacity, teach music
34. Periodically evaluate the effectiveness of its policies and programs
35. Ensure systematic interaction with its membership concerning the goals and objectives of the conference

*Priority objectives

NOTES

1. Daniel Boorstin, *The Seekers* (New York: Random House, 1998), 6.

2. *Member Handbook,* 1996–97 (Reston, VA: Music Educators National Conference), back cover.

3. Charles Gary, telephone interview with author, 18 December 1998. Gary was the executive secretary of MENC at the time of the Tanglewood Symposium.

4. Allen Britton, "Music in Early American Public Education: A Historical Critique," in *Basic Concepts in Music Education* (Chicago: The National Society for the Study of Education, 1958), 207.

5. This germinated in the Contemporary Music Project, the large MENC curriculum project of the 1960s.

6. From "Goals and Objectives for Music Education," *Music Educators Journal* 57, no. 4 (December 1970): 24–25.

7. Michael L. Mark, "The GO Project: Retrospective of a Decade," *Music Educators Journal* 67, no. 4 (December 1980): 42–47.

8. Mary E. Hoffman, "Goals and Objectives for the Eighties," *Music Educators Journal* 67, no. 4 (December 1980): 48–49, 66.

9. National Commission on Instruction, *The School Music Program: Description and Standards* (Vienna, VA: Music Educators National Conference, 1974).

10. Hazel Nohavec Morgan, ed., *Music Education Source Book* (Chicago: Music Educators National Conference, 1947); and Morgan, ed., *Music in American Education: Music Education Source Book Number Two* (Chicago: Music Educators National Conference, 1955).

11. "MENC Forms Two Commissions," *Music Educators Journal* 57, no. 8 (April 1971): 47–48.

12. Affective Response, Community and Adult Music, Creativity, Early Childhood, Gender Research, General Research, History, Instructional Strategies, Learning and Development, Measurement and Evaluation, Perception, Philosophy, Social Science.

13. Richard Colwell, ed., *Handbook of Research on Music Teaching and Learning* (New York: Schirmer Books, 1992), dust jacket.

14. Nelson B. Henry, ed., *Basic Concepts in Music Education*, Fifty-seventh Yearbook of the National Society for the Study of Education, part I (Chicago: University of Chicago Press, 1958). This was the second NSSE yearbook that involved MENC. The first was the Thirty-fifth Yearbook, part II, entitled *Music Education*, published in 1936.

15. Charles Leonhard and Robert House, *Foundations and Principles of Music Education*, (New York: McGraw-Hill, 1959).

16. Bennett Reimer, *A Philosophy of Music Education* (Englewood Cliffs, NJ: Prentice-Hall, 1970), 2.

17. Howard Gardner, "Who Owns Intelligence," *The Atlantic Monthly*, February 1999: 70.

18. For example, the Copyright Law, reductions in funding for music programs, the reauthorization of the Elementary and Secondary Education Act; the establishment of the Cabinet-level Department of Education; the 1979 White House Conference on the Arts; the Career Education Act of 1978; legislated authority to conduct a baseline survey of the status of arts education in the schools, which resulted in the publication of the book *Toward Civilization*; and the need for a White House Conference on Education in 1980. MENC also provided expert witnesses to testify at several congressional hearings. One, "The Arts Are Fundamental to Learning" (1977) was a joint hearing before the Subcommittee on Select Education of the Committee on Education and Labor, U.S. House of Representatives, and the Special Subcommittee on Education, Arts, and Humanities of the Committee on Human Resources, U.S. Senate. Another was entitled, "To Permit the Use of Title IV-B ESEA Funds for the Purchase of Band Instruments," after which Congress agreed to permit the purchase of band instruments with Title I funds.

19. Samuel Hope, "The Need for Policy Studies in Arts Education," in David Pankratz and Kevin Mulcahy, *The Challenge to Reform Arts Education: What Role Can Research Play?* (New York: American Council for the Arts, 1989), 74.

20. John T. McLaughlin, ed., *Toward a New Era in Arts Education* (New York: American Council for the Arts, 1988), 7.

21. Pankratz and Mulcahy, xi–xiii.

22. "National Music Education Summit Participating Organizations," *Teaching Music* 2, no. 3 (December 1994): 48.

23. National Commission on Instruction, ix.

24. Paul R. Lehman, *The School Music Program: Description and Standards*, 2nd ed. (Reston, VA: Music Educators National Conference, 1986), 7.

25. Hoffman, 48.

26. June Hinckley, correspondence, 21 March 1999.

Chapter Two

Why Do Humans Value Music?

Commission Author: Bennett Reimer

Bennett Reimer is the John W. Beattie Professor of Music Emeritus at Northwestern University in Evanston, Illinois.

Committee Members:
John Buccheri
~ Karl Bruhn
Roy E. Ernst
Terese M. Volk
Iris Yob

Response: Robert Glidden

I. INTRODUCTION: SETTING THE STAGE

Whenever and wherever humans have existed music has existed also. Since music occurs only when people choose to create and share it, and since they always have done so and no doubt always will, music clearly must have important value for people. What is that value?

Throughout recorded history some people have spent enormous mental effort trying to answer that question. It is a fascinating question because attempts to answer it force one to grapple with the nature of humanity itself. If we can explain why humans need music, we may learn something profound about what it means to be human. We know that humans need food, clothing, shelter, language, social interaction, belief systems, and so forth, and that these needs help define the human condition. But why do they also appear to require music, which seems, on the surface, to be only remotely related to human survival rather than central to it? As Howard Gardner frames the issue,

> Precisely because [music] is not used for explicit communication, or for other evident survival purposes, its continuing centrality in human experience constitutes a challenging puzzle. The anthropologist Levi-Strauss is scarcely alone among scientists in claiming that if we can explain music, we may find the key for all human thought or in implying that failure to take music seriously weakens any account of the human condition. [1]

Why should music educators try to explain why music is valued by people? Why not just get on with our responsibility to teach it? After all, people will no doubt continue to need music whether we or they can explain why. Is it really necessary for music educators to have such an explanation? The answer is emphatically "yes," for several compelling reasons. First, professional music educators should have a convincing rationale for why the work they have chosen to do is important. Second, the profession as a whole needs a sense of shared aspiration to guide its collective endeavors. Third, the people to whom music educators are responsible—students and their communities—must understand that their need for music is being met by professionals aware of what that need is and competent to help fulfill it. Fourth, teaching can only be judged effective when it enhances cherished values: not being clear about what those values are insures ineffectiveness. Fifth, the ongoing attempt to define those values keeps music education on track toward maintaining its relevance to its culture. So, difficult as it may be, the attempt to continually clarify why humans value music is necessary if music education is to be successful.

A Single Value or Many Values

Can the value of music be identified as one particular contribution it makes to people's lives? Some have thought so. Music has been claimed to be, essentially, a force for morality, or a special way to experience the world, or a unique way to exercise creativity, or a way to "know" what cannot otherwise be known, or an instrumentality for political/social change, and on and on with claims for a singular, distinctive benefit music bestows on people.

The rationale for seeking a single, essential value of music is that finding it will mean that the "essence" of music will have been discovered. If that is too much to hope for, at least the quest will get us closer to that essence, allowing us to identify, and focus our efforts on, values more fundamental to music than those which are peripheral.

Opposed to this orientation to musical value is one that claims that a singular, essential value for anything in human life, including music, does not exist, and asserting such a claim misrepresents the diversity and complexity of human reality. Further, trying to focus on a single musical value inevitably causes other important values to be unjustly neglected in favor of those a society privileges. Rather than search for some imagined essence of music we are better advised to abandon any hopes of locating what does not exist, and instead, include in our aspirations for music education any values we can possibly identify. We can then make a variety of contributions to human welfare.

A focus on diversity of values rather than on a single, defining value has arisen over the past several decades. Many thinkers now argue that human history demonstrates that our lives and our beliefs cannot be reduced to singular, ultimate solutions. For every human belief, assumption, or value, according to this view, opposing beliefs, assumptions, and values exist, each contending for truth. We can no longer expect definitive answers to our questions, but only an ongoing attempt to address old and new perplexing dilemmas, causing us to adopt an attitude of openness to all possibilities. The search for essences, in this view, has not only been unproductive, it has been harmful to human welfare, by excluding competing values rather than embracing them. What is lost in certainty, security, and faith by giving up the quest for essences is made up for by the higher values of inclusiveness, creative tension, and ongoing responsibility to invent useful solutions for particular problems.[2]

The conflict between beliefs in (1) reliable answers and secure values, and (2) ongoing contradictions among answers and the relativity of values is among the most characteristic factors in contemporary intellectual life.[3] Music education is not exempt from this conflict, and we cannot excuse ourselves from it because of our shared devotion to what the Tanglewood Declaration called music's "integrity as an art,"[4] as if there was no dispute about what that phrase actually means. We, as all others in the intellectual/artistic community, must reconcile ourselves to the difficulties of both holding significant values and being open to their uncertainty. Estelle Jorgensen summarizes our dilemma:

> Rather than attempting to bring conflicting ideas or tendencies into reconciliation, unity, or harmony, music educators may sometimes need to be content with disturbance, disunity, and dissonance. Things in dialectic do not always mesh tidily, simply, or easily. Nor necessarily ought they. The resultant complexity, murkiness, and fuzziness of these dialectical relationships, however, greatly complicate the task of music educators.[5]

Forming a "Community of Belief"

The "task of music educators" referred to above is shared by all professions and by all humans: to forge a meaningful basis for cooperative endeavors based on shared values, while at the same time recognizing that values are subject to alteration or even abandonment if they lose their validity. The argument that there should be no commitment to beliefs is, after all, one particular argument: the need, even the necessity, for a consistent, foundational belief system is as forcefully and convincingly argued for by as many as those who deny its possibility. A healthy culture, nation, religion, profession, or person, according to this widely held view, requires strongly held beliefs, based on complementary values, providing a basis for effective action.[6]

Music educators in the United States, along with their colleagues around the world, share many convictions about the values of music, convictions that enable them to make consistent choices about why and how to teach music. These convictions need not be, indeed must not be, regarded as dogmas incapable of criticism, change, or replacement. As in a healthy democracy, differing viewpoints and diversity of opinions are inevitable, exhilarating, and rejuvenating, serving an essential role in the well-being of the larger organism. The viability of the music education profession, at any particular period in its history and in any particular cultural setting, may well depend on the existence of shared values upon which effective initiatives can be based, and acknowledgment that complete unanimity is neither likely nor desirable. The codependence of harmony and dissonance, after all, is something music educators know a good deal about, and it is as relevant in the field of values as it is in music.

The following examination of dimensions of musical value demonstrates that it is possible to identify values widely held in common, which can provide a basis for professional aspirations, planning, and action, and also recognizes that tensions among and uncertainties about claimed values are inevitable, reminding us of our continual need for individual and professional critical self-examination.

II. DIMENSIONS OF MUSICAL VALUE

The dimensions of value explained in the following discussion are conceived with music in mind. But each claim for the value of music can be claimed also by other human endeavors. Is there anything unique to music, setting it apart as having a distinctive identity?

In her search for an answer to the question "What is art for?" (another way to ask the same question would be "Why do humans value art?"), Ellen Dissanayake concludes that an essential characteristic of the arts is that they provide a mechanism for creating objects or events that "place the activity or artifact in a 'realm' different from the everyday."[7] (Emphasis in original.) That is, the arts, in unique ways, "make special." Other ways of expressing this idea are that the arts exist to make the seemingly ordinary extraordinary, or to make the seemingly insignificant significant. Whatever other values the arts bestow, their distinctiveness as a valuable human endeavor is their powerful capacity to accomplish such transformations.

Adopting this idea as one useful way (among others) to regard the arts, we can express the distinctiveness, or uniqueness, of music as being its use of sounds to accomplish its task of "making special." In music, sounds, so constant and useful in human contact with the ordinary world, become "special," extraordinary, and significant, transforming the commonplace into what is remarkable. As philosopher of the arts Francis Sparshott puts it, "It is more nearly true of music than it is of anything else that it offers an alternative reality and an alternative way of being."[8] Sounds created to provide an alternative sense of meaning, or an alternative sense of significance, are an essential ingredient if the result is to be regarded as "music."

This constitutes both the power of music and its limitations. Music cannot do what, for example, poetry, or painting, or dance, or theatre, or film can do, although it can contribute to them. Similarly, none of the other arts can do what music can do, although the other arts can be allied with music in a variety of ways.[9] Whenever sounds, by themselves or as an integral component, are being used to "make special"—to achieve significance—music is doing what it does, offering its values in its unique way. This foundational idea will be assumed throughout this paper.

Five dimensions, or aspects, of music will be identified as a way to organize the numerous values claimed for music, and to emphasize that many (but not all) of them can be considered to be complementary. Each dimension calls attention to a wide range of musical values related by similarity of focus. No assumption is being made that these five exhaust all possibilities, although they do claim to be important aspects of music's value. They also serve as an example for how other dimensions can be identified and explained by those interested in doing so.

1. Music Is End and Means.

This dimension of musical value focuses on the question "where does one go to find whatever is of value about music?" One location of musical value recognized throughout history is within music itself—within the sounds of music as every culture creates and shares them. In this view, the experience of musical sounds, whether through composing them, performing them (in this paper the term performing will refer to the performance of composed music), improvising them (which requires a substantially different set of competencies from performing composed music), or listening to them, as well as associated involvements such as conducting, arranging, sound engineering, moving, and so forth as various cultures provide them, is taken to be, in and of itself, the end, or purpose, of music's existence.

The difficulty with the "music as an end in itself" view has always been to explain just why sounds, arranged in ways cultures deem appropriate, are valuable for people. That they are indeed valuable—often supremely valuable—is evident. Cultures have often, even routinely, regarded their music as a profoundly important dimension of their identity, to be protected and treasured, in and of itself, as among their greatest achievements. But why are musical sounds, which are, after all, just sounds, so deeply valued?

As explained in the Introduction, it is unlikely that any single reason will adequately account for the high value humans have always held for musical experience itself. Yet several reasons have been taken very seriously over the centuries, and remain convincing, or at least credible, among those who pursue this matter professionally. As Wayne Bowman puts it in his detailed and exhaustive book on the subject,

> Just what is music? And what is its significance or importance? Or, more concisely yet, What is the nature and value of music? These seemingly simple questions have generated, and indeed continue to generate, an astonishing array of responses. But amidst the striking diversity there do exist discernible patterns, convergences of perspective, recurrent disputes and problems. [10]

In the discussions of dimensions of musical value following this one on music as end and means, an attempt will be made to explain some of the influential convergences of beliefs about the values of musical experience. Enhancing the musical experience has been and remains a central justification for the need for both music education and for professional music educators. Creating musical sounds through composing, performing, and improvising them, and sharing their meanings through listening to them, are among the most challenging and satisfying endeavors in which humans choose to engage themselves. To assist with those challenges, and to heighten those satisfactions, requires high levels of expertise, both in music itself and in the teaching of it. Music educators are those professionals whose expertise has been, is, and no doubt will continue to be, primarily devoted to those values that musical experiences themselves characteristically satisfy.

A different view about musical value is that it exists as something separate and distinct from musical experience itself. Involvements with music serve as a means, or instrumentality, for achieving a variety of associated values. Here the focus is not on the experience of musical sounds themselves, but on the effects music may be said to have as an enhancement of or influence on some other activity.

The problem with the "music as means" view has always been to explain how it is that musical sounds can cause the enormous number of effects that have been claimed for them throughout history. Many of those effects are claimed entirely out of faith, with little or no evidence that the cause-effect relationship actually occurs. Some effects seem to be substantiated by reliable evidence. But how do sounds, which are, after all, just sounds, cause the claimed effects?

An important distinction must be made here, a distinction seldom given adequate attention. There is a crucial difference between the many positive consequences resulting from involvement with musical experience itself, and the use of music as a means to secure values not dependent on musical experience itself. Consequences of musical experience, in addition to the sheer pleasure and fulfillment brought about by creating and sharing musical sounds, include the sense of deepened individuality it yields, the societal beliefs it enables to be embodied and shared, the breadth and depth of feelings it adds to our inner lives, the awareness we gain of both the universality and cultural specificity of the human condition, the dimension of depth (or "specialness") it adds to our experience of life, the fulfillment of an inborn capacity to create and share the meanings expressive sounds afford, and on and on with the many values attained as a consequence of being involved with the sounds of music.

Using music as a means, to the contrary, focuses on producing outcomes unrelated to the quality and depth of musical experience itself. For example, the claim has been strongly made recently that certain involvements with music enhance spatial-temporal reasoning abilities. The enhancements are not a consequence of deeper musical experience as defined here. They are results of particular opportunities some music and some involvements with music provide to manipulate patterns similar in some ways to the patterns underlying spatial-temporal reasoning tasks. The high value our society holds for spatial-temporal reasoning can then become the reason music should be valued—for its utility as a means to achieve that particular result. The implications for music education practice of pursuing this value would be far-reaching, in transforming its focus on learnings related to musical experience, such as the National Standards for music education define,[11] to a focus on only those activities pertinent to improving spatial-temporal reasoning.[12]

The example above yields a criterion for distinguishing among values for music as an end or as a means. To the degree a claimed value is dependent upon and a consequence of involvement in the ways music is experienced and learned, such as the Standards represent, it can reasonably be identified as an end of musical involvement. To the degree the attainment of a value suggests or requires that musical learnings and involvements be altered in the direction of that value, weakening or eliminating musical learning and experience, it can justifiably be regarded as focused on music as a means.[13]

In many if not most cases, the values claimed for music as a means, no matter how farfetched they might seem to be, and as unrelated to musical experience they might seem to be, are assumed to occur naturally from musical learnings, musical involvements, and musical experiences. There is usually no intent that the musical focus or content of such learnings, involvements, and experiences be weakened in pursuit of the claimed value. In such cases the value(s) claimed may be considered to be complementary to those of music as an end, adding still other benefits to those resulting as consequences of musical experience.

Music educators are fortunate that the pursuit of musical learnings seems to enhance a variety of positive complementary values: this provides additional arguments for the value of music education. Judgments have to be made as to the ever-present risk that pursuing such values would require significant changes in the focus of the music program. In cases where no risk is evident, or where accommodation to these values can be made with little change to a musically focused program, it is likely to be to the advantage of music education to be gracious and positive in embracing them. When music is forced to serve ends incompatible with the values of musical learning, professional expertise to deal with the issue must be brought into play. Fortunately, such conflicts of values seldom occur.

The remainder of this paper will be devoted to an explanation of significant values of musical experiences and the positive consequences such experiences bring about.

2. Music Encompasses Mind, Body, and Feeling.

For much of Western history, and especially since the influential thinking of the philosopher-mathematician Rene Descartes (1596–1650), mind, body, and feeling have generally been considered to be separate components of human functioning. Descartes was driven to identify an absolutely reliable basis for knowledge, in which all doubt was dispelled. He found that basis in the idea of pure intellect, especially pure mathematics, in which the unreliable, confused, and imperfect senses and emotions have, as much as possible, been eliminated so they are unable to exert their negative influences.

The "highest" values, then, are the values of the disembodied intellect, and the "highest" subjects—those of most value—are the ones in which intellectual capacities are given full opportunities to develop. As a result, the subjects most valued in education, the "basics," are those that require the greatest exercise of the intellect, or intelligence, such as mathematics, languages, and the physical and social sciences. Subjects such as the arts, which are based on feelings, emotions, physical sensations and actions, and certainly not on "pure thought," are decidedly secondary in value, according to this conception. Their values are desirable, worthy of support after the basics have been attended to, pleasantly supplementary to the real work of education, but not, after all, central to or necessary for the solid foundation education is required to build.

The belief that the intellect, or intelligence, is separate from and of higher value than the body or the feelings has so pervaded Western culture for so long as to be, for most, a "given," no longer subject to examination. So long as this belief system endures, it is highly unlikely that music will be regarded as playing much more than a minor role among far more important intellectual endeavors. No amount of "advocacy," of impassioned pleading, of desperate attempts to somehow attach music to values higher on the scale as if that will rescue it from its lesser status, is likely to do much more than win occasional battles for sheer survival, necessary as it may be at present to fight such battles. Something else is needed if music is ever to be regarded as equal in value to the basic subjects required to be studied by all who are to be considered "educated." That something is a sweeping shift in people's understanding of the nature of mind, body, and feeling. That shift is now well under way.

From a variety of scholarly disciplines, including psychology, physiology, philosophy, neuroscience, anthropology, sociology, and education, powerful, converging arguments are being made for a fundamental transformation in the ways we understand the nature of the human condition. Contrary to Descartes' conception of a disembodied, emotionless intellect, it is rapidly becoming clearer that human cognition, or intelligence, is (1) demonstrated in diverse forms, (2) intimately tied to the body and the ways it functions, and (3) pervaded throughout with feeling. Far more complex than Descartes and his followers could have imagined, the human capacity to know, think, feel, and act—what we call "mind"—requires the interaction of dimensions previously believed to have little to do with one another. The implications for our understanding of music, both as to its nature and its value, are profound.

1. Intelligence Is Demonstrated in Diverse Forms.

There is no single, proper, correct form in which human thinking occurs. Instead, a variety of forms of intelligent functioning—of ways to create and share meanings—coexist. Different explanations of the diversity of modes of human thought have been offered, such as Philip H. Phenix's "Realms of Meaning" (Symbolics, Empirics, Esthetics, "Synnoetics" [personal meanings], Ethics, and Synoptics); Howard Gardner's "Frames of Mind" (Linguistic, Musical, Logical-Mathematical, Spatial, Bodily Kinesthetic, Interpersonal, Intrapersonal, Naturalist, Spiritual or Existential); and the authors in Elliot Eisner (ed.), "Learning and Teaching the Ways of Knowing" (Aesthetic, Scientific, Interpersonal, Intuitive, Narrative/Paradigmatic, Formal, Practical, Spiritual).[14] All point to the conviction that thinking, or intelligence, is not limited to the two forms previously conceived to be the only ones in which it could genuinely take place—the verbal and the mathematical.

Musical intelligences, manifested distinctively in each musical role such as composing, performing, improvising, and listening, require "thinking in sounds," the special form of human cognition fulfilled by music. Thinking musically—creating meanings through sounds formed in ways cultures have devised—is an act of intelligence, reason, thoughtfulness, rationality, intellect, and mindfulness. That these words may sound inappropriate when applied to music, as if they somehow render music "academic," or "abstract," or "theoretical," is testimony to how captive we have been to the idea that these words are limited to the linguistic or mathematical thinking modes. Music, as much as those and other modes, as precisely, as accurately, as powerfully, as logically, as broadly and deeply, as genuinely, is a demonstration of the human capacity to think—to be intelligent. Each musical role a culture provides requires a particular way to think in sounds, creating meanings only musically organized sounds are capable of bringing into being. All humans are capable of thinking in musical sounds. It is a fundamental capacity of the human mind.

2. Intelligence Is Intimately Tied to the Body and the Ways It Functions.

Thinking in sounds requires the engagement of the body, as all thinking does. The bodily basis of human reality—the influence of our bodies on how and what we can know and imagine—is becoming clearer through a variety of scholarly enterprises, explained and summarized most usefully, perhaps, in Mark Johnson's *The Body in the Mind: The Bodily Basis of Meaning, Imagination, and Reason.*[15] As Johnson explains, *"Any adequate account of meaning and rationality must give a central place to embodied and imaginative structures of understanding by which we grasp our world"*[16] (emphasis in original). Imagination is the power all humans have to perceive things and events as being connected in some way, whether by similarity or difference. It is the power to achieve patterned, coherent experience. Without the imaginative capacity to make connections among what we experience, our lives would be chaotic, completely without form. Meaning would be impossible, as would purposeful action. Human imagination is at the core of human thinking and doing.

In a great variety of ways, human imagination is dependent on the realities of the human body. The body's structure and functions give us the bases for the various ways connections are made within and among our experiences, including what many have regarded as "pure thought," as if human thinking of any sort could take place elsewhere than within the realities of our bodies. (Johnson gives detailed descriptions of the many ways human thought is "embodied.") Music is a prime example of thinking as being body-centered. Sounds themselves are experienced not by some sort of isolated brain but by the fullness of the brain's connection to the entire body. The "dynamic" qualities of sounds, their movement/energy/vitality characteristics as imagined by composers, performers, improvisers, and listeners, are qualities intimately connected to the movement/energy/vitality of life itself as experienced in and through the body.[17] No wonder music "makes special," touching us, moving us, energizing us, creating coherent, patterned sense of body-mind experience.

3. Intelligence Is Pervaded with Feeling.

The picture of music's value for creating meaning is still not complete. Human intelligence, in addition to taking many forms beyond the verbal and numerical, and in addition to being centered in the realities of the human body, is pervaded throughout with feeling. Although this is not a new idea, it is receiving important support from recent work in neurology, the most dramatic explanation coming from brain researcher Antonio R. Damasio's *Descartes' Error: Emotion, Reason, and the Human Brain.*[18] Taking direct aim at Descartes' argument for the separation of thinking and feeling, and its negative influence on science over the centuries, Damasio argues that "contrary to traditional scientific opinion, feelings are just as cognitive as other percepts. . . . Feelings form the basis for what humans have described for millennia as the human soul or spirit."

> I see feelings as having a truly privileged status. They are represented at many neural levels, including the neocortical, where they are the neuroanatomical and neurophysiological equals of whatever is appreciated by other sensory channels. But because of their inextricable ties to the body, they come first in development and retain a primacy that subtly pervades our mental life. Because the brain is the body's captive audience, feelings are winners among equals. And since what comes first constitutes a frame of reference for what comes after, feelings have a say on how the rest of the brain and cognition go about their business. Their influence is immense.[19]

The growing recognition of the role of feeling in human cognitive functioning—in the human capacity to be intelligent—shifts the grounding of music's value from the "merely pleasant" to the profound. (See the discussion of Dimension 5 below.) The long-recognized special powers of music to explore, embody, and illuminate the depths and breadths of human feeling are now being recognized as central to human knowledge and understanding.

As a primary way in which mind, body, and feeling are unified in acts of meaning-making, musical endeavors represent a pinnacle of what the human condition exemplifies. The values of music stem from its contribution of special meanings to human life. These meanings are unavailable except through the unified experiences of mind, body, and feeling that music affords. Such involvements, in turn, inevitably have many positive affects on the quality of the interrelated mental, physical, and emotional dimensions of human life.

3. Music Is Universal, Cultural, and Individual.

Since music has existed everywhere that humans have existed it is natural to wonder what values it has bestowed on all humans universally. Are the values of music generic to humans despite the many differences among them (in time, place, race, gender, age, belief system, and so forth)? Conversely, are all musical values specific to particular times, places, races, genders, and so on? Or are musical values entirely individual, each human being uniquely creating and experiencing the values music confers?

Some thinkers, interested in the broadest, most widely shared values of music, have suggested that many universal values of music can be identified. Among these are the values of emotional expression; aesthetic enjoyment; the need to structure reality; the need to share musical experiences and meanings with others; entertainment; spiritual fulfillment; validation and stabilizing of social norms, beliefs and institutions; probing, challenging, and changing cultural norms; providing connection with the vast web of humankind over the ages; expanding the meanings humans are capable of grasping; and on and on with values transcending particular times and settings.

Other thinkers prefer to focus on the cultural basis of human values. They explain the values of music as being tied to the particularities of beliefs and ways of living in each culture and each subculture. To understand why music is valued by humans, in this view, one must examine the belief system—the value system—each culture has devised, and how music contributes to the values particular to that culture. Music, in this view, is essentially and necessarily a product of singular communities of people, who have created their own norms of what counts as valuable. Without understanding the particular system of values, ideology, and politics in which music exists it is impossible to identify or cultivate musical values, which are always situated in the specific circumstances in which humans live out their lives.

Still another set of ideas about musical value focuses on individual experience. Human reality is, at bottom, unique to each person, a function of each person's ways of thinking, feeling, acting, making meaning, and constructing a sense of place or context. Only individuals, after all, compose, perform, improvise, and listen, even if they do so in cooperation with others. "Cultures," "groups," "families," "races," "nations," "genders," "religions," are all abstractions. What is real is the specificity of the experience an individual has when undergoing it. If music has value it must be explained in terms of each person's particular configuration of mind, body, and feelings comprising that person's selfhood. In acknowledging and honoring each individual's musical values we create a mutually respectful basis for exploring the values of other individuals and other cultures.

What can we make of these different positions about the value of music? Each seems to have validity: each calls attention to a persuasive set of claims. While it might seem that a choice must be made among them, it is possible to reconcile them with an inclusive conception—that all human beings are, at the same time, like all other human beings, like some other human beings, and like no other human beings.

This paradoxical condition is the basis for many of the dilemmas humans face, as when one dimension so dominates as to diminish or even threaten the others. If we concentrate too heavily on universal values we may compromise the validity of and necessity for group identification, with all that such identification adds to the value of our lives. We may also threaten the specialness—the uniqueness—of each human's experience, a quality much to be treasured and protected.

However, if we focus all efforts toward values situated within particular communities we can erect walls that separate, implying that cross-community sharing of values is impossible or undesirable. The bloodiest conflicts in human history have occurred because of over-zealous identification with particular cultural values, trampling on alternative cultures and on individuals with alternative values.

And if we so emphasize individual needs as to forget that every individual is also a member of the larger human community, and of particular communities within it, we can amplify qualities of selfishness and alienation, depriving people of the preciousness of communal membership.

Difficult—perhaps impossible—as it may be to perfectly balance the universality, cultural connectedness, and individuality of the human condition, music educators must continually recognize the validity of the values claimed within each level. The values of all three must be represented because music powerfully serves an essential need in each: (1) the need to experience meanings shared by all members of the species "homo sapiens," (2) the need to experience those meanings fashioned by various communities with similar value orientations, and (3) the need to experience them within the full individuality of selfhood. A person with a healthy musical identity understands music to be a common possession of humans, honors and delights in the distinctiveness of the musical communities of which he or she is a member as well as the musics of other communities that widen and enhance meaningful musical enjoyments, and treasures the personal responsibility to seek musical fulfillments as relevant to an internalized, self-determined value system.

That music so powerfully fulfills values at each level of the human condition is testament to its necessity as a factor in the living of a humane life. It

explains why all people have had, now have, and no doubt will continue to
have music so long as humans endure as a species.

4. Music Is Product and Process.

Many values are attached to products—the results of human endeavors and
nature's manifestations. A good loaf of bread, automobile, pair of shoes, job,
political system, tomato, sunshiny day, forest, are each, of its kind, prized
because of its contributions to human welfare. In music, successful results of
creation, whether compositions, performances, or improvisations, are similarly prized because they contribute to our musical welfare, with all the
resulting positive consequences for the quality of our lives. We treasure a
good song, or symphony, or solo by a favorite jazz musician, or performance
by a country fiddler or gamelan or Beijing opera troupe or African drum
ensemble, as a source of musical satisfaction and meaning. We honor those
musicians, whether composers, performers, or improvisers, who provide us
with their products—the outcomes of their musical efforts. In practically
every culture some people are recognized to be capable of producing outstanding musical results, and win high esteem for doing so. Often, a musical
product or body of work deemed extraordinarily successful is regarded as a
cultural treasure, among the most precious achievements of that culture.

For most people the word "music" refers to all products of the sort having
whatever characteristics they define as musical. Not surprisingly then, the
dictionary defines music to be a noun rather than a verb. This focus on music
as being a particular "kind of thing" reflects one major dimension of musical
value—the achievement of musical significance as expressed in works of
music.

Much of music education is devoted to sharing with students the treasures
of successful musical products. The songs we teach in general music classes,
or that are published in collections, are chosen partly for their appropriate-
ness for the age and abilities of those who will sing them, but also, centrally,
for their quality as successful pieces of music. Similarly for pieces chosen for
performing groups; whatever other considerations must be taken into account, the consideration of their musical value is always paramount. This
consideration also guides our choice of music to be listened to. Underlying
all choices of music is the desire to share the bounties of musical experience
available from musical products.

No product, musical or otherwise could exist without the processes that
brought it into being. Engaging people in those processes allows them to
experience the creation of the product, and therefore to understand and
undergo another essential dimension of what the product exemplifies. Experiencing music from the process standpoint, as a creator of compositions,
performances and improvisations, and as a creative participant in the mean-

ing-making of listening, shifts the identity of "music" from noun to verb. Music becomes, in addition to being a bearer of realized musical values, a vehicle for realizing those values. Being musically creative, in all the ways this can be accomplished, not only fulfills the human capacity for bringing meanings into existence as only music can do, it also deepens the perspective on the nature of musical meanings. Seen as a particular realm in which creative imagination is brought into play, encompassing mind, body, and feeling, and embracing universal, cultural, and individual levels of experience, creating music exemplifies the human capacity to be generative—to bring meaning into existence.

Every generative musical act is aimed toward an end—to create musical meaning. Without that end in view the act becomes musically meaningless. Every musical end—every result of creating music embodies the sum of the acts of making it. Without those acts there would be no result. Music is result (product) and act (process) interdependently; music is both noun and verb simultaneously. The values of music education for students of any age, but especially for young people, lie primarily in learning how to be more skilled when they are engaged in musical processes. It is natural, then, for music educators to argue that what is important in music education is the process, not the product. There is a danger in forgetting that, in music, process cannot be separated from product. The fact is, an awareness of process cannot occur without concurrent awareness of product; separating the two violates the nature of music. The widespread myth that process is what counts, not product, is examined by art educator Elliot Eisner as follows:

> This myth, related to the one on creativity, argues that what is educationally significant for children is the process they undergo while making something, not what it is that they make. It is argued further that when attention is devoted to the product rather than to the process the child's growth is likely to be hampered; one would be, so to speak, keeping one's eye on the wrong target. It's not what a child makes but how he makes it that is important. I will not take the tack that just the opposite is true. I will not argue that the product is what's important, not the process. I won't do this because I believe that dichotomizing process and product is wrongheaded to begin with. In the first place, there can be no product without some type of process. The processes we use at whatever level of skill shape the qualities of the product that will be realized, whether that product is ideational or material. Similarly the product or end-in-view that we aspire to create shapes the means we employ and provides a criterion against which choices in the present are made. Further, unless some of us here are mind readers we will never be able to see the processes the child is undergoing. What we see are the manifestations of those processes: what they produce. It is from these products that we are able to make certain inferences about process. To disregard what the child produces puts us into an absolutely feckless position for making inferences about those processes. In addition, without attention to what is produced we have no basis for making

any type of judgment regarding the educational value of the activity in which
the child is engaged. Process and product therefore cannot be dichotomized.
They are like two sides of a coin. Processes can be improved by attending to
the product and products improved by making inferences about the processes.
To neglect one in favor of the other is to be pedagogically naive. [20]

Heeding Eisner's admonition allows music educators a balanced perspective
for action and a flexibility to emphasize process or product depending on the
context. In a professional situation, such as, say, an orchestra, the musicians
are expected to have achieved such high levels of expertise that the barest
minimum of process, in this case rehearsal, is needed to produce what the
orchestra exists to produce—the finest, most polished realization of its repertoire for its audience to experience. Product orientation drives the professional enterprise, unlike the developmental learning, or process orientation driving the educational enterprise. Of course the professional orchestral musicians, no matter how high their level of expertise, must still be concerned
with process; hence their need to continually practice, rehearse, expand their
repertoire, and so forth. What differs between children performing as part of
their musical education, and professional performing, is the *balance* of process orientation and product orientation.

  · Keeping an appropriate balance is an ongoing challenge for those responsible for helping young people achieve the fullest possible value from music.
For example, music educators involved with performing groups, must, as
part of their responsibility, present to the public the outcomes—the products—of their learning. The drive to present a respectable product, especially
when doing so brings a variety of coveted rewards, can so overwhelm the
need for attention to learning processes as to seriously jeopardize the educational purposes of studying music.

  An imbalance in the other direction is just as hazardous. For example, the
widespread assumption that in music anything attempted must be, by virtue
of attempting it, considered acceptable; that "anything goes" because there
are no criteria for success or failure; that just "doing it"—having "hands
on"—is desirable whether or not *minds* are on; all reduce process to the
trivial. Connecting process to the quality of the product assures the veracity
of the process, both musically and educatively.

  The values of musical involvements, embracing the specialness of musical experience, the positive consequences of having it, the complementary
values accruing to it, and its universal, cultural, and individual dimensions,
stem from the interrelation of process and product on which the musical
enterprise depends. Achieving an appropriate balance between them is an
ongoing responsibility of music educators, no matter the age of their students
or the particular musical engagement being pursued.

5. Music Is Pleasurable and Profound.

All humans have the capacity to enjoy their lives—to revel in the immediacy of the pleasures life affords. A great deal of time and effort go into, and have always gone into, the pursuit of pleasurable experience—experience that diverts, amuses, and delights. The pursuit of happiness is, at least to some substantial degree, the pursuit of enjoyment.

Entertainment may be understood as the attempt to provide pleasurable experience. While not all entertainment requires music, much of it does. That is because music has a singular capacity to arouse or elicit experiences that are amusing, uplifting, and delightful. Musical sounds are remarkably effective in their ability to mirror, or embody, the inner qualities of enjoyment—its energy, vivaciousness, zest, and elation. When music, all by itself, is experienced as having such qualities, it entertains—it provides the value of pleasure. When music accompanies a variety of other entertaining activities it adds powerfully to their effectiveness. Music is treasured as a medium whereby humans gain joyful experience.

Along with the capacity and need for pleasure, all humans have the capacity and need to experience life at depths below the surface of the commonplace. All cultures have recognized and attempted to provide means for achieving experiences of deep meaning for their members, experiences variously termed "sacred," "holy," "soulful," "spiritual," or "profound."[21] The world's religions are, to a large extent, devoted to providing such experiences, and many aspects of secular life also strive to impart a sense of deep significance to our experiences. Such experiences, it is commonly believed, are among the most precious humans are capable of having.

Music, in its capacity to achieve a sense of deep significance by going beyond the meanings made available by words to meanings only sounds can bring into being, has always been a major source of, or an important accompaniment to, the quest for profound experience. That is why music's alliance with the sacred is so strong and widespread, and why it is so often regarded with reverence for having the power to deepen experience, the power to console, heal, and restore wholeness, or wellness. Music is an important medium whereby humans experience the spiritual.

Both the pleasurable and the profound are experienced as qualities of "feeling." As pointed out in Dimension 2 above, feeling is inclusive of the mind and the body. The term "feeling" is commonly used when discussing the quality of experience we undergo because that term comes closest to capturing the way we actually encounter experience—we "feel" it subjectively, that is, as something happening within ourselves. The human capacity to feel—to consciously experience one's self and one's world subjectively, including sensations, emotions for which descriptive words exist (love, fear, joy, etc.), and complex feelings for which no words exist—is at the heart and center of the human condition.[22] In a real sense, to feel consciously is to be human. (It is interesting, and telling, that in much of science fiction, nonhuman creatures, masquerading in the guise of being human, are found out as impostors by their incapacity to feel.)

The range of music's power to embody and display feeling is enormous, encompassing the lightest, most fleeting diversions, the most complex and weighty profundities, and everything in between. *No point along that vast continuum of feeling is exclusive of or entirely separate from, implications from other points.* That is, there is significance in the pleasurable and joy in the profound. We would not, and could not, exist at any one level of feeling to the exclusion of others: to do so would be to live a unidimensional life. Music serves human needs to feel by capturing and exhibiting feeling across the entire range of its possibilities. No single experience of musical feeling excludes or diminishes the importance of, and need for, any of the others.

Further, music does not simply imitate, or reproduce, those feelings available from all the other activities and engagements in human life. Music's ability to create feeling and make it available for experiencing inevitably transforms feeling into the materials and processes of which music is created —sounds organized in culturally provided configurations. That is, feeling, at whatever point in the continuum of its possibilities, is transformed by music into "feeling-as-musical," just as feeling in poetry is transformed into "feeling-as-poetic," feeling in painting into "feeling-as-visual," and so forth for all the arts. Musical experience, as all artistic/aesthetic experience, both dwells in the realm of human feeling and transforms that realm into its particular way of being.

In doing so, music is able to add a unique dimension to the capacities of humans to feel. Music goes beyond—makes special, or transforms—the feelings in nonmusical life, adding another dimension to the human capacity to feel, a dimension not available except through music. Music is an essential way to expand, deepen, and vivify the feelings humans are able to experience. It is among the most powerful means humans possess to fulfill their need for an abundantly feelingful life.

No single, particular music is more or less capable of providing significant experiences than others. While evidence is scant about which musics tend to cause deep experiences of feeling, indications are that such experiences take place "within a well-defined community of musical expectations,"[23] in which familiarity and self-identification play important roles. "Soul music"—music in which people find a sense of identity, of selfness, reaching to the core of their personal/communal experience of the world—is a precious, self-defining, and self-realizing possession. While some are likely to "find soul" in the music of the Western classical tradition, because of their societal context, experience, and training, many find their deepest musical satisfactions elsewhere. Fully recognizing this reality, and legitimizing it by respecting and including for study and experience the many musics treasured by people, including but going beyond those of traditional Western styles, remains a pressing agenda for the music education profession.

The need for rich and diverse feelingful experience, so powerfully fulfilled by music, exists throughout our lives. At every age, including infancy, a life being "well lived" is a life being lived with the fullest possible richness of feeling. Whatever the quality of feeling music affords, from the amusing to the soulful, from the fleeting to the indelible, from the frivolous to the passionate, all are precious contributions to a central value humans seem to share—the value of life being fully lived because it is being abundantly experienced. At bottom, this value, with all its ramifications for and support of the many values complementary to it and arising as consequences of it, is likely to provide a foundation on which music educators can build a community of belief, allowing them to act effectively and in solidarity toward helping people benefit from the significant values of music.

III. SUMMARY AND CONCLUSIONS

The question of why humans value music has eluded all efforts to answer it conclusively despite many attempts throughout history. However, useful explanations have accumulated over time, serving well to provide enough agreement, or persuasiveness, to allow communities of people, such as music educators, to feel that they share a common belief system upon which they can build cooperative actions.

One significant orientation to the values of music has been toward its role in enhancing the depth, quality, scope, and intensity of inner human experience in ways particular to how music operates; ways that distinguish music from other human endeavors. This orientation has preoccupied philosophers of music, whose interests tend to be directed toward understanding the "nature" of music—its particularity as a human creation and the values it serves as such. Taking a philosophical stance, two characteristics of music may be suggested as bases for its values in human life.

1. Music makes human experience "special." It aims to achieve a level of experience different from the commonplace. Music makes ordinary experience extraordinary, or insignificant experience significant. Music creates an alternative to the reality of the everyday; an alternative to the ordinary way of being.
2. Music, unlike all the other arts, depends on the use of sounds, organized in ways various cultures sanction, to create the sense of specialness it adds to human experience. Music is unique in its use of ordered

sounds as the basic material by which it accomplishes its "transformation" (passing over from one form to another) of experience.

Five dimensions of musical value may be identified as related to its distinctive nature.

1. Music Is End and Means.

1. All the various ways to be engaged in musical experiences—such as composing, performing, improvising and listening—enable both the creation of musical meanings and the sharing of musical meanings with others. The value of doing so is in making available an endless source of significant experiences uniquely gained through music. To seek the meaningful satisfactions of musical creating and sharing is to pursue musical value as an end. This end of musically meaningful experience has been sought by humans throughout history.
2. Many positive consequences grow out of the pursuit of musical meaning as an end. To be human is to make meaning and seek meaning. A life full of meaning, including musical meaning, is a life fulfilled in one of its primary needs. The consequences of such fulfillment are a sense of wholeness, wellness, and satisfaction. Effects on individuals' physical, emotional, psychological, and spiritual health are profound. These effects radiate outward to the health of families, communities, nations, and cultures, all of which depend, ultimately, on the well-being of their members.
3. Many values not dependent on the uniqueness of musical experiencing are believed to be gained as a result of involvements with music. When the pursuit of these values requires that musical experiences and learnings be diluted in order to achieve them, music is being used as a means. In most cases the achievement of these values does not require any change from the pursuit of musical values as an end. Such values may then be considered complementary to musical ones, and can be regarded as welcome, positive contributions of programs devoted to musical learnings. Music educators may choose to promote such values to gain additional support for music study.

2. Music Encompasses Mind, Body, and Feeling.

1. The long-standing idea that "thinking" is the supreme capacity of the human mind, and that thinking is separate and distinct from the body and the feelings, is giving way to the recognition that thinking, knowing, and understanding—what is generally called "intelligence"—

takes place in a variety of forms and necessarily includes involvements of the body and feelings.

2. Human intelligence occurs in multiple forms beyond its traditional association with verbal and mathematical thinking. Musical ways of thinking demonstrate intelligence in the fullest sense of that word— the mind functioning in a reasoned way to create meaning. The capacity to think musically is inborn in human beings.

3. Intelligence requires the involvement of the body, and the body-centered imaginative power to form connections among experiences. Musically intelligent functioning is grounded in the body's capacity to undergo the dynamic qualities of sound and their interconnections as imagined by composers, performers, improvisers, and listeners. Sound is a particularly powerful medium for engaging the body in acts of creating meaning.

4. Human intelligence, in addition to taking many forms beyond the verbal and numerical, and in addition to being centered within the realities of the human body, is saturated with feelings that vivify and color life. Musical meaning arises from the feelings music allows us to create and share. The unification of mind, body, and feeling in the creation of musical meaning adds an indispensable source of value to human life.

3. Music Is Universal, Cultural, and Individual.

1. At one level, musical meaning is universally sought by all humans and is cherished universally for the values it adds to life. Music can be conceived, at this level, as a generic possession of the human species.

2. At another level, music can be regarded as a phenomenon particular to the culture in which it exists, both reflecting and creating the values and ways of being in that culture.

3. At still another level the values of music can be understood as the possession of individuals. Only individuals create and respond to music, even if cooperatively. "Universals," or "cultures," are only abstractions from individual experience.

4. These three dimensions of musical value need not be conceived as contradictory. All humans are, at the same time, like all other humans, like some other humans, and like no other humans. All three levels of the human condition must be acknowledged as contributing to the values of musical experience: an awareness of all three adds immeasurably to the depth and quality of musical valuing. That music fulfills values at all three levels helps account for its indispensable contribution to the quality of human life.

4. Music Is Product and Process.

1. Successful musical products, whether compositions, performances of them, or improvisations, are precious for the benefits they offer to people as sources of significant meanings. Often a particularly excellent musical product or body of work is considered a cultural treasure, representing the highest achievement of which humans in that culture are capable. Much of music education is devoted to sharing with students the bounties of musical meaning embodied in successful musical products.
2. No product, musical or otherwise, can come into being without the processes that create it. Acts of creative musical imagination, involving mind, body, and feeling, and encompassing universal, cultural, and individual dimensions of experience, engage musical intelligence deeply and powerfully in generating meanings. The experience of musical creativity profoundly satisfies the human need to be generative.
3. Music as process and as product are interdependent: one cannot exist without the other and the values of each depend on the values of the other.

An overemphasis of either, at the expense of the other, weakens musical experience and diminishes its value. Effective education in music continually aims toward a balanced representation of both product and process.

5. Music Is Pleasurable and Profound.

1. At one level, music is an essential source of pleasurable experience, either by itself or as allied with a variety of other pursuits of enjoyment. The capacity of music to express the energy, zest, and elation of pleasure is endless, causing music to be treasured as a means for gaining the values of life experienced as joyful.
2. At another level, music serves the need for experience below the surface of the commonplace, in which deep meanings are uncovered— meanings often called sacred, or profound. Such experiences of soulfulness, of spiritual significance, are commonly believed to be among the most precious of which humans are capable. Music's alliance with this level of experience has been acknowledged throughout history as adding a profound realm of value to human life.
3. Music *creates* possibilities of feeling available only from music. It does not simply imitate or reproduce joyful or profound experiences available in other ways. No single kind or style of music has sole possession of this capacity; all musics can serve and have served the

values of significant experience. The need for such experience exists for all humans, at every time of life from early childhood to old age.

Music education exists to make musical values more widely and deeply shared. While no single explanation can completely and ultimately define music's values, sufficient agreement to provide a basis for communal action is possible and desirable. At this time in history, a viable belief system for music educators may be achieved if an attitude emphasizing inclusiveness rather than exclusiveness is taken. In this paper an attempt has been made to explain that musical values can be regarded as both end and complementary means; as encompassing the mind, body, and feelings; as being universal, culturally specific, and individual; as deriving from musical products and processes; and as embracing experiences across the entire spectrum of human feeling as made available by the entire array of the world's musics. Each music educator has the responsibility to forge a persuasive professional position from this and other attempts to solve the age-old puzzle of why humans value music.

NOTES

1. Howard Gardner, *Frames of Mind: The Theory of Multiple Intelligences* (New York Basic Books, 1983), 123.

2. A penetrating explanation of recent views in opposition to the search for essences, as exemplified in music, is given in Wayne D. Bowman, *Philosophical Perspectives on Music* (New York Oxford University Press, 1990), chapter 8, "Contemporary Pluralist Perspectives," 356–409.

3. For discussions of the influences of the value dilemmas of contemporary philosophy on visual art education, see Suzi Gablik, *Conversations before the End of Time: Dialogues on Art, Life, and Spiritual Renewal* (London: Thames and Hudson, 1995), and Ronald W. Neperud, ed., *Context, Content, and Community in Art Education: Beyond Postmodernism* (New York: Teachers College Press, 1995). An argument for foundational values of art in face of pluralist views is given in Ellen Dissanayake, *What Is Art For?* (Seattle: University of Washington Press, 1988).

4. Allen Britton, Arnold Broido, and Charles Gary, "The Tanglewood Declaration," in *Documentary Report of the Tanglewood Symposium* (Washington, DC: Music Educators National Conference, 1968), 139.

5. Estelle R. Jorgensen, *In Search of Music Education* (Urbana, IL: University of Illinois Press, 1997), 69.

6. Interestingly, an influential set of arguments for the necessity of a foundational value system, based on the existence of an underlying human nature, has arisen recently in the scientific community, exemplified by Edward O. Wilson, *On Human Nature* (Harvard University Press, 1978), and *Consilience: The Unity of Knowledge* (New York: Alfred A. Knopf, 1998).

7. Dissanayake, note 3 above, 92.

8. Francis Sparshott, "Aesthetics of Music: Limits and Grounds," in *What Is Music?*, ed. Philip Alperson (New York: Haven, 1987), 89.

9. Bowman, note 2 above, 2.

10. *The School Music Program: A New Vision* (Reston, VA: Music Educators National For a wide-ranging and insightful explanation of the similarities and differences among the arts, see

the classic book by Susanne K. Langer, Feeling and Form: A Theory of Art (New York: Charles Scribner's Sons, 1953).

11. Conference, 1994), 9–26.

12. This particular situation is the topic in Bennett Reimer, "Facing the Risks of the 'Mozart Effect,'" *Music Educators Journal* 86, no. 1 (July 1999): 37–43.

13. For a detailed examination of the dangers of arts education being forced to pursue political agendas rather than artistic values, see Constance Bumgardner Gee, "For You Dear—Anything! Omnipotence, Omnipresence, and Servitude 'through the Arts,' Part 1," *Arts Education Policy Review* 100, no. 4 (March/April 1999): 3–17, and "For You Dear—Anything! Remembering and Returning to First Principles, Part 2," *Arts Education Policy Review* 100, no. 5 (May/June 1999): 3–22.

14. Philip H. Phenix, *Realms of Meaning* (New York: McGraw Hill, 1964); Gardner, Frames of Mind, note 1 above; Elliot Eisner, ed., *Learning and Teaching the Ways of Knowing* (Chicago: University of Chicago Press, 1985).

15. Mark Johnson, *The Body in the Mind: The Bodily Basis of Meaning, Imagination, and Reason* (Chicago: University of Chicago Press, 1987). For an insightful analysis of the role of the body and the imagination in aesthetic experience see Mike Dufrenne, *The Phenomenology of Aesthetic Experience* (Evanston, IL: Northwestern University Press, 1973), chapter 11, "Presence," 335–44, and chapter 12, "Representation and Imagination," 345–69.

16. Ibid., xiii.

17. An explanation of the particular role of the body in performing is given in Bennett Reimer, "Is Musical Performance Worth Saving?" *Arts Education Policy Review* 95, no. 3 (January/February 1994): 2–13. For an exhaustive account of the involvement of the body in music listening, see Marian T. Dura, "The Kinesthetic Dimension of the Music Listening Experience" (Doctoral diss., Northwestern University, 1998).

18. Antonio R. Damasio, *Descartes' Error: Emotion, Reason, and the Human Brain* (New York: H. P. Putnam's Sons, 1994).

19. Ibid., xv, xvi, 159–60. Also see Dufrenne, note 15 above, 370–425, on the role of feeling in aesthetic experience.

20. Elliot Eisner, "Examining Some Myths in Art Education," *Studies in Art Education* 15, no. 3 (1973–1974):11.

21. For a discussion of the widespread existence of beliefs in music's capacity to provide profound experiences, and a definition of the experience of profundity in music as "being moved deeply in response to music," see Bennett Reimer, "The Experience of Profundity in Music," *Journal of Aesthetic Education* 29, no. 4 (Winter, 1995): 1–21.

22. Definitions of "affect," "feeling," and "emotion," and an extended account of the role of feeling in intelligent functioning, are given in W. Ann Stokes, "Intelligence and Feeling: A Philosophical Examination of These Concepts as Interdependent Factors in Musical Experience and Music Education" (Doctoral Diss., Northwestern University, 1990).

23. Reimer, note 21 above, 5.

Chapter Three

Response to Bennett Reimer's "Why Do Humans Value Music?"

Commission Author: Robert Glidden

Robert Glidden is president of Ohio University in Athens, Ohio.

Let me begin by offering commendations to Professor Reimer for an excellent paper. Like a good piece of music, this paper reads better and my understanding is enhanced with each successive reading. It is well crafted and it is highly comprehensive for its relative brevity. In other words, it is concise, efficient, and effective! I would expect no less from Bennett Reimer, having known and admired him and his work for some thirty-five years.

In this response I will try to add to, rather than refute or refine, anything Professor Reimer has presented. His five dimensions of musical value are comprehensive in scope and obviously reflect a lifetime of thought and study on these matters. I will very briefly suggest some additional values from my own experience and perspective—a kind of overlay of my words over his—and then offer some thoughts about why humans may find even greater need for musical knowledge and skills in the future.

ADDITIONAL "VALUES"

The Combination of Intellect and Emotion

In answering for myself the question "Why do humans value music?" I have long believed that we are drawn to music because it is the most powerful combination of intellect and emotion that we know. Do I believe that most people intentionally seek out intellectual qualities when they invest their time in musical experiences? No, not most people. But as Reimer has said in his presentation at this conference, humans have a need to find meaning. The search for meaning in music naturally includes a search for more than pure emotion.

Music is the most abstract of the arts, and in the combining of emotion and intellect music's abstractness is an advantage. While it may be true that some kinds of music can be experienced as predominantly intellectual and others as predominantly emotional, it is impossible to separate intellect from emotion in music of substance. If we think of intellect and emotion as opposite poles on a continuum of objective to subjective, even our strongest emotions are not devoid of rationality, and our purest intellectual endeavors are not entirely objective and devoid of emotion.

It is possible that some of the satisfaction one derives from a substantive musical experience is the fulfillment of our need to combine intellect and emotion. And certainly, when we analyze and make normative judgments about music, we are attending to the effective combination of thought and feeling. As Reimer has stated in his paper (p. 29): "The growing recognition of the role of feeling in human cognitive functioning—in the human capacity to be intelligent—shifts the grounding of music's value from the 'merely pleasant' to the profound."

Reimer also makes a critically important point for music educators and for anyone who cares deeply about the place of music in formal education in discussing the dimension of musical values that he labels "Music encompasses mind, body, feeling." He says (p. 27): "The belief that the intellect, or intelligence, is separate from and of higher value than the body or the feelings has so pervaded Western culture for so long as to be, for most, a 'given,' no longer subject to examination. . . . Something else is needed if music is ever to be regarded as equal in value to the basic subjects required to be studied by all who are to be considered 'educated.'" The problem here, of course, is that most people, and certainly most educators, define "intellect" or "intelligence" as having to do only with verbal and quantitative skills and knowledge. We are indebted to Howard Gardner and his theory of multiple intelligences for shedding light on this subject, but I fear that Gardner's theory has not been generally understood nor accepted by the educational, establishment in general.

Expression of Our Most Intense Emotions

Observation would lead us to believe that music is virtually a *requirement* for expressing our most intense feelings of joy, or our most intense emotions of sadness or grief. Music as an expression of intense feelings supersedes verbal expression, perhaps partly because most of us are not capable of satisfactorily expressing those intense feelings verbally, and partly because in those moments we do not *wish* to express ourselves verbally. We refer again to music's ability to combine intellect and emotion. As we seek to express our most intense feelings we recognize that the capabilities of our verbal language are too limited. Reimer, discussing the dimension he calls "Music is pleasurable and profound," says (p. 35), "Music, in its capacity to achieve a sense of deep significance by going beyond the meanings made available by words to meanings only sounds can bring into being, has always been a major source of, or an important accompaniment to, the quest for profound experience."

Music as a Mental Discipline

For some, music has value strictly as a mental discipline, as a mental exercise. This, of course, is dependent on one's knowledge and musical skills. For those who can realize it, the value of music as an exercise in mental discipline is learned, but like mathematics, there is beauty in the structures and organization of music that brings great satisfaction to people who have the opportunity to learn music in that way.

Communal Value

Music has great communal, meaning "shared experience," value for many people. This is certainly true for those who perform music with others. The experience of sharing communication and understandings of musical meaning through ensemble performance is a special one. Musicians, who have had the opportunity to play chamber music, or to sing in a barbershop quartet, or to participate in any nonconducted ensemble, recognize the unique thrill of communication that occurs in the process of making music together. The same may be said of social dancing, whether ballroom or folk dancing. Dancers communicate with each other, with rhythmic coordination and through the mood of the music, and the shared experience is unlike any other for most people.

The communal value is powerful for listeners as well. The powerful emotions and stimuli that each one of us feels as an individual is enhanced by the belief that others are sharing that same experience. Perhaps this is made all the more powerful because we cannot express that satisfaction verbally. It is impossible to describe in words our reactions and responses while listening to music, yet we know, or at least we assume, that fellow audience members are experiencing many of the same responses. The communal experience of listening to music in a concert situation is special—it is just one of the reasons that live concerts continue to bring greater satisfaction than listening privately to even the most perfect recordings.

An Outlet for Creative Energies

For many people, music has great value as an outlet for their creative energies. This is true not just for those who compose or those who improvise, but also for those who perform and interpret music. Musicians understand the special thrill of discovery when they have created something original. Originality in this case may pertain only to their own experience, but a new discovery expressed musically is nonetheless a satisfying accomplishment, whether while singing in the shower or performing in a jazz club. It is my belief that most of us, perhaps all of us, have the ability to be musically creative if we are given the encouragement and the right environment in which to exercise our creativity.

A Medium for Communication

Because music can express feelings and emotions in ways that defy precise verbal definition, it has intrinsic, communicative value. It crosses barriers of verbal language, certainly, although the oft-heard reference to music as a "universal language" may be exaggerated. Cultures do not all share the same musical understandings. While it is true that for those within one cultural set—those who at least share a common musical vocabulary—there is a universality about music as a means of expression, it is also true that for people who have not benefited from musical education, the music of another culture can be quite strange indeed. We can learn to be crosscultural or multicultural in our tastes and understandings, but such appreciation is definitely a learned skill and attitude. This is a special challenge for music educators, not just to teach the music of cultures outside Western culture but also to teach respect and understanding for musical expressions that emanate from subcultures within our own culture.

ADDITIONAL THOUGHTS

The question "Why do humans value music?" is probably less pertinent here than the question "Do we value music enough to teach it to our young?" There seems to be ample evidence that music is fundamental in people's lives, at least for societies collectively even if not for every individual. As Bennett Reimer points out (p. 24), "Cultures have often, even routinely, regarded their music as a profoundly important dimension of their identity, to be protected and treasured, in and of itself, as among their greatest achievements." I also recognized that music must be important in contemporary society when I heard on NPR's *Morning Edition*, on Labor Day of this year, that MP3 (CD audio-quality sound files) had replaced Sex as the most searched for item on the Internet.

Is music, however, so fundamental to our quality of life that we should teach it thoroughly to our young? Or does it suffice to let our youngsters absorb what they will through popular culture? In other words, are skills and knowledge important. enough to justify precious school time, or do we assume that a casual approach will suffice?

The question of music's value, more appropriately stated for our purposes, has to do with its social and quality-of-life-enhancing value for all people. We recognize, certainly, that the very talented, the very interested, will, can, and do learn a great deal on their own without formal education. But we also know that *most* will not learn enough useable skills without some formal instruction and encouragement. So, does music have sufficient value for our society that our schools should assure musical learning for all?

A tribal society that *uses* music in its daily life—a society that relies on music as fundamental in the rituals of ordinary life—would not take the chance of neglecting to teach the practice of music to its young. In "more developed" societies throughout the world, certainly in our U.S. society, we seem to assume that music is a casual thing, a recreational or entertainment pursuit that is not fundamental to our intellectual or social health. Therefore, there is little importance placed on learning how to "do" music. I can testify from firsthand listening experience, speaking as one who lives in the middle of a campus, next door to a fraternity house, that today's young people are *not* learning to sing.

The notion that music is no more than a casual pursuit is one that we must challenge vociferously. First of all, even if music's value for most people is no more than recreational, as the world becomes more and more technology assisted and information-driven, one of our principal concerns should be, will be, about how we will find humanizing influences. I have read the prediction that by 2020, perhaps sooner, 60–80% of the workforce will be working at home in front of a computer. If and when that occurs, what experiences will we truly share as human beings? What experiences or activities will help us to know ourselves, to relate to others through stimuli that evoke common feelings and reactions?

Perhaps if we think about music in a tribal culture we can learn why it is so important to us as humans. Music provides a common framework whereby people can engage together for the common, shared celebration of joy, for dance or movement activities, for worship or contemplation, or for shared expressions of grief. It is simpler than text in many respects, yet more complex in others and certainly more emotive. Music is important because it affords us another common language through which to express our emotions—individually as well as collectively. We need that humanizing influence.

At some point, we as a society may come to realize how critical the nonmaterial values are to our quality of life. At the present time technology continues to drive us (and our economy) by intriguing us with what *can* be. The ease and immediacy of communication is wonderful today and will only be enhanced in the future. But at some point all this technology will "settle in," as the automobile and electric power have in the past. We will take for granted the ease and immediacy of communication, and then what?

I suggest that music as a means of "communication" (i.e., the sharing of emotions and common reaction to expressions of joy, of triumph, of grief, of serenity)—as intellectual stimuli, or romance, or humor, you name it—will be all the more important as our connections with each other become more and more technologically based.

Music will change as people change, of course, but what better link to traditions or styles of the past do we have? The music of popular culture has the capacity to take each of us back to our youth. Whom do you know who doesn't like the music of his or her youth? For many, *that* is their favorite music, for all time. But further, for the learned, music provides a reflection of style and perspective of past generations, of past centuries. We learn and feel something about people who lived centuries ago because we can recreate their music.

Technology has made music more ubiquitous, after all—whether in elevators or supermarkets and shopping malls or in our personal compact disc collections of music of all ages and all genres. How many could have imagined, at the turn of the last century, that we could have individual collections of music, from many centuries ago or newly composed last year, at our fingertips for listening whenever the whim captures us? And while that is wonderful, it is also a situation that tends to numb us. We do not listen as carefully because we are constantly surrounded by musical stimuli and our choices are almost limitless. We will not change that, of course, and in one respect the ubiquity of music is simply further testimony to the value that it holds for people—all people. But it does present another special challenge for music educators: the teaching of listening skills.

Whether or not we should teach musical skills and knowledge to our young is not, after all, a philosophical question—it is a political and economic one. Can we afford to teach music? Of course we can. The real question is, can our society afford *not* to?

Most of us would agree that we would like our schools to give more attention to the life of the mind—to intellect for its own sake, to higher expectations of learning for our young. I submit that the teaching of music is entirely consistent with that. We should not rely on arguments for music as a "mental ability enhancer," the so-called Mozart Effect, but neither should we be shy about promulgating musical activity as intellectual in nature, as a great connector between the intellectual and the emotional in our thinking processes.

I will not enter into arguments about what music we should teach, or *how* we should teach it. That is left to others at this conference. Furthermore, although I once had strong feelings about that, I am now more concerned about fundamental skills. I am sorry to report that from my observation, we have *lost ground* since the Yale Seminar of 1963, the report of which intrigued me to the point of passion about the prospect of teaching the literature of music in schools on a par with teaching the literature of the language. That was a dream then that I did not think unrealistic, but unfortunately we are farther from the realization of such a dream now than we were in the 1960s. I am now convinced that we must focus on teaching our young basic musical skills—like how to sing (even if not how to read) and how to "feel" and emote through music. We have much too much to lose in humanizing influences for future generations if we fail to do that.

Chapter Four

Why Study Music?

Commission Author: J. Terry Gates

J. Terry Gates is an associate professor of music education at the State University of New York at Buffalo.

Commission Members:
Ed Calle
Jennifer Davidson
Jack Heller
Daniel Scheuerer
David Shrader
Larry Williams

Response: Samuel Hope

We can achieve well and have fun simultaneously.—Katie Davidson, age 17

I. "WHY STUDY MUSIC?" IS A DISTURBING QUESTION

We have all confronted skeptics who claim that musical skill can be learned without planned, sequential instruction. Furthermore, most people, early in their lives, develop strong preferences for a few types of music. We don't need to be "taught what to like." And if people follow those strong preferences with action, they gather detailed knowledge about the music that they invite into their lives, most of it without conventional instruction. In the face of these beliefs and others, what rationales support planned programs of music study and how do these programs benefit our society and our people? What ethical basis is there for interfering with these natural human processes?

Our profession rests on the assumption that music study is not only valuable but necessary. "Why study music?" is a question that invites professional risk. So, why bring it up?

One reason is that there are so many positive, enthusiastic, and convincing answers. Music study is defended in curriculum documents, in appeals for more time or money for school music, in parent conferences when a good student plans to drop out of music study, in recruiting presentations, in advocacy brochures, and more. These defensive arguments have a special urgency about them that arises from the general belief that music education programs are at risk and that we need constant assurances that music study makes sense. Perhaps that is why there are so many answers. The skeptic asks, "Why do you work so hard at justifying the worth of your discipline? If it has always been so hard to justify music study in American schools, why don't you just give up?"

Another reason to bring up the question is that there are so many exceptions. We must respond to evidence that music study is unnecessary: We hear that Irving Berlin could not write down the music he composed. We hear that most popular music stars, even a few famous opera singers, "can't read a note." The skeptic asks, "If these accomplished musicians didn't need to learn through music study, why should I bother to study music, or why should I support such a program for others?"

We are forced to bring up this question because there is so much music around us. Recorded music is readily available for purchase, and good playback equipment is relatively cheap. Whole channels of television and, increasingly, cable radio products and Internet sites are devoted to music presentation. Broadcast media companies use music to draw targeted audiences to advertisers through the music policy decisions that they make. "Music study seems redundant," says the skeptic. "In this mediascape, I can find all I need, so why push me into music I don't need? And, why should I learn to perform it when there is little reason for me to make my own music anymore?"

We should address this issue because it is common for people to say to musicians something like, "I can't sing a note, but I love music anyway." There are many explanations for this negative and unnecessary claim, but it ultimately relieves the speaker of musical responsibility. Many of these people cite negative events during music study as the cause of that effect.

Finally, people at a young age tend to have very stabilized tastes for music they like and eventually support financially, through media purchases or direct support individual freedom supports personal choice in matters like music. The reasoning goes: "To know what I like, and I like what I know, so what gives you the right to challenge that? What gives schools the right to select music for me or my child? Why should other people create a list of music officially supported by public policy through government agencies such as schools?"

Can We Answer the Skeptics?

The skeptic's questions are not easy to answer well. The simplest response to all of them is that virtually everyone is drawn to music of some kind. Music is complex enough to reward lifelong study, and people tend to return to behavior that is reinforced. Music that rewards attention over one's lifetime requires study, and study improves the range and subtlety of meanings we can derive from musical experiences. The skeptic comes back: "But there is much in life that is interesting, complex, and rewarding; we don't study many of these things as deliberately as you think people should study music." Converting a virtue like meaningful music into a necessity in public policy is as difficult to explain intellectually and politically as it is agreeable socially and personally. Music study is easy to defend but hard to rationalize.

Another simple response is that universal, conscious study of music springs from traditional European-American values, and the function of public education is to indoctrinate the young with those values. Proponents of this view often say, "We should not question such important traditions. They have served us well, and they continue to produce a healthy variety and an unending flow of new music to hear, to perform, and to enhance the events and rituals in which we participate." Does this leave too little room for the empowerment of the individual? Do we socialize music study too much, and is this problematic in a society that values and even depends upon individual creativity?

Now that the arts are part of the education core, not only in *Goals 2000* but also in most states' education policies, we have some quick work to do. Music education and education in the other arts are in competition for funds and policymakers' attention during the rapid development of high-stakes, standards-based graduation examinations in so-called basic subjects. School administrators attend workshops on how to motivate teachers to raise standards, usually understood to mean that test scores in reading or mathematics, and so on, should go up. They are hearing the policy assertion, "If it isn't among the graduation tests, it doesn't belong in the school." Alas, many are listening. Within the current generation of school leaders' lifetimes, business and industry visionaries have created a management outlook that favors plans to "focus the organization," downsize, outsource optional services, and go to the bottom line for validation. This is not lost on school managers. People from business and industry are on school boards. For many of the school managers who are accountable to these people, the bottom line is test scores.

We must meet the skeptic's challenges and glib, obvious responses to them with new, better understandings of the effects and benefits of music study—psychological, educational, cultural, social, and (even) economic. We must also look ahead, to see if we can frame our deliberation of this challenging question in such a way that new questions can enter the professional debate and new understandings can contribute to the answers as they emerge.

The purpose of this document is to meet these social and cultural conditions with some extended, research-informed thinking about music study. We will confront some of the thorniest issues related to the topic and develop reasoned answers to some of the most difficult questions asked of us. Although oriented to the learner, this paper will also envision stronger rationales for planned, sequential music study and better music teaching practice for the coming generation. At the beginning of each section below, there are some questions that guided the writing. At the end of the paper, I've summarized the complex ideas that form the six-part answer to the question "Why study music?"

II. MUSIC STUDY: THE ISSUES

When One "Studies Music," What Does One Do?

We learn all the time merely by living our lives. This is *incidental learning*, and it occurs in most of life's situations; our environments, including the people around us, shape the ways we approach other, less familiar, environments. Humans *study*, on the other hand, with the assumption that they are capable of shaping themselves in some predictable way—intentionally and mindfully to broaden the experience upon which they live in the future or to deepen it, usually both. Study is deliberate, planned learning. The distinction is in the planning, predicting, and goal setting, not in the results. We learn a great deal of unplanned content through incidental learning. Planning not only allows us to guide our learning, but also gives us the potential to accelerate our learning processes, to learn more quickly and efficiently.

In this paper, *study* refers to what individuals do to learn deliberately, in self-guided musical growth as well as in "formal" and "informal" settings for study, in and out of schools. The orientation of this paper is the person because, regardless of the setting, it is the person who learns; this paper attempts to describe the process "from the inside out." Learning is always personal; one does not learn for someone else. This is true in study as well as in incidental learning. But a person can learn something in order to guide the learning of others—a common occurrence, in music teaching as well as in music making.[1] Regardless of what one does with what one has learned, learning is an individual process and, as we shall see below, study is the way we deliberately change ourselves. Learning is the necessary condition and foundational assumption of study.

When someone studies music, she or he intentionally engages music and music-related materials and ideas to reconstruct and improve some of the skills, knowledge, evaluative insights, and cognitive capacities used in musical experiences. The learner then arrives at new encounters with music as a changed person, more capable than before. Study, then, consists of actions designed to produce personal learning. Incidental learning lacks the focused intentionality of study. Because this paper's principal audience consists of music teachers in educational institutions, much will be said about schooling. However, a proper understanding of musical study ignores barriers between the sources of learning; the reader should not assume that the setting for music study is confined to or focused primarily on schools.

Four Interactive and Overlapping Types of Change Occur in Music Study.

Cognitive capacity: Study depends upon a person's capacity to construct and recall information, but cognitive capacity is not confined to this. With music, the source of the information disappears after the sound dies away, but we are equipped to deal with this well. Perception is the neurophysiological process that both enables and is shaped by cognition. But, perception is not a passive process. We construct what we perceive, and our prior experience shapes what we notice about a situation. cognitive capacity expands when we do this. With mindful, alert repetition, we notice more; our experience becomes richer. As an ever-expanding result of music study, then, there should be noticeable increases in the amount of information one can construct during a musical experience. Alas, we cannot yet measure this capacity directly. Intuition is perhaps the most closely related indicator of human cognitive capacity, and music study increases the range and improves the validity of one's musical intuitions.

Repeated experience and intuition can also be limiting if we become comfortable with their current state, for such comfort is the foundation of bias. Since perception is an active process and shapes what we notice, it takes some effort to keep expanding one's perceptual field with new musical experience so that mere habit or, worse, boredom does not result from repeated experience with music. Not only does study depend on expanded perceptual capacity, but the effort to expand it pays off in richer information, better intuition, and greater cognitive capacities.

Evaluative insight: Everybody has experiences that repel, attract, or leave them unmoved. Expanding our cognitive capacities, chiefly through repetition with the same or similar experiences, leaves us with the sense that some of these experiences are better than others, even though they might be similar in general. Five performances of the same music vary enough that our inclination is to rank them, or at least rate their effectiveness. Rarely are they equivalent.

Through music study, there should be noticeable increases in the personal development and use of criteria related to musical and human value. These can be noted and shared through one's estimates of goodness or fit between musical events and human capacities, needs and wants. The person, through music study, should explore the potential and actual results of musical actions at deeper and deeper levels of subtlety and import.

Knowledge: This much-maligned term always needs to be defined in analytical contexts. I will use the term to mean analytical abilities and the precision of the terms that support them. In this context, knowledge includes things such as musical terminology, analytical strategies and principles, even "rules" for tone production. Knowledge has been gained when there are observable increases in the precision, communicability, and usefulness (really, *validity*) of terms, strategies, and principles; and an improved speed and accuracy in recalling such things. One can increasingly use memory as a reliable source of schemes useful in analysis.

Sharing musical experiences when the causes for them (the musical situations) have disappeared requires language and many other symbol systems, even conductors' gestures. As our musical experiences grow in variety and complexity, and as we communicate with each other about them, the validity of the terms, strategies, and principles about music becomes tested against that of others.

Skills: I will use a narrow definition of the term *skills.* In this analysis the term skill is not analogous to more inclusive or general uses of the term, such as expertise, or (as used in schools) *library skills,* or *writing skills.* Expertise involves more than psychomotor or manipulative abilities.

Here are some analogous terms used in educational and psychological writing and discussions: techniques, psychomotor learning, manipulative abilities, executive functions, or execution. These terms mean about the same thing as skill, and it would not be necessary here to analyze the variations. Skill is an important result of music study.

Expanding or increasing one's musical skills results in changes in human characteristics useful for musical purposes. These include characteristics such as strength, accuracy, predictability, endurance, flexibility, control, and speed in one's use of a musical instrument, including the human voice, as well as computers and any other means of producing sounds used in music.

At its best, music study occurs during and through authentic participation in music. In this way, then, music study differs little from practical music making and listening. Skilled music teachers, however, design musical settings that create a patterned, efficient, sequenced, and thorough development of musical abilities in learners. To the student, learning music and doing music differ little. The pedagogical process that is promoted here is similar in general to good teaching in mathematics, social studies, or language arts instruction; i.e., the instructional and learning strategies have an authentic quality. However, musical experience is not equivalent to these others. It is unique and important. Bennett Reimer's paper develops the idea that musical knowing is not only different from mathematical knowing and the rest, but also equals their importance to living a human life well.

Does Music Study Add Up to Anything?

The best reason to study music is that it gives people a reliable, thorough, and efficient way of becoming expert at creating, communicating, and deriving meaning musically in the world of humans. Musical expertise "matures"—becomes embodied—when a person naturally and effectively mobilizes his or her best musical resources in musical situations without prodding from someone else. It is important to understand that this need not be institutionally related to age.

As noted above, however, it is too common for people in the United States to abandon active music making or excuse away their nonparticipation. A major cause for this is that many musicians have made a wall out of expertise, and some have set themselves up as gatekeepers. We must now lead people to define expertise dynamically and personally, not as some sort of barrier to a musical life. The gap between school music and what I call "life music" can be narrowed by redefining expertise as an action one initiates mindfully that synergizes one's skills, knowledge, evaluative insight, and cognitive capacities in practical, authentic musical situations.

There is no need to certify expertise any more than we do now, but there is a need to help people to diagnose their musical expertise and motivate them to expand it. National and state standards help music teachers to identify and diagnose some aspects of musical expertise, but standards should not be used to "evaluate musicianship." Musicianship is much broader, more fluid, more varied in its expression among people than any list of competencies suggests. This does not negate the value of standards. Music teachers can learn how to use standards diagnostically, and use these diagnoses with other data to support their critical leadership function in the musical and educational health of our society. [2]

The distinction between an *expert* and a *novice*, in music or in anything else, cannot be based on the identification of a threshold that separates people. The terms novice and expert merely represent ends of a continuum that can be abstracted from life when we bring our learning to bear on a problem. We find ourselves somewhere along the novice/expert continuum in just about everything we do. *Musical expertise*, then, is the term I will use to refer to a characteristic of all persons that represents the aim of music study—the embodiment of musical skills, knowledge, evaluative insight, and cognitive capacities, coupled with the capacity to self-diagnose them, to expand them effectively and efficiently, and to use them synergistically in musical situations of all kinds.

Most people have musical profiles that describe their levels of expertise in the several "components" identified by whatever assessment of expertise is being used. Such assessments, by definition, limit the diagnosis of expertise to the components designed into the assessment tools. All such tools are like stencils, letting information flow only through whatever "windows" were put there.

Moreover, people expect reports of the results of the assessment. In K–12 music performance assessment, it is common to locate six levels on the novice/expert continuum, generally defined by the artistic difficulty of a large body of musical literature. Music performance competitions and other third-person evaluations produce ratings or rankings. When required to do so, music teachers give grades.

There are other grounds for a diagnosis of musical expertise than musical difficulty. Based on a series of studies in England and other countries, Keith Swanwick and his associates described an eight-level diagnostic scheme for assessing expertise in music composition, performance, and listening, the synergy of which Swanwick calls musical knowledge or musical understanding.[3] David Elliott suggested a five-component orientation to analyzing musicianship and assessing musical growth.

There is still another view. Thomas Regelski sees musical expertise as a life process undefined by stages or types, but defined instead by the person living and participating musically in his or her world.[4] *Expertise* is a term not applicable in this formulation, except as each person becomes interested in defining it; and one does not "study music" in the sense normally used to refer to the deliberate development of one's skills, knowledge, evaluative insight, and cognitive capacities in relative isolation from each other. Rather, notes Regelski, "In music, then, this comprehensive, functional, and basically tacit 'know how' is what is called artistry, functional musicianship, musicality, virtuosity, or creativity—usually all are implied" (p. 47).

Such *know how* develops naturally through action. Levels of know-how can be described at any given point. However, descriptions vary with the person, the assessment instrument, the level of know-how, and the musical task of the moment.

An important distinction arises here between assessing musical expertise diagnostically and evaluating it against some standard described in advance, regardless whether such standards were defined by others or by oneself. Doing curriculum or making predictions about levels of expertise depends upon some generalized view of how humans study and learn music. Programmatic (or even curricular) efficiency comes from grouping people with similar know how together, predicting how the diagnosis might go at various stages or making some other accommodation to diversity among developmental profiles. The term *efficiency* again rises to the surface.[5] Programmatic efficiency, however, is a weak personal motivator at best.

Unfortunately, the discussion of various musicianship patterns of growth above slights the personal nature of music study. People test their expertise in ways unique to their musical interests. Personal motivation and study are intertwined, of course. When a person confronts a musical situation that is interesting enough to motivate attention and, at the same time, is challenging or disturbing, baffling, too difficult to manage easily, and so on, one studies. The person is not likely to be motivated to study if he or she does not value a better outcome enough to do what it takes to meet the difficulty with better personal tools—to determine a way to make things better and to learn how to do it.

People challenged in this way attempt to analyze the difficulty in order to focus the learning, to make the learning efficient as well as effective. The most lasting and liberating motivations come from within the musical situation. As a result of the analysis of the musical difficulty, one forms plans, gathers materials, and takes action, usually to change one's current profile of skills, knowledge, standards of quality (evaluative insight) and what one notices (cognitive capacities). One studies. Then, people enter (create) the musical situation again mindfully, aware of an improved capacity to have the musical benefits at a higher level. The person diagnoses and assesses learning, a marker of expertise.

In incidental learning, all of this happens intuitively and often instantaneously, without much deliberation. We can thank our pedagogues, philosophers, and psychologists for the current state of our ability to slow the process down enough to find out how it can be improved. To the learner, however, in music study or not, musical curiosity is a natural motivator: "What would happen if I . . . ?" Curiosity, as well as our growth as people, motivates music study. What we valued and sought to experience as children no longer satisfies when we are older because we have changed as people. Music rewards study because there is always music to meet the needs of persons of any age or stage in life. Music teachers should intervene in this process only if they can make it better.

What Happens to the Learner during and after Music Study?

By now, nearly everyone interested in children has heard of the "Mozart Effect" and the findings from research that support it.[6] Symposiums,[7] books, recordings, workshops, governors' gifts to new mothers, and convention sessions are devoted to its promise. It is good that musical behavior and its human effects are being seriously studied by psychologists and neurologists, and, as Clifford K. Madsen told the American Music Therapy Association in 1998, "We hope that further investigation confirms these preliminary investigations."[8] All music teachers share that hope. Bennett Reimer (most recently, 1999) and his philosophical predecessors such as Charles Leonhard, Harry Broudy, and James Mursell argue for a music-based rationale for music study, rather than a justification based on extramusical benefits. This, also, is a value that music teachers share. These are not competing values if we are clear what we mean by the term music.

Because music is fascinatingly complex, its study is rewarded, but research into music learning mechanisms moves slowly. This is becoming apparent not only in music but in other disciplines. Although researchers have increasingly better equipment and better research designs, work in music research is still in its early stages, and it will take time for definitive answers to musically human questions to emerge. Teachers and policymakers must stay in touch with such research and put what is learned into the musical and educational perspectives arising from their professional situations.

The distinction between incidental learning and deliberate musical study is important in such research. Above, I asserted that music study involves planned increases in musical skill, knowledge, evaluative insight, and cognitive capacities. Incidental learning—learning by participating in the musical traditions in one's life-space—may result in these increases, but such things are seldom planned. For research, assessment tools must be sensitive to one or the other. Studies of music achievement most often test the efficacy of teaching-learning procedures. Incidental learning can complicate the conclusions if it is not "controlled for" in some way. Conversely, studies of incidental learning are seldom "uncontaminated by" deliberate attempts of subjects to grow musically.

However, for general assessment purposes in music education, it is increasingly important that assessment instruments be sensitive to both. That is, music teachers must base instructional plans on what people actually know and can do in music, not on what the teacher thinks she or he taught them. Once a clear diagnosis of the student's musical characteristics is made, the teacher can determine how to guide further musical studies.

This paper is about music study, but we must continually emphasize that planned music study and incidental music learning accumulate and support each other in the development of musical expertise. Some hypotheses about music study are supportable:

- The ability to organize acoustic events into patterns (construct schemata, derive meaning from sound) grows with music study.
- Learning time compresses with skilled management of the learning process as well as with age and experience. That is, learning how to learn improves naturally, but teachers can accelerate the process even more.

- Music study, used as a contingency, ". . . is an effective reinforcer for academic behaviors like math [*sic*] or verbal learning, as well as social behaviors like attentiveness."[9]

Newer theories of human functioning integrate factors that once were separated. For example, mind and brain are no longer seen as separate entities, studied by putting one or the other in the foreground. Subject and object (subjective "vs." objective) are no longer viable divisions of reality. Even the right brain-left brain metaphors have lost their power to organize our thinking about how we use our capacities. Mental processes (mind) are no longer separated from physical processes (body) since their synergy is a much more powerful way of thinking about human beings. The nature-nurture question is no longer asked seriously; we now know "it's both." In general, the "or" and the "versus" are disappearing from the way we explore human ecology. Things are not either this or that; they are "both," in some form of integration. Moreover, theories of music are emerging that view music as a unique and liberating form of embodiment.[10]

When researchers looked at musical behavior in these integrative, "both-and" ways, they found some interesting things.

- More of the brain is engaged during musical experiences than during rest or linguistic communication.[11] Musical participation, including listening, seems to arouse other brain functions, such as spatial reasoning, attention, and perception. Music can, as a result, carry other information, such as the letters of the alphabet, the steps to a dance, the procedures in an industrial assembly line, the brand names of manufactured products in jingles, and the place names in popular songs.
- There are more developmental patterns in music besides the changing voice and certain kinds of music aptitude.[12] Composition and improvisation, listening abilities, and the ways musical performance is integrated with the rest of one's life also exhibit developmental patterns.[13]

Music study, then, changes people.[14] It expands the brain's electro-chemical activity in the presence of music and since the brain is an active part of perception, and because perception and cognition are integrated processes, what one notices in music expands. Our understanding of the extent to which this affects other human functions is increasing, and there are few simple answers.[15]

The following are some ways that music study can support various abilities useful to the student in reaching several important educational goals:[16] analyzing documents, analyzing performances and other actions, brainstorming, classifying, comparing and contrasting, creating a product, decision-making, defining context, developing and applying craftsmanship, develop-

ing personal commitment, discovering/generating patterns, evaluating, se-
quencing, synthesizing, valuing uniqueness and diversity.

As a result of our growing knowledge, we have a more thorough appreciation of the complexity of our capacity to make sense out of our world. This
is liberating because unwarranted beliefs lead more often to division between
people than to understanding, tolerance, and collaboration. Music study and
learning provide independent, personal, expanded ways to experience life.
This is empowering because, with study, we are each able to construct an
acoustical environment that includes an ever-expanding store of personally
meaningful music, rather than an environment limited by the musical taste of
other people.

III. PERSONAL EMPOWERMENT—SOCIAL COMPLICATIONS

There are ethical problems with the personal-power argument for music
study, however. If we turn for guidance to tolerance and understanding,
rather than to competition and dominance, we soon realize that in the personal-power argument we are setting up a scenario in which we are "reacting"
against others who are, themselves, merely exercising their rights to create
personal musical environments. Musical space is as important for others as it
is for ourselves. We devalue other people's interest in expanding their cognitive capacities, evaluative insights, knowledge, and skill in music at the risk
of losing their tolerance for ours. We must learn to value musical commitment in ourselves and in others. A music study program that motivates musical expansion and personal choice accompanied by tolerance and creativity
produces diversity of the richest kind.

What Personal and Social Benefits Are Unique to Music Study?

Personal motivations for music study do not explain what we know about
musical life, however. If personal music cognition were all there were to the
phenomenon, few traditions would emerge and we could not explain the
power of music to become treasured and to unify whole societies. Music
study, then, includes not only our own meaning making but also a study of
the meanings that others find and create in their music. Patterns emerge and
habits form from this, usually through incidental learning. As Howard Gardner points out about learning to read:

> By the age of third grade almost every kid in America can read. . . . The
> question is Why don't kids read? The answer is because their parents don't
> read, and that includes many teachers. . . . So, kids are going to like music and
> be involved in it if their families and the people around them are involved in
> music. [17]

If music is learned through living, then, what about schooling? Is institution-alized music study—school music—merely a neo-liberal attempt to wrest control of students' musical lives away from their families and friends, and shape their preferences for them "for their own good"? After all, guiding the music learning of others requires that the guide, not the learner, make deci-sions about musical experiences, and these decisions are based on the de-fendable and well-considered belief that the musical experience selected for the learner was appropriate.

Is there a personal corollary to this; If we insist on our personal preroga-tives, isn't that enough? Why study music that lies outside of the music found meaningful by our family, our friends, and ourselves? The short answer is not a liberal one, but a libertarian one: We should reserve the right to exercise musical options, even when these options seem to compete with the collec-tive taste. And, we cannot exercise options that we do not know are there. We should also reserve the option not to exercise our independence but to con-nect musically with a social group. This, too, is a natural process, but some seek belonging through music systematically. Poignantly, many teenagers go to extremes to learn the dances and purchase the recordings and videos that some desired group of their peers finds fashionable, whether or not they are personally meaningful as music to the teenager. People make sacrifices of money, time, and personal freedom for the purpose of belonging, and music is part of this picture. This is familiar to anyone who joins a religious or spiritual group, school, club, or organization that uses music in its rituals. Expanded to whole societies, belonging through music is the reason we teach children in America our repertoire of songs. We should continue this process, but that is not all.

E Pluribus Unum

Partially to promote community, we plan music study for others not only so that their musical experience is similar—so that they have the option of belonging through music—but also so that their musical options increase beyond those easily available in their personal surroundings. Music study contributes to what some call the *ecology of schooling*, or the complex "land-scape" that the school presents to learners. Unity and diversity are both important parts of this landscape in compulsory schooling, and music makes both unity and diversity audible in ways that language does not. Planned well, music study can uniquely give reinforcement to the many person-group relationships that the school is designed to build. If competition is held up as the primary motivator for music study, unity and diversity are lost. Competi-tion reinforces conformity. Conformity is not the same as unity, and diversity is seldom valued in musical competition. Unity, on the other hand, is an important quality, felt rather than directed, and music can be part of it. There is not a good English word for the German word *gemütlich*, the good quality of community that people experience during events that promote unity rather than conformity.

In the ecology of schooling there is much use made of competition. The same students who study music compete in other arenas of their school lives, and, to be sure, there are competitions in music. On the whole, for most students, however, the competition values of these other school experiences are set aside in good music study. The emphasis is on creativity and sharing knowledge, insight, and skill. Out of the diverse contributions of musical students in a good music program comes an especially vibrant unity that reinforces their certainty of belonging, and this certainty increases their tolerance for diversity.

Music study, then, models an *ecological* approach to schooling through its infinite variety of worthy traditions and its real-time integration of process with product, a feature common to all music. Physical knowing (skill) in music contributes to and is supported by other forms of knowing in good musical practice. Through music study, however, we learn to separate the forms of knowing from each other, to improve on them, and then to re-integrate the result in a musical whole again. In this way, music study is a metaphor for the ways of knowing found scattered and largely separate throughout the student's day.

Not only in the social sense, then, but also in the curricular sense, diversity of ways of knowing and varieties of creative contributions become unity in music study. *E pluribus unum.*

Why Should All People in the United States Study Music?

No society lasts for long that fails to maintain a complex and diverse culture and neglects to use it in the general education of its young. The value that we call "free speech" lies at the core of America's strength, and we interpret this now to include all forms of symbolic expression, artistic behavior, and communication. Though this value protects disturbing expression, sometimes, it also permits an open flow of insights. People who sense that change is needed communicate something about their views. Music and the other arts participate in this "landscape of insight." People who are in touch with this landscape, but whose feelings aren't so well formed, can sense when someone else is expressing similar needs. There is communion. Sensitive people can connect, participate, reject, revise, communicate, and advance the insight for themselves and others. They can avoid the feeling of being alone with their inchoate perceptions.

This cultural process and the exercise of free expression are critical to the health of our society. The larger, industrialized twentieth-century societies that attempted to control and limit their people's cultural resources by the

censorship, repression, and politicization of music, the other arts, and religion have collapsed.

However much people often express regret that "things aren't as they
used to be" in today's musical participation, we must recognize that culture—music—remains stagnant at the risk of losing its meaning and importance as a social and cultural resource. In fact, school music programs should
emphasize musical change and personal creativity. Doing so will go further
to strengthen our society and preserve the importance of music in schools
than the mindless preservation of bygone skills and repertoires.

Preservation need not be mindless. Our heritage contains monuments of
human thought that some call the canon of western civilization, a cultural
store that is deemed valuable enough that it ought to be preserved by teaching. Through music study, students gain access to the musical minds of
geniuses such as Bach, Mozart, and Beethoven. If music teachers emphasize
musical processes that challenge all students to share their musical
thoughts—including their musical recreations of the masterworks—through
their skills, knowledge and evaluative insights, then music study, even study
of the masters, can have a new, stronger focus.

There is an important view that schools should transmit the complex mix
of values that define the cultures within our borders, including those values
reflected in their musics. At the same time, we expect schools to deliberately
model and teach social conventions such as waiting in line, staying to the
right, neatness, punctuality, "walk, don't run," polite speech, personal space,
empathy for someone hurt, patriotism, individual contributions to group outcomes, and many more. If part of the school's function is to promote a civil
society, then these are laudable habits for children to form, whether or not
they know why they are forming them. Perhaps music programs reflect a
mindless approach to learning social conventions when they emphasize technique over critical insight in learning to perform the musical canon. For
example, reinforcing correct, accurate performance and ensemble conformity
and discipline at the expense of musical insight, or emphasizing slick public
performance as the principal focus of music study for all children may reflect
the broader "school values" listed earlier in this paragraph. Alas, in doing so,
such programs model for children a disdain for valued musical actions that
go beyond correct, prepared performance. Lost are the social and personal
values growing out of improvisation, composition and revision, experimenta-
tion with musical ideas, and pushing the envelope of one's cognitive and
perceptual capacities through music. People who promote correctness and
uniformity are disturbed that students can challenge social conventions
through the arts. To people disturbed by the authentic music produced by
students—much of it exploratory—individual expression is not what these
school values and social conventions support. There are good, practical rea-

sons and functions for social conventions; teaching social conventions mindlessly miseducates children on such points.

Musical actions are metaphors of this problem, and music study helps children and young people negotiate the issues that arise from it. Through a good music program, one that emphasizes both individual and group accomplishment, both personal insight and recreative skill, all students can grow in that special value that supports our group preservation of individual "free speech" or, in its more contemporary formulation, "freedom of expression." Music study requires and reinforces individual action that alternatively creates and recreates, expresses and replicates. People who study music for extended periods learn how and when to be themselves and when to be a good group member.

This encourages children to form the dual habit of individual expression and group accomplishment. These interact. Neither trumps the other in our culture. All should study music because there are few other places in their early life experiences where personal sensitivity and contributions to the group are in such consistent, close, and powerful synergy.

At its best, then, music study is both an individual and a communal process. There are many valued musicians (people call them "self-taught") whose study is largely one of individual exploration not only to increase their skills, but also to increase their knowledge of other musicians whose music making they admire. Individual taste guides their study, and some of these musicians contribute significantly to the musical monuments of our culture. Indeed, all active musicians, regardless of the external sources of their expertise, contribute to the society's "landscape of insight" to which I referred earlier.

Far from denigrating the contributions of self-taught musicians, our society values these models and marvels at them. It is instructive that they are held up against the kind of "musical training" that stereotypes many school programs. The fact that self-taught musicians are contrasted with institution taught musicians should be a warning that music education institutions are losing credibility to the degree that individual musical impulses of children are subjugated to some mistaken notion of group values. We must know more than we do about the music learning strategies of self-taught musicians and bring such strategies into our pedagogy rather than reject them. After all, once we leave "formal" instructional settings, we become self-taught. Musical expertise is oriented to self-guided musical study and music making.

For these and other reasons explored here, all persons should study music in a program that challenges both individual musical initiative and communal (group) achievement. In this way, the cultural value that marks our special brand of individual/group integration is modeled for children and practiced by them, and is therefore preserved in the schools.

Should Every Person Travel a Similar Music-Study Path?

Music is ubiquitous, and it is part of being human. Being identified with our culture through music study requires that we start any episode of study wherever we "are" musically. Teachers who intervene in this process can take the student from there to levels of musical expertise that provide lifelong avenues for individual growth. Music teachers can provide efficient learning of the essentials of the music currently being created and used, and thereby help individuals to compress the time it takes to act effectively on their musical impulses. Building multiple paths to reaching a mature, self-generated expansion of musical expertise is critical if all are to contribute, and the corollary values of respect, tolerance, and empathy for others' insights are built by sensitive teachers along the way.

If music study is to be efficient and effective both for the person and for the group, then there is a path. There are music-study patterns that the profession has found effective. The "content" of music study can be outlined as it is below,[18] and there are sequences for study within the various parts of the outline that the profession has found efficacious.

Elements of Music Learning That Are Common to All Paths:

Tonal development

- deliberately produce and discriminate pitch changes
- derive meaning from pitch/loudness/timbre
- create and decode notation for pitch/loudness/timbre

Rhythmic development

- maintain and respond to steady beat
- derive meaning from rhythm
- create and decode notation for rhythm

Interpretive/expressive development

- compose and improvise meaningful music
- derive meaning from gestures of conductors, performers
- gain insight from multiple musics
- evaluate musical validity of compositions and performances by self and others
- move musically (dance)

Process

- experience music
- practice for mastery and enjoyment
- orient skill increases to tonal, rhythmic, and expressive expertise
- analyze, evaluate, and produce music
- study music's many social, cultural, ethnic contexts
- find and use multiple sources and settings for musical learning
- recognize and use varied instructional sources

The music teacher will be able to guide and accelerate learning for the twenty-first century by emphasizing the following characteristics of teachers: motivator, facilitator, diagnostician, critic, evaluator, organizer, questioner, researcher, scholar, and (most important) active musician. The teacher's contribution to music study is to accelerate and guide learning. The teacher's musical expertise gives guidance to students, and the teacher's pedagogical expertise accelerates their learning.

IV. PUBLIC MUSICAL HEALTH

What Is the Likely Future Relationship between Professional Music Teaching and Music Study?

Although space does not permit a full exploration of the issue here, there is a research base supporting pedagogical training.[19] Such preparation professionalizes intuitive music teachers by making their instruction deliberate and better adapted to the diverse needs of the entire population, including those who are uniquely motivated to study music. Learning for all becomes accelerated and more efficient. Teachers converse about pedagogy, and there is efficiency in any specialized professional vocabulary. In pedagogical communication, common goals emerge along with shared strategies for reaching them. New knowledge of learning processes employs deliberate alternatives to the skills-dominated methods of intuitive learners, "self-taught" musicians.

What would music in society be like in 2020 if all music instruction programs were closed tomorrow, from kindergarten through graduate school? Would people still study music? Would America be better off? What are the unique functions of professional music teachers? How do sources for incidental music learning such as mass media or the Internet contribute to music study? How do these differ in their contributions to the "musical health" of our society?

Of course music study would continue if music schools and music in public schools disappeared. What replaces them would be an idiosyncratic mix of parallel musical universes that mirror the many categories of expertise and interest that cover our landscape now, from religious sects to motorcycle clubs.

The argument against musical eclecticism as a public policy is that we risk our society's cultural and social health by leaving music to the entertainment industry. As I have said elsewhere[20]

> If education is in trouble at the systemic level . . . then we must immediately begin to draw folks into action in large numbers or risk—what? Perhaps, we risk abandoning music education to some cultural processes that represent disturbing futures:
> . . . to cultural processes such as the mass media that demand too little of general education,
> . . . to cultural processes such as advertising that convince people to buy musical products that diminish rather than expand human musical potential,
> . . . to cultural processes such as many government leaders' political interests that push us back to a tribal, xenophobic approach to musical living, when the information age moves us in just the opposite direction, and
> . . . to cultural processes such as retailing and commercial broadcasting that indoctrinate us with the commercial view: that musical insights should be no deeper than one's childhood appetites and no wider than the personal borders of one's convenient lifespace.

Music teachers can meet these challenges by adopting what might be called a "public health" approach to their work. That is, K–12 music teachers, especially classroom music teachers, are in professional contact with the entire population. In addition to the expertise that the teacher provides directly to students, he or she has the tools and should have the motivation to discover and evaluate the community's musical resources. Music teachers, more than any other occupational group in music, have the professional expertise and the opportunity to equip both future citizens and whole communities for liberating, powerful musical lives.

How Can the Institutionalization Process of Music Study Be Strengthened in Our Society?

The public policy justification for music study revolves around only a few basic questions, some of which were addressed above. One that remains is: At what developmental point should music study become deliberate and professionally guided?

Music study for infants, a policy in parts of northern Europe, and practiced informally in families everywhere, is becoming increasingly institutionalized in America. The "Mozart Effect" has given new impetus to infant and toddler music education, and we have long known that sound imprinting occurs before birth.

Music teachers know professionally that an early start in music has life-long benefits not only to musical growth, but also to general functioning. This and the growing body of music research accumulates to suggest that we adopt a "public musical health" perspective, where music teachers engage not only K–12 students but others—parents of infants, to name one group—as part of the work.[21]

Today, there are literally hundreds of well-written publications that promote music education. In spite of this, we are asking "Why study music?" This is evidence that we sense some gaps.

What is missing are ways to document the overriding importance of the individual- social musical process, and to de-emphasize the current focus upon various kinds of products, whether stated as "testable" outcomes, music performed in public, or changed brains. We need to find ways to convince others in the world outside our profession of the essential benefits of the process of music learning, investing them with enthusiasm for "walking the path" of music study.

As a whole profession, we must redefine instructional efficiency in terms of musical health, individual and societal, before we can be better advocates for our collective pedagogical insights and expertise. To do this effectively, we must remove the "either-or" formulation from our professional arguments. There is weak logic in an argument that forces choices—either the person or the society; either performer or listener; either producer or consumer; either curricular or extracurricular; either pop music or classical music. People whom we must persuade to our cause do not recognize these dichotomies as important. Music is "both-and," and our collective advocacy must be inclusive.

So, Why Study Music? What Does Music Study Do for Us as Persons and as a People?

Music study contributes uniquely both to the general and specialized education of people.

1. People create, communicate, and derive unique meanings from music. Musical actions are open-ended constructions. They arise from people's sense of meaningfulness. It takes study to broaden and deepen our ability to use music along with other ways to communicate our insights with and among people.
2. In music making, *product* is uniquely and intimately related to *process*. In both small units of musical behavior and large, the process of making music contains immediate and constant feedback, sets the foundation and generative impulse for subsequent actions, and rein-

forces both individual and communal actions by setting up musical products as problems or hypotheses rather than as ends in themselves.

3. Music study empowers all people. Music making of a high degree of insight and complexity is possible with a wide range of materials. Resources needed for music making are readily accessible, and deep musical experiences can evolve from free resources. The human voice and environmental materials afford primary means for making music, and study helps people to learn how.

4. Music study results in, depends upon, and rewards personal excellence. Music making puts craftsmanship in the foreground at every level of expertise. Expanding and growing skillfulness occupies a natural and prominent place in all degrees of musical complexity. In music making, evaluation is clear and public, and the standards are both personal and sociocultural. Music study and music making are unique person-group settings for personal growth.

5. In spite of the public nature of music making, musical goals and the means to reach them are ultimately personal. Reaching musical goals confirms personal efficacy as it rewards disciplined action, sometimes over long periods of time. For all students, music study affords an expanded means of personal efficacy. For some people, music study is a crucial, primary pathway to personal development. Music study rewards self-discipline in a uniquely integrated experience of process with product and a uniquely powerful synergy of being with belonging.

6. Part of compulsory education's purpose is to promulgate cultural values, promote community, integrate people with society largely through cultural and social means, reduce isolation, and promote an advanced tolerance for diversity. Music study integrates these purposes in single actions. Good music study requires people to learn several important musical traditions, to engage the masters of these traditions, and to embody the means and the motivation to contribute to our culture's future by giving effectively to its present.

If there is a "bottom line" to all of this, we study music to give us as persons a reliable, thorough, and efficient way of becoming expert at creating, communicating, and deriving meaning musically in our human world. Musical expertise "matures" when we take charge of our own music learning program. We deliberately expand the range of musical experiences, and naturally and effectively mobilize our best musical resources in musical situations of a wide variety. The professional task for music teachers is to stay learner-centered, nurturing this human process until it flowers in a society full of musically expert people.

NOTES

My thanks go to the people who contributed to the foundations of this paper: The Commission—Ed Calle, Jennifer Davidson, Jack Heller, Daniel Scheuerer, David Shrader, and Larry Williams; and others who reacted to earlier drafts—especially, Mary E. Bickel, Paul Lehman, Michael Mark, and Thomas Regelski. Although the writing and the responsibility for the viewpoint are mine, their contributions were critical to whatever success this document has.

1. In this paper, "music making" means music performance, composition, and improvisation. "Musicing," as used by Elliott (1994), and "Musicking" by Small (1998), include also dancing and listening. For a further discussion of this issue, see Gates (1991).

2. Paul Lehman's chapter in this publication expands on the issue of teaching toward the Standards.

3. See Swanwick (1991, 1994), Swanwick and Franca (1999), and Swanwick and Tillman (1986).

4. Regelski uses the term "praxis" for this way of seeing musicality. Praxis generally means "mindful action" or action based on judgment. As Regelski puts it (Spring 1998, p. 32): "Praxis, in this view, amounts to theory, judgment, wisdom, and knowledge put into action by and as a rational phronesis of 'good' or 'right results' for particular circumstances." Action, of course, suggests a contribution of skill; otherwise, the results Regelski describes would happen accidentally. However, musical technique building, in the praxial view, occurs in the process of doing music ". . . for particular circumstances . . ." not developed in the abstract, isolated from music making with the implication that one is building skills that someday one might find useful. Praxially built skills are applicable to future music making but are not abstracted from it in "scale studies" or "technic-builders." That said, where weak skills block musical expression, the learner diagnoses this and attacks the problem, perhaps with help from others; but he or she does so intentionally, with a musical application in mind. He or she studies. The term phronesis refers to the application of judgment through the options that occur naturally and become guiding in a mindful act before, during and after the action. See also Regelski (Fall 1998).

5. Smith (1997) challenged the relevance of most available music research to our understanding of novices. He found that most "music science" used musical experts, rather than novices, as the point of reference in the rationales, and he proposes new directions, including a re-examination of such beliefs as octave equivalence.

6. For a brief summary of the current intelligence/music rationale, see Gromko and Poorman (1998). See also Rauscher (1997).

7. Two recent symposiums are the Ithaca Conference'96: Music as Intelligence (Brummet, 1997) and The 1999 Charles Fowler Colloquium—Enlightened Advocacy: Implications of Research for Arts Education Policy and Practice (16–17 April 1999, at the University of Maryland, College Park).

8. Clifford K. Madsen, personal correspondence, 9 April 1999.

9. Abeles, Hoffer, and Klotman (1994, p. 262). Here, they are summarizing findings from Madsen, Greer, and Madsen (1975), and Madsen and Prickett (1987).

10. Wayne Bowman, Lucy Green (1997), and Eleanor Stubley are among those developing newer theories of musical embodiment, taking musical experience and human functionality to new levels of integration.

11. Studies in support of this use technologies that include neural mapping, brain chemistry studies, blood flow studies, using PET, MRI, EEG, CAT, etc. See Hodges (1996), ch. 7, for a solid overview. Both Hellmuth Petsche and John Holahan and their collaborators have published various studies using such technology, as have Donald Hodges and others in the Institute for Music Research (IMR) at the University of Texas, San Antonio. Michael Wagner also works in this arena.

12. See Gordon (1987) and Walters and Taggart (1989) for definitions and accounts of what Edwin Gordon calls developmental music aptitude.

13. See Swanwick (1991, 1994), Swanwick and Tillman (1986), and Swanwick and Franca (1999) for crosscultural research in music composition and listening development. See Green (1997) and Kemp (1996) for thorough explorations of musicians' personalities in Western music's "schooled" traditions. Alas, few psychological studies of this scope are available in the "unschooled" tradition, but see Keil and Feld (1994) for what will prove to be a groundbreaking ethnographic and social psychological analysis of vernacular musical behavior.

14. See Howard Gardner's discussion of how this works in Brummett (1997, pp. 1–30).

15. See Searle (1994) for a good analysis of the brain-mind issue and Dissanayake (1988, 1992) for applications of genetics to the arts.

16. Thanks go to Jennifer Davidson for suggesting and contributing most of this list.

17. See Brummett (1997, p. 21).

18. See *National Standards for Music Education* (Consortium of National Arts Education Associations, 1994; and Music Educators National Conference, 1996) for more detailed lists. See also chapters in this book by Paul Lehman and Cornelia Yarbrough.

19. See Colwell (1992).

20. Gates (1998).

21. John Feierabend, Donna Brink Fox, Edwin Gordon, Lili Levinowitz, and other leaders in the practice of working with infants have developed teaching procedures based on their own research and experience, continuing a practice that builds on pioneering work by such people as Donald Pond and Robert Petzold.

SELECTED BIBLIOGRAPHY AND REFERENCES

Note: The books and articles selected here are among many of relevance to the topic, and this list is by no means exhaustive. It represents an attempt to connect the science of music learning and teaching with the belief systems of music in the Western tradition. In addition to the books, there are many excellent journal reports of research exploring a manageable number of experimental variables in music learning. The items listed here were selected from music research journals since 1992 if the primary purpose was (a) to review or critique current or recent research in music learning, or (b) to provide an extended treatment of music learning processes or developmental stages. For journal articles, the year 1992 was selected to extend rather than replace the most recent critical reviews of this literature in Colwell (1992) and Hodges (1996).

Abeles, Harold F., Charles R. Hoffer, and Robert H. Klotman. *Foundations of Music Education.* 2nd ed. New York: Schirmer Books, 1994.

Brummett, Verna, ed. *Ithaca Conference '96 Music as Intelligence: A Source Book.* Ithaca, NY: Ithaca College, 1997.

Colwell, Richard, ed. *Handbook of Research on Music Teaching and Learning.* New York: Schirmer Books, 1992.

Consortium of National Arts Education Associations. *National Standards for Arts Education.* Reston, VA: Music Educators National Conference, 1994.

Demorest, Steven M. "Sightsinging in the Secondary Choral Ensemble: A Review of the Research." *Bulletin of the Council for Research in Music Education* 137 (Summer 1998): 1–15.

Dissanayake, Ellen. *What Is Art For?* Seattle, WA: University of Washington Press, 1988.

———. *Homo Aestheticus: Where Art Comes from and Why.* New York: The Free Press, 1992.

Dowling, W. Jay, and Dane L. Harwood. *Music Cognition.* Orlando, FL: Academic Press, 1986.

Elliott, David. *Music Matters.* New York: Schirmer Books, 1994. Fiske, Harold E. *Music and Mind.* Lewiston, NY: Mellen Books, 1990.

———. *Music Cognition and Aesthetic Attitudes.* Lewiston, NY: Mellen Books, 1993.

Gates, J. Terry. "Music Participation: Theory, Research and Policy." *Bulletin of the Council for Research in Music Education* 109 (Summer 1991): 1–36.

———. "International Theorizing in Music Education: The MayDay Group and Its Agenda." Presented at the International Society for Music Education, Pretoria, South Africa, 25 July 1998. (For the text, see http://members.aol.com/jtgates/maydaygroup/ on the page titled The MayDay Group Agenda.)

Gordon, Edwin E. *The Nature, Description, Measurement and Evaluation of Music Aptitudes.* Chicago: G.I.A. Publications, 1987.

Green, Lucy. *Music, Gender, Education.* Cambridge: Cambridge University Press, 1997.

Gromko, Joyce Eastlund, and Allison Smith Poorman. "The Effect of Music Training on Preschoolers' Spatial-Temporal Task Performance," *Journal of Research in Music Education* 46, no. 2 (Summer 1998): 173–81.

Hargreaves, David J., and Adrian C. North, eds. *The Social Psychology of Music.* Oxford: Oxford University Press, 1997.

Hennion, Antoine. *Comment la Musique Vient aux Enfants: Une Anthropologie de L'Enseignement Musical.* Paris: Anthropos, 1988.

Hodges, Donald A., ed. *Handbook of Music Psychology.* 2nd ed. San Antonio, TX: The University of Texas at San Antonio, 1996.

Keil, Charles, and Steven Feld. *Music Grooves.* Chicago: University of Chicago, 1994. Kemp, Anthony E. *The Musical Temperament: Psychology and Personality of Musicians.* Oxford: Oxford University Press, 1996.

Kjelland, James M., Jody L. Kerchner, and Marian T. Dura, eds. "The Effects of Music Performance Participation on the Music Listening Experience: A Review of Literature." *Bulletin of the Council for Research in Music Education* 136 (Spring 1998): 1–55.

Krumhansl, Carol L. *Cognitive Foundations of Musical Pitch.* New York: Oxford University Press, 1990.

Madsen, Clifford K., R. D. Greer, and Charles H. Madsen. *Research in Music Behavior.* New York: Teachers College, 1975.

Madsen, Clifford K., and Carol A. Prickett, eds. *Applications of Research in Music Behavior.* Tuscaloosa, AL: University of Alabama Press, 1987.

Music Educators National Conference. *Performance Standards for Music: Strategies and Benchmarks for Assessing Progress toward the National Standards, Grades PreK–12.* Reston, VA: Music Educators National Conference, 1996.

Rauscher, Frances H. "A Cognitive Basis for the Facilitation of Spatial-Temporal Cognition through Music Instruction." In *Ithaca Conference '96—Music as Intelligence: A Sourcebook,* edited by Verna Brummett, 31–44. Ithaca, NY: Ithaca College, 1997.

Regelski, Thomas A. "The Aristotelian Bases of Praxis for Music and Music Education as Praxis." *Philosophy of Music Education Review* 6 (Spring 1998): 22–59.

———. "Schooling for Musical Praxis." *Canadian Music Educator* 40, no. 1 (Fall 1998).

Reimer, Bennett. "Facing the Risks of the 'Mozart Effect.'" *Music Educators Journal* 86, no. 1 (July 1999): 37–43.

Searle, John R. *The Rediscovery of the Mind.* Cambridge, MA: Massachusetts Institute of Technology, 1994.

Small, Christopher. *Musicking: The Meanings of Performing and Listening.* Hanover, NH: University Presses of New England, 1998.

Smith, J. David. "The Place of Musical Novices in Music Science." *Music Perception* 14 (Spring 1997): 227–62.

Swanwick, Keith. "Further Research on the Musical Developmental Sequence." *Psychology of Music* 19 (1991): 22–32.

———. *Musical Knowledge: Intuition, Analysis and Music Education.* London: Routledge, 1994.

Swanwick, Keith, and Cecilia C. Franca. "Composing, Performing and Audience Listening as Indicators of Musical Understanding." *British Journal of Music Education* 16 (1999): 5–19.

Swanwick, Keith, and June Tillman. "The Sequence of Musical Development: A Study of Children's Composition." *British Journal of Music Education* 3 (1986): 305–339.

Walters, Darryl L., and Cynthia Crump Taggart, eds. *Readings in Music Learning Theory.* Chicago: G.I.A. Publications, 1989.

Wilson, Edward O. *On Human Nature.* Cambridge, MA: Harvard University Press, 1972.

Woodford, Paul G., ed. *Critical Thinking in Music: Theory and Practice.* London, Ontario, Canada: The University of Western Ontario, 1998.

Chapter Five

Response to J. Terry Gates' "Why Study Music?"

Samuel Hope

*Samuel Hope is executive director of the
National Association of Schools of Music.*

It is particularly challenging to respond to a comprehensive and thoughtful paper in a few words. Professor Gates, supported by his commission members, has provided us with what the French call "a tour of the horizon." What a grand intellectual tour it is, taking us from the inner processes of music itself to broad contextual issues to various heights of scholarly perspective. There are contrasts, often poignant, between assertions of the committed and the skepticism of bystanders and critics. Many of the problems of educating for culture in a free market democracy are considered. The paper is written with precision. It argues with poise. It reflects a deep understanding of multiple perceptions about the question of its title.

Given all of these attributes, what is a responder to do? To reinforce certain points does not move us beyond or even into questions raised by the paper itself. To quibble over nuances of interpretation is not worth our time. Instead, I want to respond by emphasizing yet another perspective, one included in Professor Gates' paper but not the center of its broader purpose. By responding in this way, I hope to provide this symposium with two kinds of answers to the question of "Why Study Music?" One is a comprehensive analysis; the other, a simple response. One is a policy investigation; the other, a primal answer. Both are needed if we are to advance the cause of music study.

There are many ways of organizing the structure of knowledge. Let me mention two. The first is to consider the basic functions of major modes of thought and action. The function of science is to tell us how the world works, the function of history is to tell us what happened, the function of philosophy is to tell us what things mean, and the function of art is to make new things or to make old things new. These modes of thought and action are present in every discipline, no matter what category. However, in gaining a basic education, it is more effective to learn these modes by acquiring the basics of the core disciplines of science, history, and art, and at the appropriate developmental stage, philosophy. Elementary and secondary students study science as science, history as history, art as art, in order to gain basic information and to understand how these basic modes of thought and action work. Music is one of the core disciplines in the arts category.

Another set of organizers describes the way that human beings communicate with each other. Beyond touch, taste, and smell, I can think of five: letters and words, numbers and associated symbols, still images, moving images, and abstract sound. When we put letters and words together, we have language. When we put numbers and symbols together, we have mathematics. When we work to create still images, we produce the work in the fine arts, architecture, and design. When we work with the moving image, we produce dance and film. When we work with abstract sound, we create music.

We can conclude from these two series that music is worth studying because it is a core exemplar of one of the four basic modes of thought and action, and because in itself, it is one of the five basic ways that human beings communicate with each other.

What could be more fundamental than that? Music is a basic way of knowing and doing because of its own nature and because of the relationship of that nature to the human mind and intellect.

Beyond the fact that music is hardwired into our basic mental, emotional, and intellectual equipment, the pursuit of music through study begins to produce many other things beyond an understanding of its fundamental uniqueness. As Professor Gates' paper includes and indicates, there are many lists of these benefits. But everyone here who has studied to create or perform music for a long time, knows that such study teaches things that nothing else teaches. Take organization, for example. Many kinds of study teach us about organization or how to organize. However, nothing but music study teaches us about organization in terms of abstract sound. Organization in sound comes out differently than organization with words; it requires a different thought process, a different technique. The Romeo and Juliet of Tchaikovsky is not the Romeo and Juliet of Shakespeare. Neither creating them, presenting them, or receiving them is the same. The different thing about music study is its use of the material of sound rather than other material, and all that this implies for developmental learning. When we are working in the studio, or in rehearsal, or in analysis, struggling to make sound make sense, we are connecting a fundamental mode of thought with a basic means of communication using knowledge, intellect, and physical skill. We are solving sound design problems. We are doing something unique. This is what Professor Gates is talking about when he suggests that the product and the process are one. These connections are made from the simplest levels of capacity to the most complex. At the summits of achievement, these connections produce incredible intellectual and emotional results. As is true in all disciplines, these high achievements confirm music's fundamental position, its revelatory powers, and its place in basic education.

Without question, we live in a context that can be explained from many perspectives. We can consider and argue politically, economically, sociologically, promotionally, and so forth, but none of these perspectives produce a note of music. Virtually none of us are music professionals, because at some time in our past, we made a sociological analysis, much less an economic or political one. At base, we are musicians and teachers of music because our own study has taught us something so valuable that we can do nothing else with our lives except try to pass that value and that opportunity on to others. Our culture regularly invites everyone to feel guilty and walk away from hard focused work and great achievement, to reject that which we don't enjoy immediately. Our policy future on behalf of music study needs to reject these invitations. We must ask and answer the question "Why Study Music?" not because we don't have the answers, or even an understanding of other people's answers, but because so many other people don't have the answer, or don't want to hear it, people who make decisions that affect us and our mission of substance. Some want to use the power of music but not give others access to this power. Others want to use music or arts education purely for political, economic, or other purposes. There are hundreds of nonsubstantive agendas.

We satisfy these agendas at the peril of our cause and our professional lives and honor. We will never answer all of the skeptics. Despite all evidence, we in the arts will never convince everyone that intellectual work can be pursued through the still image, the moving image, and sound, as well as it can be pursued through words and numbers. But no matter what anyone says, no matter what anyone funds, no matter what anyone does, the facts of nature, the facts of history, and the facts derived from our own experience reveal fundamental truths about music and its position as a human basic in terms of brain, mind, and heart. As such, everyone who is to be educated must have an introduction to the world of communication, thought, and achievement that is music. Study is the only way to gain a fundamental understanding of this world. Music is no different in this regard than any of the other basic modes of thought and action or means of communication. If we are wise, we will render unto politics that which is political; to economics, that which is financial; to sociology, that which is sociological; to demographics, that which is demographic; to advocacy, that which is promotional; and to technology, that which is technical. However, in doing all of these things, we will never forget that the center of our purpose is to render unto music that which belongs to music.

And so, as we move forward with the great responsibility for music that we hold in trust for civilization, let not our knowledge of a problematic context, the admonitions of nay-sayers, or the manipulations of pundits and politicians destroy our faith. Rather, let us use our understanding of difficulties and arguments and opposing forces as the basis for strong tactical decisions that advance our grand strategy so that what we know to be true from thought, study, experience, and evidence can be brought into the lives of many, many others. How can music, among all the others things that it is, also be about learning? How can we help students to more of music? How can we build a bridge between what they know music to be and what music can do? How can we build a bridge from self-absorption to broad engagement? These have always been our great tasks. They are our great tasks now. The answer to our question for this hour is in music itself.

Chapter Six

How Can the Skills and Knowledge Called for in the National Standards Best Be Taught?

Commission Author: Paul Lehman

Paul R. Lehman is professor emeritus of music in the School of Music of the University of Michigan.

Commission Members:
William Anderson
Ronald Brandt
Kimberly Burns
Willie Hill
Will Schmid
Regina Zakrajsek

Response: Jane Walters

Music makes a difference in kids' lives. It exalts the human spirit. It enhances the quality of life. Since the 1930s it has been taught in almost every school in the nation. Although the quantity and quality of music instruction vary widely, generations of young people have learned a basic repertoire of music and have learned to understand and appreciate music in school. Many students have learned to sing and play instruments, sometimes at a very high level.

Still, the music program that was acceptable in the twentieth century will be inadequate in the twenty-first. Both the nature of society and its expectations for its schools are changing. This chapter will describe a vision for music education in the year 2020. It is not a prediction of what will happen but a summary of what educators should aim for.

Defining a music program for the future involves describing not only the curriculum but also the learners, the teaching staff, the preparation of teachers, and teaching materials and strategies. The expectations expressed here are intended to apply to all students and all schools. They are intended to ensure both equity and quality in music education. Although they may be unattainable in the short term, these expectations are appropriate for a democratic society and, with the necessary political will and public support, are in fact attainable eventually. The auxiliary verb "will" is used throughout rather than "should" to emphasize that this description represents a clear and distinct vision for the future and that these expectations are feasible. The expectations are intended to suggest opportunities and not rigidity or authoritarianism.

BACKGROUND

The program described here is based on the National Standards for Music Education[1] and on those state and local standards that are themselves based on the National Standards. These standards seek to ensure that the music curriculum in every school is grounded in high expectations and an optimal learning environment for all students. They reflect the best practices found in current schools. It is these practices that should provide the models for schools in 2020.

The National Standards for Arts Education,[2] which include the National Standards for Music Education, were published in 1994 by the Music Educators National Conference. Developed under the guidance of the National Committee for Standards in the Arts, they were designed to represent a national consensus of the views of organizations and individuals representing educators, parents, artists, professional associations in education and in the arts, public and private education institutions, philanthropic organizations, and leaders from government, business, and labor. The standards specify what every student should know and be able to do in music at the end of grades 4, 8, and 12. They provide a coherent vision of what it means to be educated in music; a foundation for building a balanced, comprehensive, and sequential curriculum in music; and specific assistance in improving the music program. They apply to every student through grade 8 and to every student enrolled in music beyond grade 8.

The National Standards include nine content standards in music:

1. Singing, alone and with others, a varied repertoire of music

2. Performing on instruments, alone and with others, a varied repertoire of music
3. Improvising melodies, variations, and accompaniments
4. Composing and arranging music within specified guidelines
5. Reading and notating music
6. Listening to, analyzing, and describing music
7. Evaluating music and music performances
8. Understanding relationships between music, the other arts, and disciplines outside the arts
9. Understanding music in relation to history and culture

The National Standards were intended as models for states and local districts, and almost every state has now developed standards, frameworks, or statements of expectations in the arts. Although the terminology may vary from state to state and year to year, the concept of standards, expressed as statements of what students should know and be able to do as a result of instruction, will likely continue to exert a strong and positive influence on education in the United States. The term "standards" in this chapter refers to whatever standards—national, state, or local—provide the basis for the music program in a particular state or school district.

Sarah, age 14, is beginning her first year at Kennedy High School. Since age 5 she has studied violin and played in school and community youth orchestras. As she enters her new high school, she is fascinated by the variety of small ensemble options that are part of the school's music program. In addition to playing violin in the high school orchestra, she will, at various points along the way, have the option of playing acoustic or electric violin in a mariachi ensemble, a small jazz combo, a string quartet, a rock group, a bluegrass band, a Cajun group, and a blues band. She also likes to sing and looks forward to using that talent either as a soloist or a backup singer in some of these groups. A year ago, when she was in the eighth grade, she had been thinking about dropping out of the music program, but after attending a concert at Kennedy she decided to continue because these options were just too attractive to pass up.

THE NATURE OF SOCIETY

The social conditions that can be expected to shape or influence education in 2020 are described in greater detail elsewhere in this publication. The following conditions are considered of particular relevance to this chapter:

1. The settings in which music instruction is delivered will be more numerous and more varied than ever before, including, for example, charter schools, home schools, for-profit schools, other alternative schools, and distance or distributed learning centers. There will be more opportunities within the community for both students and adults to make music and study music. There will be greater cooperation between schools and other community agencies in coordinating these offerings in order to increase the range of opportunities available and to broaden access to those offerings.

2. The demands placed on schools for improved and expanded services will exceed the availability of financial resources. There will continue to exist a serious mismatch between the expectations of both legislators and the public and their willingness to provide the necessary fiscal support. Because new responsibilities will continually be placed on schools while none are removed, it will become increasingly necessary for schools to set priorities, and the competition for resources will be intense.

3. Although the availability of technology may be uneven and inequitable, its role will be increasingly prominent in every aspect of education. Technology can make virtually unlimited quantities of information available to every student. The dramatic effect it will have on the delivery of instruction will parallel the effect it will have on the nature of music making.

4. There will be great emphasis on interactive and collaborative learning. Ways will be sought for students to work together on group projects to reflect the ways in which much work is accomplished in the adult world. The important contributions of music instruction to the skills and knowledge valued in business, industry, and the professions will be recognized and emphasized as valuable ancillary outcomes.

5. The student population will be more diverse than ever before in many respects, particularly in the ethnic and cultural backgrounds represented. Each of these groups will seek to ensure that its own cultural traditions, including its own music, have a place in the school curriculum. Schools will be recognized increasingly as microcosms of the society they serve.

Many of these conditions reflect external influences over which music educators will exercise relatively little control. All will affect the content and methodology of music teaching. Music educators must be prepared to meet these challenges and to take advantage of the opportunities they represent.

The teaching/learning process is a complex, interactive process heavily dependent on the context in which it occurs. Good schools require the understanding and support of all segments of society. Education is important to everyone because no other institution has more impact than the school on the economic, personal, and social well-being of our nation and its inhabitants.

Terrell, age 12, and his mother are selecting his course options for the seventh grade. Although he has always loved music, he didn't choose to begin the study of a band or orchestra instrument in the fifth grade, when the opportunity was offered in school. But now he has found several six-week music modules available in seventh grade that interest him very much. One option is Guitar. He has heard that the students in that class can learn to play both acoustic and electric guitars, and even electric basses. (A neighbor who took the class last year even started his own band with some other students.) Another interesting option is Computers and Music. Terrell had a taste of this in sixth grade and discovered that he could write his own songs and carry out cool multimedia projects. Another option is World Music Drumming. He tried drumming recently with a group at the Boys and Girls Club and did well enough that he was asked to play a solo over the other kids' rhythms. One of his girlfriends has studied African dance, and he hopes that she might take the course with him. Still another option is Keyboard. Terrell admires his church organist as well as some of the keyboard players he sees on TV. Last month a friend taught him how to play the bass line to "Heart and Soul." He thinks that he could learn to play with both hands, and he can picture himself as the center of attention at parties.

THE NATURE OF THE MUSIC PROGRAM

The program described here for 2020 will require many changes from typical current practice. Some of these changes can be undertaken by music educators acting individually or collectively. Others will require initiatives for which music educators must depend on other decision-makers. In every such case the need and rationale for change must be stated clearly and concisely. Music educators must participate actively in the public and professional forums in which education reform is debated, and they must act positively and constructively to preserve and enhance the opportunities for music learning available to the nation's youth.

Diana, age 8, loves to sing. When she was a baby, her parents sang to her every day. Later they taught her the songs and musical games they learned in their parenting classes. There was an electronic keyboard and a ukulele in their house, and she quickly learned to play her favorite songs on both instruments. Since she was three she has participated in various programs at the Sunrise Valley Child Care Center, where she has regular opportunities to sing, listen to music, and play instruments. People in the area have donated a variety of instruments to the center, and she has recently been teaching herself to play the xylophone with only a little help. When she was seven she enrolled for keyboard lessons with a woman who has a studio in her home. When Diana practices, her performances are uploaded automatically onto her personal Web page, which her parents, her piano teacher, and her school music teacher can access. She is sometimes surprised that her teachers and parents seem to know so much about what she is doing, and she occasionally longs for the "good old days" when, she has heard, parents and teachers didn't talk with each other nearly so much. The man from Keyboards R Us, where her family bought its keyboard, regularly sends her information about new music and new opportunities for learning music at the store and throughout the community.

The content of the music curriculum will reflect these principles:

Comprehensiveness

The goal for the year 2020 is that every school will offer a comprehensive, balanced, and sequential program of music instruction of high quality designed to achieve the standards and to meet the needs of students. The schedule will provide sufficient time and sufficient flexibility to ensure that every student has access to instruction in music. Students in the middle and high schools will have a wide array of opportunities in addition to band, orchestra, and chorus for participation in music. Although certain music courses may carry prerequisite requirements, access to some music instruction, including performance instruction, will be available to every student in every grade without prerequisites. Small ensembles, including mixed ensembles, ethnic ensembles, and popular music ensembles, will play an important role in the music program. All students will have access to a Web-based learning environment.

Every student will be able to express himself or herself through singing, playing instruments, improvising, and composing. Every student will be able to listen to music intelligently, critically, and knowledgeably, and to understand what is heard. Every student will be able to analyze and evaluate music and to move to music with fluency and ease. Aural skills will be emphasized. Every student will demonstrate an understanding of the relationships between music and the other arts, and between the arts and other disciplines. The best composers in each genre will be encouraged to write music for school use, and the distinction between classical, folk, and popular music will be increasingly blurred or eliminated. Every student will be able to learn new music independently, and every adult's life will be enriched by the skills and knowledge acquired in the study of music.

Every course in music, including performance courses, will include instruction in creating, performing, listening to, and analyzing music, in addition to focusing on its specific subject matter. The balance will depend on the nature of the course, but every course will include some instruction in each of these skills. The artificial dichotomy between performing and creating music will have largely broken down and the two functions will be seen as intimately related, as they were throughout most of music history.

Technology will alter in profound and irreversible ways the manner in which music is taught and learned, just as it has altered in profound and irreversible ways the roles that music plays in the lives of human beings. Computers, electronic keyboards, synthesizers, samplers, CD-ROMs, and other MIDI devices will enable every student to be actively involved in creating, performing, listening to, and analyzing music without necessarily mastering the traditional prerequisite skills. It is especially important that the media and technology used for teaching music in the school include the media and technology used to produce and experience music outside the school.

David, age 19, is a sophomore in music education at Reston State University. At last week's lesson he showed his trumpet professor his analysis of the Purcell Sonata for Trumpet, which he is preparing for a recital, and the professor offered a number of helpful comments. This week he asked his music history professor, who plays bass at a local supper club, to help him with the intricacies of the baroque ornamentation. Their conversation led to a stimulating comparison of baroque ornamentation with those used in jazz by legendary players such as Miles Davis. On the Internet David located some background information on the clarion trumpet, for which the Purcell piece was originally written, and he downloaded several period recordings of clarions, including one of the Bach Brandenburg Concerto no. 2. During his wind ensemble rehearsal yesterday the conductor pointed out that one of the contemporary pieces the group was working on is a concerto grosso, a form used by Bach in the Brandenburg Concerto he had just been listening to. David is finding that what he learns in one class can often help in other classes. He is interested in all kinds of music, and he is determined not to erect artificial barriers between the styles and genres of music in his professional life.

Diversity

Music education in 2020 will reflect the wide range of diversity that exists in the United States. The musical repertoire used in the schools will represent the broad spectrum of music cultures found across the nation and throughout the world. Curriculum planning will take into account the educational contributions of other institutions in the community including, for example, churches, private studios, professional organizations, commercial and for-profit institutions, youth groups, families, and self-instructional media.

Musicians and music institutions of the community will be utilized, when available, to enhance and strengthen the school music curriculum. Teachers, students, parents, studio teachers, community agencies, business leaders, and others will serve as partners in the teaching/learning process. Students in alternative schools, including home schools, will have the opportunity to acquire the skills and knowledge called for in the music standards. Students with disabilities and students with limited English proficiency will have the opportunity, to the fullest extent possible, to participate in music on the same basis as other students. Special programs and opportunities will be available to meet the needs of students who are talented in music.

Assessment

Implementing the standards will require meaningful assessment of the achievement of every student. Student assessment will reflect progress toward acquiring the skills and knowledge called for in the appropriate standards.[3] Assessment will support, enhance, and reinforce learning. Planned before rather than after instruction, it will be viewed by both students and teachers as an integral part of the learning process rather than an intrusion or an interruption of learning. Assessment will be based not on the skills and knowledge that are easiest to assess but rather on those that are most important for students to learn. It will be authentic in that it will be built around the essential nature of the skills and knowledge being assessed.

The assessment of musical skills and knowledge will be a cumulative process continuing throughout the student's career as a learner. Assessment will be broadly conceived, to include, for example, not only assessment by the teacher but also self-assessment, peer assessment, and multiple-teacher assessment. It will include small-group projects as well as individual work, and it will reflect process as well as product. Students will be aware of what they are expected to know, how they are to be assessed, and what criteria will be used to judge their achievement. This information will also be available to parents and other interested parties.

The New Curriculum

In summary, the curriculum to which music education should aspire by 2020 will differ from the traditional curriculum in several important ways, including the following:[4]

1. The curriculum will be conceived not as a collection of activities in which students engage but rather as a well-planned sequence of learning experiences leading to clearly defined skills and knowledge.
2. The music studied will reflect a broad range of genres, styles, and periods, including music from outside the art music tradition, music from the various cultural and ethnic groups that the United States comprises, and authentic examples from the various music cultures of the world.
3. Because of their fundamental importance in music learning, improvisation and composition will be an important part of the curriculum for every student.
4. Learning tasks will emphasize problem solving and higher-order thinking skills and will relate to the world of music as it is experienced outside the school.
5. Although music must maintain its integrity and be taught primarily for its own sake, there will be an emphasis on interdisciplinary relationships and upon the unique usefulness of music in providing a framework within which to teach a wide array of skills and knowledge, especially in language arts and social studies.
6. Electronic technology will be used to individualize and expand opportunities for music learning and to enable every student to be actively involved in creating, performing, listening to, and analyzing music.
7. Every school will develop reliable, valid, and usable techniques for assessing student learning based on explicit objectives derived from the skills and knowledge called for in the standards.

THE POPULATION OF LEARNERS

Music education will encompass learners of all ages from birth to death. Schools will become community-based agencies providing a wide variety of services, including music instruction, to persons of all ages. Music-making and music study will make a major contribution to the quality of life for every individual and every community.

Recognizing the critical importance of early childhood development, parents, caregivers, and teachers will provide an abundance of high-quality music experiences from infancy through the years of early childhood.[5] Every adult will have opportunities to acquire the skills and knowledge called for in the standards, if not acquired earlier, or to raise those skills and that knowledge to a higher level. New music offerings will be designed to meet the special needs of aging adults.

Preliminary research has shown that music instruction in the early years can have positive effects on the brain functioning of young children, particularly on their visual-spatial ability.[6] Recent studies suggest also that music-making by older adults can minimize the effects of aging and exert a significant positive effect on their health and well-being.[7]

These findings, if confirmed by further research, will have enormous impact in expanding the demand for music instruction beyond the traditional school-age population.

THE MUSIC TEACHING STAFF

Music educators in 2020 will need a broad repertoire of skills, knowledge, and experience. They will understand the developmental processes that their students are undergoing, and they will be skilled in diagnosing student needs in music and prescribing suitable instructional remedies. They will be prepared to design and participate fully in a comprehensive and balanced music program. They will themselves possess the skills and knowledge called for in the standards, together with the ability to teach those skills and that knowledge not only to school-age students but also to the very young and to adults, including older adults.

Teachers will be aware of the stylistic differences among the various genres and periods of music. They will be able to use media and technology to compose, notate, perform, and study music; and they will be skilled in planning instruction for students. They will be able to relate music to the larger concerns of society and to teach music in a cultural and historical context.

Maria, age 4, is enrolled in the preschool program at the Sunrise Valley Child Care Center, which she enjoys very much. She especially likes being able to sing and listen to music every day. She's enthusiastic about playing the recorder and the other instruments that are available to her. She doesn't get to see her grandparents often because they live more than 800 miles away, but she has gotten to know many of the older people who come regularly to the town's Adult Learning Center, where her father works. A group assembles once a week to sing together at the Adult Learning Center, which is near the Sunrise Valley Child Care Center and is managed by the same community agency. Maria likes very much to sing along with them. They know many songs she doesn't, but she's already learned quite a few of them. One of the ladies taught her a song about her cat, Don Gato. She especially enjoys listening to the New Horizons Band, which rehearses weekly at the Adult Learning Center, because they seem to enjoy what they are doing so much. She sings along as they play. She asks questions about the various instruments, and there's nearly always someone around who can answer her questions. She wants to learn to play as many instruments as she can.

Teachers will have a broad knowledge of assessment techniques and materials in order to select or create the most appropriate assessment strategies for each learning task, and they will be skilled in interpreting and utilizing assessment data for the purpose of improving learning. They will have access to tools that will enable them to assess where students fall along the continuum of achievement for each learning task. Various agencies, including, for example, professional organizations and representatives of the music products industry, will collaborate in the production of assessment materials.

The population of teachers will represent a broad diversity of ethnic and cultural backgrounds. Music educators' concern for diversity will include, for example, attention to differences in learning style, cultural or ethnic background, age, gender, emotional needs, physical needs, and family structure.

Regardless of his or her field of specialization, every music teacher will be able to teach courses open to students lacking the time, background, or interest to participate in the school's select performing groups. Because oral traditions and aural learning are key to most of the musical styles of the world, awareness of these traditions and facility in teaching them will be essential for music educators.

Preservice Teacher Education

Every prospective teacher will be expected to demonstrate not only the skills and knowledge called for in the standards, including skills and knowledge in improvisation and composition, but also the ability to teach those skills and that knowledge. Teacher education institutions will provide models for integrating composition, improvisation, performance, and analysis in their theory, history, studio, and ensemble classes.

The development of musical and personal flexibility is an important goal of preservice music teacher education. Accordingly, every prospective teacher will be expected to be able to perform in at least one performance tradition in addition to the European tradition, to develop skill in teaching students with diverse learning styles, and to be receptive to new repertoire and new musical styles that reflect changes in the music cultures of the United States and the world.

Inservice Professional Development

New and expanded opportunities for professional development for music educators will be increasingly necessary. Teachers will be expected to update their skills and knowledge on a regular basis to reflect changes in the philosophy and practice of music education. They will be expected to have knowledge of the current styles and genres of music that exist outside the school in order to select the best music from each genre, traditional or new, as appropriate, for use in the curriculum.

MATERIALS AND STRATEGIES FOR TEACHING MUSIC

It is obviously unrealistic to expect students to acquire skills and knowledge in music unless they are provided with adequate opportunities to learn. This means not only that qualified teachers and sufficient time to learn must be made available but also that the necessary instruments, materials, equipment, and facilities must be provided. Every school must offer a learning environment in which students have a reasonable opportunity to achieve the skills and knowledge called for in the standards.[8] In many schools this will require an increase in the time and resources allocated to music.

Teaching Materials

The Standards specify what students should know and be able to do, not the methodology or specific teaching materials to be employed. Those decisions are left to school districts and individual teachers. In any given setting some materials will be more effective than others in achieving the skills and knowledge outlined in the standards.

One of the most important principles in selecting teaching materials is that only materials of high quality will be used. All teaching materials selected must be among the best of their genre at that level of difficulty. For every genre, style, and historical period some works are of better quality than others, and, while knowledgeable persons may disagree about criteria, quality is always a basic consideration.

In selecting teaching materials for use in their classrooms and rehearsal halls in 2020, teachers will be guided by the following principles:

1. Materials will be developmentally appropriate for the students. The age, background, and experience of the students are important considerations in selecting teaching materials that will be effective.
2. Materials will be appropriate for the teaching strategy employed and for the instructional setting. Even the best materials may be ineffective when used with teaching strategies for which they are unsuited or in instructional settings where they do not fit.
3. Music repertoire will be varied with respect to genre, style, historical period, and cultural or ethnic origin. This variety is important in helping students to understand the broad and basic role that music plays in the lives of human beings and to realize that there are many different but equally valid forms of music expression.

4. Music repertoire will contain both elements that are familiar to the students and elements that are new and challenging. If there is nothing in the materials that relates to music with which the students are familiar, they will have difficulty understanding the materials and will be slow to accept them with enthusiasm, while if there is nothing new or challenging, the materials are probably of little educational value in that setting.

5. While the music repertoire selected must all be of good quality, the same criteria for selection need not be applied to every work. For example, some works may be chosen because they have withstood the test of time; some may be chosen because they are particularly useful in teaching technique or musicianship; some may be chosen because of their usefulness in teaching aspects of history, geography, sociology, languages, science, or other disciplines; and some may be chosen simply because they are especially appealing to students and audiences.

Teaching Strategies

Like teaching materials, teaching strategies must be developmentally appropriate and suited to both the instructional setting and the content being taught. They must be varied in recognition of the varied learning styles of individual students. Also, they must be sprinkled with new and imaginative practices on a regular basis in order to improve the teacher's effectiveness and to ensure the personal growth and development that lie at the root of professionalism in teaching.

These proposed guidelines are based on the fundamental premise that if teachers use good music, and if they teach it well, students are likely to be engaged and to learn. More important, they are likely to be motivated to continue to seek out and to learn music throughout their lives.

The year is 2020. Jennifer, age 46, her husband, Brian, 48, and their two children, Laura, 22, and Matthew, 17, all sing in the local Community Chorus cosponsored by the school district and the Adult Learning Center. The chorus, which meets one evening a week, has sung in shopping malls and retirement homes as well as on local access TV. Jennifer played flute in the band when she was in school. She takes pride in her large and expanding collection of CDs, which features folk music from around the world and which provides background music as she works at home in her part-time job designing Web sites. Brian attended a small school that offered little music, but he studied piano privately, he still plays jazz keyboard, and he enjoys listening to a local classical music station during his forty-minute commute to and from work. Laura had been away at college but returned to the area this year to teach first grade in a nearby community. While in high school she especially enjoyed her courses in Latin American music and music technology. She became very skilled in improvising on the wind controller, and a composition of hers received a superior rating at the state festival for high school composers sponsored by the state music educators association. In the undergraduate course in music methods she was required to take, she learned to use the guitar to accompany classroom singing, and she employs that skill to good effect with her first-graders. Matthew, a senior in high school, took minicourses in recorder ensemble and keyboard in middle school and is now taking a course in American popular music. Last year he took music theatre and managed to sing in the school musical while also playing in a citywide soccer league. Although Laura and Matthew have had many more opportunities than their parents to study music in school, music plays a very important role in the lives of the entire family. The Community Chorus provides an opportunity for them to participate in music together, and they are enjoying it enormously.

THE CHALLENGE

This chapter describes a music program for 2020 characterized by universal access to instruction, a comprehensive curriculum, an adequate learning environment, utilization of community resources, and continuous inservice teacher education.

The music program outlined in the standards and described further in this chapter can play an essential role in providing a rewarding and satisfying life for every man, woman, and child in the nation. It can truly enhance the quality of life for every individual—but only if it is implemented. Implementing this program will require the cooperation and support of all who value the arts and all who share a commitment to providing a high-quality education for every young person in the United States.

NOTES

1. Contained in *National Standards for Arts Education* (Reston, VA: Music Educators National Conference, 1994) and in The School Music Program: A New Vision (Reston, VA: Music Educators National Conference, 1994).

2. Consortium of National Arts Education Associations, *National Standards for Arts Education* (Reston, VA: Music Educators National Conference, 1994).

3. For suggestions, see *Performance Standards for Music: Strategies and Benchmarks for Assessing Progress toward the National Standards, Grades PreK–12* (Reston, VA: Music Educators National Conference, 1996).

4. For further information, see *The School Music Program: A New Vision*, 1–7.

5. Standards for music in prekindergarten (ages 2–4) are not included in the National Standards for Arts Education but are found in *The School Music Program: A New Vision*, 9–12.

6. See John W. Flohr, Daniel C. Miller, and Diane C. Persellin, "Recent Brain Research on Young Children," *Teaching Music* 6, no. 6 (June 1999): 41–43, 54.

7. Ted Tims, "The Impact of Music on Wellness," unpublished paper, conference on "Music Medicine: Enhancing Health Through Music," sponsored by the School of Medicine and School of Music, University of Miami, Miami, Florida, 23–24 April 1999. S. For further information see Opportunity-to-Learn Standards for Music Instruction: Grades PreK–12 (Reston, VA: Music Educators National Conference, 1994).

8. S. For further information see *Opportunity-to-Learn Standards for Music Instruction: Grades PreK–12* (Reston, VA: Music Educators National Conference, 1994).

Chapter Seven

Response to Paul Lehman's "How Can the Skills and Knowledge Called for in the National Standards Best Be Taught?"

Jane Walters

Jane Walters is executive director of Partners in Public Education and former Tennessee Commissioner of Education.

It is a great privilege to read all the papers that have been written for this symposium, but it is a particular privilege to respond to Paul Lehman's paper. In his paper Dr. Lehman lays out a very clear explanation for the history and the content of the National Standards as well as a vigorous defense for the implementation of both national standards and state and local standards. He also talks about the considerable attention that we need to give to training teachers and preparing them for the classrooms of 2020. All of us are aware of the value of original sources, so when we think about the beginning of the standards movement, it is very special to have with us the person who chaired the effort for the music educators. For the graduate students here, that is hard to beat!

When we talk about the nature of societal changes, there are many things that are reflected in this paper that we have seen in actual practice. One topic Lehman discusses is the idea of general music classes in secondary school. Since that was also a major thrust of the Housewright Symposium keynote speech by Libby Larsen, I wonder about the implications this has not only in the training of secondary school music teachers, but also in the spirit of what they believe about music. I come from a state where there was legislation passed in 1992 that requires a fine arts credit in high school for students on the college preparatory path. It has been in law now long enough for us to see the results of the requirement on enrollments in classes. The enrollments have increased noticeably in the visual arts, but the increase in music classes has been far less dramatic. If you ask the children why, they will tell you that they do not have to audition for visual art class. There seems to be a mind-set, at least with a great many young people, that in order to participate in music in high school, you have to be a special, "talented" youngster. You have to be the one who can perform, which students define in the formal sense. The present emphasis on performing groups in high school, which borders on obsession, gives us considerable food for thought if we are serious about music education for all children.

Another critical point in Lehman's paper is the number of choices in music classes that we will have in the next twenty to twenty-five years. One of the problems for schools in providing these choices is the increasing emphasis on smaller schools with more personal attention for students. Large high schools with several thousand students are often viewed as impersonal and unable to meet the needs of students in the next century.

If parents and communities continue to support the trend to smaller and more intimate school settings, it will be more and more difficult to offer the wide variety of music class choices Lehman envisions. Another trend that has mushroomed in the last ten years is the concept of home schooling. During my years as state Commissioner of Education in Tennessee, I saw personally the enrollment increase in home schools. One of the things that I found interesting was the role of community organizations in providing so-cial experiences for home schooled youngsters, particularly in music. In many areas where there is a relatively large percentage of home schoolers, there will be a church or community organization that establishes a program for these youngsters to participate together in music. They will form a choir, a band, or some other sort of performing group. Many times they are not the traditional groups that we have in many of our secondary schools. For exam-ple, I have not seen a single marching band of home schoolers. Maybe they miss having a football team to run through their halftime show; I am not sure! At any rate, they do perform; they set up small instrumental ensembles, small choir groups, anything in which they can get a reasonably cohesive group of youngsters to work together. Such groups give these children the socialization their parents are often looking for, as well as musical training and experience. Quite often church musicians include working with these groups as part of their job responsibilities.

This movement is having a real impact on what we do in schools, particu-larly in regard to certification of teachers. Many of these church musicians and private teachers do not have the traditional certification required of school music educators, yet many of them have excellent credentials in mu-sic as well as experience and training in working with students.

There are other issues in education that are providing challenges for traditional music education programs. Charter schools, for example, are providing parents with another choice for the education of their children. Technology, with classes available on the Internet, provides still another choice. While attending school on the Internet is not as widely accepted as either home schooling or charter schools, it is a choice that is just beginning to come into its own. The Virtual High School in Florida is a concept that will become increasingly popular everywhere. The enrollment in all of these alternatives to traditional schooling is growing exponentially, and the more choices parents and students have, the more different strategies we are going to have to develop to provide music education for youngsters. Only one thing is sure; none of these issues is going away. We have reared a generation that expects instant gratification. It is unreasonable to think that in a society in which you have become accustomed to a wide variety of choices, even in relatively insignificant things like selecting a pair of jeans with the "correct" brand name to sit on your fanny, you will be willing to give up choosing where your child goes to school. Choice is a big issue with all of us.

Another major issue discussed in Lehman's paper is that of teacher preparation and training. This issue has an impact on higher education institutions in two specific ways. The first is time. Everyone has a suggestion for improving teacher training, and almost every suggestion begins the same way: "Why don't we add . . . ?" The result is a "laundry list" of courses that could easily require five or more years to complete. When we view this pragmatically, we know that undergraduates are not going to spend six to seven years in training to take a job that pays a beginning salary of $30,000 a year, especially when the salary schedule tops out at $50,000 per year. Some young people are willing to begin a career at a relatively low salary if there is the potential for a much higher income as they gain additional training and experience. This is not the history of K–12 salary schedules.

The second problem is technology. Although technology has tremendous potential for allowing preservice and inservice teachers to obtain training from some of the leading experts in the country, and although they will be able to do so at a time they choose, that old devil time again rears its head. I was at a technology conference in Miami recently where they were discussing the wonderful possibilities for taking courses online. You could almost see the teachers' eyes glass over, thinking, "Oh great, now I can do inservice at 11:00 p.m. They have now made it possible for me to work twenty-four hours a day. I can hardly wait." We shall have to think very differently in the years to come about the way we structure teacher training in higher education. Some things are going to have to go away, and some of those things are "sacred cows." Many of our higher education institutions are not ready for their sacred cows to go away. Colleges and universities do not alter their form and organization easily, because their customs and modes of preparation are deeply ingrained. Worthy traditions, such as tenure and academic freedom, while having unquestionable value for institutions of higher learning, also can lead to the tradition of making a nest that time cannot penetrate.

One of the threads that runs throughout Lehman's paper is that of a multicultural approach to music education, which affects teacher training and curriculum, both in K–12 schools and higher education. As musicians, many of us think (as most people in the world do) that a good education is what we had. A good education therefore, reflects the kind of music we know and were taught, and which we expect to teach to our students. We will, therefore, continue to teach western European music to children who have never seen western Europe, who have no family that was ever in western Europe, and who believe they can live a full, rich life and never see western Europe. No one denies the contribution made to music by the western European tradition. Scarcely anyone would recommend eliminating the study of western European music from a comprehensive music curriculum. I think, however, we kid ourselves when we assume that a commitment to teaching quality music of other cultures in a meaningful way is supported by most schools and communities. One of the values that the National Council for Accreditation of Teacher Education (NCATE) subscribes to is that of multicultural education. I have had the experience of dealing with a barrage of letters asking if our state required NCATE membership of our higher education institutions. The reason for the letters was that the authors objected to the multicultural requirement. If you believe that multiculturalism is a war that has been won, I submit you are naive. It may have been won in a few communities, but we have a great many communities where the majority of the citizens do not even consider it an issue.

I was at the Tennessee Arts Academy not long ago, sitting in the back, and they were talking about different performances of "The Star-Spangled Banner." They played a tape of Whitney Houston singing it, and it was an impressive performance. I was dismayed to hear a teacher say, "Well you know, I am sorry, but that is not my 'Star Spangled Banner.'" That statement came from a teacher—a teacher who cared enough to come to an arts academy and spend a week. It was a music teacher. So if you think the multicultural war is over, and that it has been won, it has not even started. We give nods to it. We do the politically correct thing, but in our heart of hearts we often do not embrace the concept. This is an issue that we are going to have to make truly conscious efforts to deal with because everyone's music is important. Everyone's music contributes to who we are as a people. These are the kind of things that are going to be such challenges as we enter the next millennium. If we can solve some of these problems, it will make such a difference to our children.

Another issue in Lehman's paper is that of assessment. Today assessment often is decided in state legislatures. Legislatures love to pass what they can measure, and what does not cost too much! Many times when we talk to legislators about assessment, they think that we are talking about being able to prove who is doing a good job, instead of proving whether or not children are learning and in what ways they are learning, and how we can improve the areas in which they are not learning. The same thing is true when we talk about school reform. Often legislators and community officials are concerned about school districts as "jobs programs" for adults instead of education programs for children. Too often jobs in the education arena, particularly in K–12, are held hostage as political patronage. We still have school districts that put employment opportunities for relatives of elected officials ahead of the best interest of the children of the district. It happens regularly, not just in one state, but in communities in every state.

So these are the kinds of hard issues that we face when we talk about making things different in the new millennium, not only in music education, but also in all education. If we can learn to deal with choice, if we can learn to deal with each other as equals, accepting and understanding the joy of everyone's music, if we can learn to work with political organizations to put the child's welfare and education first, and if we can work with our professional organizations to make continuous improvement a reality, we are getting closer to the goals we are setting for 2020. We need to ask ourselves the hard questions about equity, excellence, and effectiveness.

These are the kinds of thoughtful questions that I think will take a prescription like Paul Lehman has written and make it possible for us to truly see a difference in music education. I hope so, because there is one thing we all know about music. There are times when you do something in music that you cannot explain and you can't tell why, but you know you have made a joyful noise. That is very special. It is our job to be sure that all children in 2020 have the kinds of instruction in music that allows them to experience that joy.

Chapter Eight

How Can All People Continue to Be Involved in Meaningful Music Participation?

Commission Author: Judith A. Jellison

Judith A. Jellison is the Mary D. Bold Regents Professor of Music at the University of Texas at Austin.

Commission Members:
Chelcy Bowles
James Byo
Richard Chronister
Craig Johnson
Anne Miller
Marvelene Moore

Response: Warrick L. Carter

INTRODUCTION

I was looking forward to an address by a nationally prominent politician who was known to music educators as a supporter and advocate for the arts. After he gave a few preliminary remarks praising the work of the thousands of music educators in attendance, it happened again. Never losing eye contact with his audience and in a strong voice, this polished, articulate, generous, intelligent speaker proudly admitted, "I was 'tone-deaf' in music classes . . . and still am . . . never played an instrument. But (voice growing louder) my wife sings . . . beautifully!" (applause).

Is there a problem? His wife sings beautifully and he supports the arts. But the tone of his voice, his lack of embarrassment, and the message he conveys is disturbing, particularly since this scene is not new. Wouldn't he and all the other men and women who "don't sing" (play an instrument, go to concerts, listen to classical music, etc.) really love to participate successfully in the music experiences that seem to bring so much joy to many of us? What happened to this man when he was an eager and intelligent young boy in school that led him to confidently declare himself a "tone-deaf" adult?

This paper is about learning. Moreover, it is about how *all* learners acquire music knowledge and skills through their school experiences and the impact of school music experiences on their adult musical lives. What music experiences are meaningful for school and adult life? Are there commonalties among meaningful music experiences in school and out of school? How can participation in meaningful music experiences in school transfer to adult life? How can all people continue to participate in meaningful music experiences?

This paper is also about all adults and all future adults (present children). I chose the language "adults and future adults" to blur the traditional separation between school and out-of-school contexts. Many of the salient characteristics of school and out-of-school contexts (physical and social setting, instruction and support provided by individuals, behavior of peers, and the inherent norms and expectations) are in fact different, but there exists an implicit assumption that school music programs provide students with the knowledge and skills that will enable them to participate successfully in a variety of meaningful music experiences in adult life. But many children do not choose to participate in the adult music experiences we may have intended for them.

What can we observe in adults' music knowledge, skills, and attitudes that are products of their school music experiences? Are adults living the musical lives we intended for them, and if not, how can we prepare future adults more successfully? How can we replace feelings of apathy or embarrassment among adults who are "not good at music" with skill, knowledge, and feelings of accomplishment and happiness? Consider these scenarios:

- Bill is a college economics major who loves music but admits that he has never gone to a classical concert because he just doesn't like to wear a tie and get dressed up. He has more than 150 CDs in his collection—mostly rock and country. He's considering buying keyboard but hasn't gotten around to it.
- Helen is a successful young professional woman who wishes she could still play her trumpet. She feels guilty that she hasn't given it to a beginning student. She just does not have the time to play and is afraid of the community band audition process. Sometimes when she is alone, she

plays her trumpet solo from *El salon Mexico*, and it brings back fond memories of her high school band performance at contest. She proudly remembers getting a "1."

* Carlos agrees that playing an instrument could be fun, but he never did because he just wasn't talented. If his young son shows any talent, he might suggest that he join band because he remembers that someone in their family owns a clarinet that isn't being used.

* Mary is 78 now and lives in a retirement community. Her school had a choir and a band; she's sorry she never participated. A friend suggested she join the Monday night recorder group. They take beginners. She'll try it, thinking that she surely could learn an instrument she heard her grand-daughter play, although admittedly the songs her granddaughter played were not that interesting. She wants to learn to play folks songs from her native country—some that she could play, and even sing, with her grand-daughter.

Music educators know these individuals—they are neighbors, relatives, or friends. We have experienced social situations when conversations turn to music, and friends or acquaintances comment, without concern and some-times quite proudly, that they know nothing about music and can't sing or play instruments. We have observed adults sing (or not sing) "Happy Birth-day" or "Auld Lang Syne," or play one of the parts for "Heart and Soul" on the piano. In these situations, we often make judgments about the music knowledge and skills of these adults and their previous experiences in school.

Some of the adults we know have rich musical lives, choosing from a variety of music experiences at different times throughout their lives. Other adults' music experiences may be limited but enjoyable (e.g., listening to popular music). What kinds of music experiences did most of these adults have in school? What did their school music experiences contribute to their lives as adults?

THE IMPACT OF SCHOOL ON ADULT LIFE

Simply put, education is intended to improve the quality of life. Music edu-cators recognize the importance of a quality school music program to the quality of musical life. Adults provide opportunities for us to evaluate the success of schools and our programs, since adults are, in a sense, artifacts of education past.[1]

Many factors outside of school may contribute to an adult's "musical characteristics," although schools and music educators traditionally have the primary responsibility for formal music education. The importance and im-pact of school experiences on the quality of the lives of future generations is a familiar and recurring theme in documents ranging from school districts' mission statements to documents produced and distributed by MENC—The National Association for Music Education.

Adult life in a post–industrial society was at the heart of the issues examined several decades ago at the Tanglewood Symposium. Participants in the symposium sought to "reappraise and evaluate basic assumptions about music in the 'educative' forces and institutions of our communities—the home, school, peer cultures, professional organizations, church, community groups, and communications media."[2] Although participants recognized the importance of collaboration among the many resources and educative forces of the communities, in the final analysis, the recommendations in the Tanglewood Declaration placed the primary responsibility for curricular and instructional changes with music educators and schools.[3]

In all probability, schools of the future, no matter how they are defined, will be the institutions charged with the responsibility of preparing students for adult life, and music will be a major part of life's preparation. In a current MENC document, music in adult life is identified as the ultimate goal for school music experiences. A statement in the introduction to the document *Opportunity-to-Learn Standards for Music Instruction: Grades PreK–12* reads: "While the opportunity-to-learn standards focus on the learning environment necessary to teach music, it is important to note that the ultimate objective of all standards, all school curriculums, and all school personnel is to help students to gain the broad skills and knowledge that will enable them to function effectively as adults and to contribute to society in today's world and tomorrow's."[4]

DECIDING WHAT'S MEANINGFUL

What are the broad skills and knowledge that will enable students "to function effectively as adults and to contribute to society in today's world and tomorrow's," and, what are the broad skills and knowledge that will enable students to participate in meaningful music experiences today in school and as adults in tomorrow's society? What are meaningful music experiences?

Music educators define many forms of music participation as meaningful (e.g., performing; composing and arranging; reading music; listening to, analyzing, describing, and evaluating music; describing and analyzing relationships between music and other arts; and describing and analyzing music in relation to history and culture). All of these experiences may be considered meaningful, but the wide range of possibilities requires that teachers make curricular and instructional choices and define priorities.

Meaningful music knowledge and skills may be decidedly more difficult to define and prioritize than meaningful life skills (e.g., literacy, economic sufficiency, independent living). When adults lack life skills (e.g., are unable to read), consequences can be severe. When adults lack music skills (e.g., unable to read music), consequences are rarely considered severe by society (even in the case of professional musicians). It is difficult for most adults to define particular music knowledge and skills as high priorities when there are few obvious negative consequences for lacking the knowledge and skills. On a regular basis we observe competent, successful adults who appear happy and who contribute to society and yet have few music skills and little music knowledge. We also encounter aficionados (adults and students) of popular music who are amateur performers, who attend concerts regularly, who are avid listeners (often listening from their own large collection of CDs of popular music), and who can, after only a few seconds of listening, identify and describe a popular piece of music and also give indepth biographical information about the composer and artist. In many cases, the skills and knowledge of these aficionados were not acquired in school. What is it then that we value for our students in school and their musical lives as adults?

This problem of defining and prioritizing meaningful music experiences becomes yet more difficult knowing that today's students will live most of their lives in the twenty-first century. Technological advances, changes in demographics, educational and medical research findings, issues of diversity, and socioeconomic factors can all impact decisions. Tanglewood participants struggled with similar issues in defining priorities for music education for a post-industrial society.

The most salient issues for Tanglewood and Vision 2020 appear to be redefinition and change, but important: issues also involve reaffirmation of values that have been and will continue to be at the core of music education. New knowledge and skills may be required for new forms of music participation in the future, although many broad experiences that are valued today will probably continue to be valued in the future (e.g., singing or playing expressively and technically accurately, performing for others and attending concerts of live performances of music, listening to exemplary works of music of a variety of genre or styles, music literacy, talking intelligently about music).

The professional judgment of the individual teacher to make curricular and instructional decisions is recognized in *The School Program: A New Vision*, a publication that was developed to serve as "a model of what the music program should comprise in terms of curriculum content and student learnings" and as a resource that "identifies those skills and knowledge that should be given the highest priority."[5] Although curricular values are clearly promoted throughout the content standards in *The School Program: A New Vision*, the preface clarifies that the "publication does not constitute a curriculum," that the "determination of the curriculum and the instructional activities designed to achieve the standards are the responsibility of states, local school districts, and individual teachers," and that the standards do not "free the teacher from making professional judgments."[6]

Throughout childhood, throughout school, parents and teachers are primarily responsible for many of the decisions involving a child's learning. With adulthood comes the independence and responsibility to make decisions—decisions about employment, place of residence, social network, recreation and leisure, and music. If the musical lives we intend for adults require specific skills and knowledge, and if the meaningful music participation we intend for adults requires their time and in some cases their money, then decisions must be made as to what is meaningful for both students and adults.

Certainly music participation by children and adults in our society is booming when it involves popular music. If other kinds of music participation are valued, if we want students to have a wider variety of choices outside of school now and in the future, then *transition* must become the guiding principle for curricular and instructional decisions. Transition, simply defined, is the movement of individuals across a variety of school and non-school environments throughout life. When adults participate comfortably, successfully, and as independently as possible in meaningful music experiences, those for which they were prepared in school, then the transition from school contexts to adult contexts in communities and homes is successful.

ASSESSMENT AND MEANINGFUL EXPERIENCES, SKILLS, AND KNOWLEDGE: LOOKING AT THE DATA

In the field of education, experiences, skills, and knowledge that are defined as meaningful frequently are assessed in order to evaluate whether what was taught was actually learned. National large-scale surveys of music participation, preferences, attitudes, and experiences, as well as assessments of students' skills and knowledge, provide some information to answer questions related to transition—whether individuals are participating in experiences that are valued by many music educators and whether students have learned particular skills and knowledge that may contribute to meaningful participation now and in the future. Surveys and assessments are naturally limited by their scope; however, in many cases, the experiences, skills, and knowledge measured in these assessments have been defined by many music educators as meaningful (e.g., listening to live and recorded performances of classical music, playing instruments, singing), thus making the data relevant to issues of transition.

Data from several studies on attitudes and music participation (primarily playing instruments) by adults and family members are reported in "American Attitudes towards Music 1997," an executive summary of a survey of 1,740 individuals aged 12 and older, conducted by the Gallup Organization on behalf of NAMM.[7] Since these surveys were intended to serve the music industry by providing information that could increase product sales, areas of study were primarily limited to attitudes and experiences related to instrumental music. Consider first the generally positive attitudes towards music, music making, and music education found in this report:

- A large proportion of individuals surveyed agree that music is a very important part of life (84%); that music is a good hobby (95%); that music brings the family together (82%); that music is a part of a well-rounded education (90%) and that the state should mandate music education in schools (70%).
- A large proportion of individuals surveyed agree that playing a musical instrument is fun (88%) and that playing a musical instrument provides lifelong enjoyment (96%).

Now consider these findings from the same report:

- The proportion of households with at least one person aged 5 or older who currently plays a musical instrument has declined from 1978 (51%) to 1997 (38%).
- Only 25% percent of the individuals over the age of 12 currently play some type of instrument, and 28% of the population over the age of 12 were former players.
- Of the total number of former players, 55% stopped playing before the age of 18, and 24% stopped before the age of 35. Of the total number who currently play, 33% are aged 15 to 17, 24% are aged 35 to 49, and 19% are aged 50 and older. Piano and guitar are played by larger proportions of children (ages 5 to 17) and adults than any other type of instrument.
- A large majority (84%) of people who play instruments or were former players first learned to play between the ages of 5 and 14. Most first learned to play a musical instrument at school (44%) or by taking private lessons (35%). Fifty-seven percent of the respondents aged 65 and older believe that they are too old to learn to play an instrument.
- Forty-one percent of all individuals agree that it isn't worthwhile to invest in an instrument unless the child has demonstrated some degree of musical talent (49% of nonplayer households, 37% of player households, and 36% of former player households).
- For all current or former players, 33% report that a parent encouraged them to begin to study an instrument, and 37% report they became interested on their own. Only 14% report they were encouraged by a teacher.

The reported positive attitudes about music along with a strong U.S. economy may, in part, be responsible for the positive outcomes seen in product sales (other than school instruments) for the music industry. The growth of the music industry can be followed in *Music USA*, a yearly publication that provides statistical data on shipments and sales of music products (e.g., instruments, acoustic pianos/keyboards, printed music, CDs).[8] The annual retail value of shipments is reported to have grown steadily since 1991 from 3.93 to "a whopping 6.10 billion dollars!"[9]

Although this generally positive report from the music industry may appear encouraging, consider the following data from *Music USA* showing how consumers are spending their money:[10]

- Several products show particularly strong growth (percussion, synthesizers, acoustic pianos, sound reinforcement), although in the school music market, more brass, woodwind, and stringed instruments were shipped than sold. Purchases of new instruments are said to be significantly affected by the level of rental returns and the number of used instruments on the market.[11]
- Although sales of recorded music have shown an increase from $7.8 billion in 1991 to $12.2 billion in 1997, shipments of classical recorded music to music companies and retailers represented only 3.2% of music shipments in 1991 and have continued to decrease across the period to 2.8% in 1997. Rock, country, urban contemporary, pop, and rap comprised 80% in 1991 and 78% in 1997.[12]

It appears that adults are not continuing to play the instruments they studied as students in school, and they are not listening to the classical music they may have heard in their music classrooms. The data also suggest that they are not attending concerts of classical music and opera, and comparisons of data from older and younger age cohorts show an increasing number of nonparticipants. Consider these findings from research

reports by Peterson and Sherkat[13] and Balfe and Meyersohn,[14] which appear in the National Endowment for the Arts document *Age and Arts Participation*:

- A comparison of each age cohort between 1982 and 1992 reveals a general decline in attendance at live performances of classical music.
- The major predictor of arts participation in 1992 was the respondent's level of education: in every age cohort, those with more education participate at higher rates. However, rank orders of participation for age groups (beginning with those born in 1936 to those born between the years 1966 and 1975) show a clear and disturbing decrease, none that is attributable to

education or income. Unlike older cohorts, there is no evidence that younger cohorts increased their participation as they matured.
• Many younger people are substituting alternative forms of arts participation (television, CDs, videotapes) for live arts participation.

The results for younger age cohorts are inconsistent among different types of arts participation. After discussing data showing high preferences among younger cohorts for a narrow range of popular music, Balfe and Meyersohn explain that these young adults "are reducing their participation in core art forms that compete most directly with the popular arts, given what is known of the constraints on their time and economic pressures. With increased sophistication of performances of most forms of popular music, as well as the general informality of their venues, it is no wonder that it is classical music, jazz, opera, musicals, and theater that have suffered the large declines among baby boomers and the younger Generation X, while ballet and art museums—both arts forms and venues having less competition from those of popular music—have enjoyed increases instead."[15]

The picture of increasing audiences for the performing arts is not encouraging for those who value adults' attendance at live performances of music other than popular music. It is even less encouraging looking across generations, considering that many of the adults who are nonparticipants will be or are new parents. Parental encouragement has been found to be one of the strongest influences on adults' interest in attending concerts.[16]

In the absence of data showing that adults are participating in experiences that are valued by many in music education, we cannot assume that parental encouragement of concert attendance, or any other meaningful music experience, is present in children's lives. For a large majority of children, teachers and school music programs may be the only influences that will affect the children's current and future interest in the variety of music experiences valued by music educators, and the only opportunities for them to acquire the skills, knowledge, and attitudes that lead to broadened choices concerning the music participation in their lives.

Students who are in school now will participate in future surveys of adult participation. Ideally, they are learning the skills and knowledge that will lead to their choosing to participate in a wide range of music experiences now and in their adult lives. Perhaps one of the most visible and current sources from which we can make some predictions for the musical behavior of future adults is contained in *The NAEP 1997 Arts Report Card*.[17] The purpose of the National Assessment of Educational Progress in the arts was to assess what eighth-grade students know and can do in three areas of music, visual arts, theatre, and dance: Creating, Performing, and Responding. Representative samples of public and nonpublic school students participated in the assessment.[18]

As with most educational research reports, the NAEP report includes cautions regarding interpretation of the data. Readers are to consider effects of other factors on the results (e.g., socioeconomic, education, composition of the student body in public and nonpublic schools, parents' education levels, and parental involvement). Also, the report identifies correlations between factors (e.g., specific scores and characteristics of school programs), and the standard cautions are given against causal interpretations. Even in light of these cautions, the generally low scores, particularly in the areas of creating and performing, are disconcerting. If the skills and knowledge that were assessed are those that represent broad areas valued by many in the music profession, then the results show a disparity between what we think we're teaching and what students are learning.

Average scores were low (Responding = 150 or below on a scale of 0–300; Creating = 34 on a scale of 0–100; Performing = 34 on a scale of 0–100). Performing scores were even low for the 16% of the students whose teachers asked them to play instruments every day (average score 53), and the 13% who were asked to sing every day (average score 40). Creating and Responding scores were also low for students who reported that teachers asked them to listen to music, write down music, or make up their own music almost every day. Only 18% of the students reported playing in a band, 3% playing in an orchestra, and 22% singing in a chorus. But even scores for students who participated in school ensembles were relatively low, with ranges of 43 to 52 for Performing and 40 to 50 for Creating.

Scores were also low for students who attended a school with a music program that included one of the attributes that we tend to associate with good music programs (i.e., full-time music specialist, music instruction at least three or four times a week, a required district or state music curriculum, visiting artists, artist-in-the-schools programs, and a room dedicated to music teaching). The scores for students who attended schools with music programs that included all of the "good program indicators" were not identified separately in the report, nor were they compared with scores of students who attended schools without all of the indicators. We can only assume that scores from students who attended schools with all of the indicators would be considerably higher for responding, creating, and performing.

The results include correlations between students' scores and attributes of the music programs in which students participated. With the exception of the 9% of the students who received no music instruction, there were no significant relationships between students' average scores and program attributes. Factors that surprisingly were not positively related to scores were frequency of instruction, having a district or state arts curriculum requirement, visiting artist programs, or whether a full-time specialist or part-time specialist was teaching music. Interestingly, although perhaps not surprising to some, students who attended schools where music was taught in room(s) dedicated to music teaching had significantly higher average scores in all three areas (Responding, Performing, and Creating) than did students who attended schools where music was taught on a stage or other space not dedicated to music teaching. Perhaps this result is attributable to the fact that dedicated music spaces are often associated with schools and communities with greater financial resources.

Some of the lower scores are reported in the area of Performing (e.g., singing the song "America" with a full chorus accompaniment on audiotape and playing "Ode to Joy" and "Twinkle, Twinkle, Little Star" by ear on the MIDI keyboard). The findings for singing, although well-known in the music education community by now, bear repeating, considering the absence of adult survey data on singing and choral music. Many students were able to sing the song "America" with generally acceptable rhythm (78%) and expression (51%). Only 35% of the students sang almost all of the pitches of the melody accurately, and only 24% sang with a tone quality that was considered appropriate in most sections of the song. Only small percentages of students were able to perform the pitches of "Twinkle, Twinkle, Little Star" (25%) and "Ode to Joy" (21%) by ear on the keyboard at an adequate level or above.

Any music assessment presents challenges, particularly in the areas of performing and creating music. Readers are encouraged to examine the complete NAEP report for a deeper understanding of the process and to examine the many results that are not discussed here. Some may raise good questions about the assessment items, the number of items, or the procedures, or may have other interpretations of the findings,[19] but if we assume that the NAEP assessment is a measurement of broad areas of skills and knowledge valued in music education, then the results are disappointing.

The students in the survey are a representative sample of eighth-grade students in the nation—they represent what most eighth-grade students can do when responding to, creating, and performing music. Considering the data from these future adults, we cannot predict with any confidence that this new generation will participate happily and successfully in music experiences that require the kinds of skills and knowledge reflected in the assessment.

TRANSITION AS A PRINCIPLE IN MUSIC EDUCATION

In the face of disconcerting survey and assessment data and many of the informal observations of a large number of adults and children in our communities and schools, many teachers may be willing to entertain a different approach when teaching students—one guided by a principle of transition. Transition, defined earlier as the movement of individuals across a variety of school and nonschool environments throughout life, is a valuable principle that can guide curricular and instructional decisions and increase the probability that meaningful school experiences will continue in adulthood.

If all people are to be involved in meaningful music experiences throughout their lives' all students must first participate in realistic school music experiences that are grounded in the principle of transition. Planning for transition requires music experiences in school that are directly referenced to contexts for music experiences valued for adulthood. What would happen if, in order to teach for transition, we engaged students, on a regular basis, in activities that were similar to these music experiences valued and performed in adulthood? Consider some of the possible outcomes for the following situations:

For some teachers, playing the recorder is considered a "pre-band" experience—an early experience playing music from notation and one that may motivate students to play an instrument in succeeding grade levels. For others, recorders offer unique opportunities for students to acquire music knowledge and performing skills. The purposes may be admirable but it is unlikely that traditional practices will result in these outcomes. In reality, the elementary teacher, pressed to include everything in the curriculum, often limits students' recorder experiences to a module of several weeks in the fourth grade and limits the repertoire to ubiquitous B, A, G songs. After the recorder module, do students continue to play their recorder at home for family and friends or play with others in ensembles? As adults, do they join the Recorder Society and perform in the community or play at informal gatherings with friends? Do we see recorder as a skill that is just "good for students," hoping that the experience will transfer to other types of music learning and participation in instrumental ensembles? What are the expectations for students as a result of several weeks playing a limited repertoire?

If recorder playing is a highly valued adult music experience and transition is the basis for decisions, many of the school experiences involving recorder would be different. Consider outcomes from classrooms where students are regularly engaged in activities that are similar to the musical activities of the members of the community Recorder Society (play arrangements of Renaissance tunes with tambourines and drums, sightread simple tunes, discuss music literature, listen to performances by well-known artists and ensembles). Also, what results would occur if students experienced ongoing collaboration with members of the local Recorder Society throughout their years in the upper elementary grade levels and middle school, playing with adult mentors and performing quality ensemble music with peers? Would these types of experiences in school make a difference in attitudes, knowledge, skill, and their choices as adults to participate in these types of experiences?

Consider another situation that involves adults' singing. *If* singing (accurately and expressively) for others (younger children, other adults) is a highly valued music experience, and transition is the basis for decision making, then school experiences must involve more than those related to traditional concerts. Of course, students must frequently be engaged in enjoyable singing experiences where they are learning to sing accurately and expressively, but singing for others should occur as an integral part of those experiences. Perhaps, as an ongoing part of the music program, older students could learn to select and perform a repertoire of songs appropriate for younger students in the same school. The older students would actually learn to choose the music and sing the songs for the younger children, on many occasions, in informal settings, either in small groups or one-on-one. Given these kinds of frequent experiences, would students have more positive attitudes about singing, would they sing better, would they serve as positive role models and mentors for younger children, would they want to continue to sing for others, would they recruit lower grade level students into choir, would they sing for their younger siblings or their own children as adults?

In yet another situation involving community ensembles, what would occur if, on a regular basis, students in middle school and secondary school served as public liaisons and advocates for community performing groups and collaborated, interacted with, or performed with the adult members of community groups on a regular basis? Would these school experiences, which are similar to those of adults who are members of community organizations, lead to an increase in the number of students who participated in community performing organizations or who attended the concerts of these groups? Would more of these students contribute their time and money to benefit community (including school) music organizations when they become independent adults?

If students, as a part of most classes, reviewed program guides for their local classical radio station and selected dates and times for listening, would they, as adults, be more likely to listen to that station and lend financial support? What effects would we see if, beginning with kindergarten and continuing throughout the elementary grade levels, students shared responsibilities for turning on the radio and finding the public radio station so that their class could listen for a few minutes at the end of each day of singing and music making?

If students left elementary school and middle school having had a choir (band/orchestra) "big brother" or "big sister" for several years and had, on several occasions each year, performed with the older students, would they be more likely to join and stay in their ensemble? If elementary students spent most of their class time actually learning to sing a repertoire of songs in-tune and singing for others, would our adult survey and NAEP data look more positive? Would we informally observe more friends and members of the community engaged in music activities? And, would we hear more political speakers talk about their successes making music?

EMPIRICAL SUPPORT FOR THE PRINCIPLE OF TRANSITION

Transition is an idea. It is a principle that is overarching in its educational applications. Transition planning in music education has wide-range applicability for people of all ages, people with a wide range of abilities and disabilities, and people from all ethnic populations, cultures, and backgrounds. It can also apply to a wide range of contexts within music programs—contexts that involve a variety of experiences, knowledge, and skills. The principle of transition is also timeless. Although specific examples throughout the text of this paper may become outdated, the principle will not.

Empirical support for the idea of transition as a principle for curricular and instructional decisions comes from educational research on transfer of learning and from the application of this research to models that have been used successfully in education. Since the ultimate goal of all education is the transfer of previously learned knowledge and skill to new situations, teaching for transfer has proven to be one of the important issues in education and research. It is particularly valuable since principles of transfer apply to *all* individuals and a wide range of contexts, experiences, knowledge, and skills.

How then does transfer occur, and what research-based principles support curricular and instructional decisions based on a principle of transition? Although the transfer process is complex, multifaceted, and affected by factors concerning the task and the context, several well-established principles have emerged from the research literature that allow us to predict when transfer will probably take place.

An in-depth discussion of transfer is well beyond the scope of this paper; however, in the following section I will present four principles derived from the research literature (listed below and in italics throughout the section) that influence the extent of transfer and that provide support for the overarching principle of transition in music education. Throughout I will include several music education examples and a few necessary definitions. Although the principles are considered separately, many of the principles overlap in several of the music education examples.

The probability of transfer of valued skills and knowledge from school music contexts to out-of-school adult music contexts will be increased (1) when students participate in music experiences and learn skills and knowledge that are similar to music experiences, skills, and knowledge that are valued for adults; (2) when students have frequent opportunities to practice the same skills and tasks, and apply the same knowledge using numerous and varied examples in multiple contexts; (3) when students learn fewer things more deeply and thoroughly; and (4) when students learn meaningful principles rather than isolated facts and skills.

These principles, and much of the research literature on transfer, focus on two elements: student tasks and contexts. Tasks in the transfer literature (classroom activities, student behaviors, skills, knowledge) refer to what we can observe the student do in the classroom (compose a short piece using nontraditional sound sources, read by sight a simple melody, sing a song with expressiveness and technical accuracy, improvise an accompaniment, and demonstrate knowledge of the technical vocabulary of music in discussion with peers). Contexts in the transfer literature have come to refer to various learning settings (classroom, community, tutoring, etc.) and social/cultural settings (peers, parents, teachers, etc.). Tasks obviously will occur in contexts. The four principles with examples of music tasks and contexts are presented below.

Principle #1. The more similar two situations are, the more likely that learning in one situation will transfer to the other situation.

This principle is concerned with the degree of similarity between two (or more) tasks and contexts. Tasks naturally occur in contexts (e.g., a student plays a simple three-chord guitar accompaniment for peers singing "On Top of Old Smokey" in general music class). Consider first the original task and the original context from the guitar example. Now consider the same student playing the same accompaniment for a middle school chorus performance. The guitar accompaniment remains the same although the context is quite different from the classroom setting (different students, audience). In other situations, contexts may remain somewhat the same (regular classes with same peers, teacher), although tasks may be very different (playing a more complex accompaniment for "Smokey," playing and singing "Smokey," playing the same three chords to accompany a different song).

The more school music experiences are similar to music experiences that are valued for adult life, the higher the probability of transfer and the more successful the transition. Consider the example of students continuing to participate in music ensembles outside of school contexts. School experiences for students are more "similar" to those experiences of adults who perform in community organizations when students regularly participate in organizations' activities and have frequent positive interactions with members of the organizations—performing alongside members, successfully singing or playing appropriate parts or literature in rehearsals and in performances for audiences in their own school venue and other community venues.

At this point, readers may be thinking about the numerous prerequisites that are taught in school that are rarely if ever performed by adults. Although there are many instances in music education when learning one skill is a necessary prerequisite for learning another (holding the instrument properly and forming the correct embouchure before performing a sound with good tone), many prerequisites are not necessary for achieving a desired learning outcome (verbally identifying note names in a phrase before singing or playing the phrase accurately and with good tone). By establishing unnecessary prerequisites, precious teaching/learning time may be wasted and students may become frustrated—their enthusiasm for making music lost in the tedium. In the process of determining what students will know and do, and in what contexts, so-called prerequisites should be questioned since they may place an unnecessary delay on the students' learning and dampen student motivation. Some prerequisites may be functionally related to another skill in the hierarchy and to the ultimate goal, but many prerequisites have been erroneously established over generations of teachers and music texts.

Principle #2. The more frequent the opportunities to practice a skill or demonstrate knowledge using numerous and varied examples, the more likely it is that learning will transfer to new situations.

This principle considers the degree to which original learning is applied to a number of tasks or contexts, or the generality of the transfer. Reading music is one example of a skill that applies to various tasks and occurs in many contexts. The singing of "The Star Spangled Banner" with a large group is another example of one skill that may easily be applied to a number of school and community contexts. When a student applies original learning about practice strategies while studying piano to practicing other instruments or music, transfer has occurred across a number of tasks. When children who learn to sing in tune with a pleasing tone use these singing skills while singing a variety of songs in their classrooms, in community groups, and at home with family and friends, they have transferred their original learning to a number of tasks and contexts.

The extent to which original learning transfers to other contexts is affected by the frequency and variety of practice opportunities. The student who sings the same repertoire expressively and with technical accuracy in a small group in his or her own classroom, in other teachers' classrooms, in the principal's office, will most likely transfer those well-learned skills to singing beautifully at the PTA meeting. The students who have frequent opportunities to perform particular rhythm or melodic patterns in many pieces may independently transfer those skills to new literature. Students who use appropriate music terminology to describe numerous and varied examples of music in the classroom will not only increase the depth of their knowledge of the class examples but may transfer this knowledge and skill to describing music heard outside of class. Discussing a variety of music in different contexts (with small groups of peers outside the classroom, with the teacher, or at home with parents) increases the probability further.

Principle #3. The more deeply and thoroughly something is learned, the more likely it is that learning will transfer to new situations.

This principle is probably one of the most understandable and yet often overlooked principles for transfer—it concerns how well something is learned. Many individuals have memories of singing or playing at a concert or recital or sightreading in a testing situation when there were problems in the performance. When there was too little time for practice and rehearsal, performances were adversely affected. What was taught was not really learned.

We require children to sing for five years in the elementary schools, but are they learning to sing well? Will they choose to sing—and sing in-tune— in their homes and community choruses? Learning something thoroughly most often means repeated practice of the same skills over weeks, months, and years to the point of automaticity or habit. It is not surprising that students who reported that they were asked to play instruments or sing, notate music, or make up their own music *almost every day* had the highest average scores in those respective areas of performing and creating in the NAEP 1997 Assessment.[20]

It should be noted that learning to perform, discuss, or analyze only a few pieces of music well is not the same as learning a skill or knowledge. In some situations, students practice and learn a limited repertoire throughout the school year or can discuss and analyze only a few pieces heard in class. Learning to perform particular pieces well can be important at times, but skills and knowledge will be acquired only when students have frequent opportunities to practice, when practice is efficient, and when practice involves numerous and varied examples in a motivating environment.

Principle #4. Meaningful principles will more easily transfer to new situations than rote learning of isolated facts and skills.

Sometimes learning something well requires drill and practice, although when repeated practice is combined with a student's understanding of underlying principles for the skill or knowledge, the learning situation is made more meaningful and the extent of the transfer is greater. Students can follow a cue and learn where to breathe when singing or playing a particular piece, or they can learn how to use breath to perform expressively or adjust the pitch of a particular note. When students learn principles that explain why and how the breath affects performance, they are better prepared to make appropriate adjustments and decisions independently. Students can learn to identify forms and the periods of particular pieces, although when students learn and understand principles of composition evident in music of different periods, they are better prepared to apply the principles when identifying and talking about an unfamiliar piece of music.

Knowledgeable teachers will understand how to make learning situations meaningful, but they must also allot enough time for their students to learn thoroughly and deeply.

All four transfer principles require that teachers accept the idea that "less is more." Deciding what is meaningful and teaching fewer (highly valued) things allows time to teach those things more deeply and thoroughly, thus providing a greater opportunity for transfer of learning to occur. When deciding what to "teach deeper," one must examine the contexts for transfer. In future school or out-of-school contexts, how many music experiences require this knowledge or these skills and how frequently will they be required? For most students, opportunities for transfer to new situations are more frequent for some music skills and knowledge (performing from notation; performing with expression and technical accuracy; sight-reading; talking intelligently about stylistic features of a piece of music; demonstrating audience behavior appropriate for recitals and concerts of classical music) than for others (reading alto clef; naming all the instruments in the symphony orchestra; writing note names; playing scales; identifying by name whole, half, quarter, eighth notes).

In closing this section on transfer, I would like to restate several findings from the transfer research that have direct applicability for music education. Considering the research evidence on transfer of learning, we can predict that the probability of transfer from school music contexts to out-of-school adult music contexts will be increased (1) when students participate in music experiences and learn skills and knowledge that are similar to music experiences, skills, and knowledge that are valued for adults; (2) when students have frequent opportunities to practice the same skills and tasks, and apply the same knowledge using numerous and varied examples in multiple contexts; (3) when students learn fewer things more deeply and thoroughly; and (4) when students learn meaningful principles rather than isolated facts and skills.

Teaching for transfer is an essential part of education. When adults who have attended many years of school cannot apply their classroom learning to situations outside of the classroom, the educational system has failed. The success of education is often measured by the number of adults who are gainfully employed, who live independently, who participate as good citizens in society (parents, neighbors, etc.), and who participate in pleasurable and beneficial (mental and physical health) recreational and leisure activities. One of the most striking successes in education comes from the field of special education where the application of principles of transition and transfer has resulted in significant progress in preparing students to live, work, and play in the real world. After years of observing disheartening results from "graduates" of well-intended but often unsuccessful programs, transition needs for individuals with disabilities took on such importance that statements of transition services are now required as a part of each student's Individualized Education Program (IEP).[21]

Applications of the principles are also evident in successful models to teach problem solving in areas such as mathematics, reading, and social studies, and in apprenticeship programs and job training programs. And, although these principles have not received much study or discussion in music education, many principles of transfer are evident in the competent teaching that occurs in music education classrooms, rehearsals, and studios as children are learning specific music skills and knowledge. What is not evident in music education, however, is the application of principles of transfer within an overarching principle of transition that encompasses a child's movement throughout school years and adulthood.

DESIGNING MUSIC PROGRAMS BASED ON A PRINCIPLE OF TRANSITION

Teachers in schools, colleges, and universities who see merit in the arguments presented in this paper can immediately incorporate the principle of transition into classrooms and rehearsals, and into the course content of teacher preparation programs. The principle of transition will be most effective in music programs when (1) there is a general consensus as to the long-term goals that are meaningful for most students, (2) students are given frequent opportunities to participate successfully in appropriate related school music experiences at each grade level, and (3) students learn to make appropriate transfers of skills and knowledge within and across grade levels. Transition is also facilitated by ongoing collaboration and cooperation among music professionals within the school and collaboration with members of the community (teachers, artists, arts organizations, parents, businesses, and other supportive individuals and organizations). Individual music teachers have access to several sources of support in the community, have skills to teach for transfer, and have the freedom to develop music experiences for the same students across several years. One teacher can influence the extent of transition made by many students.

Procedures for designing music programs focus around a few key ideas. Simply stated, once it is decided what music experiences are valued for adulthood, similar school experiences need to be developed for each grade level—experiences that will then be defined and offered as a frequent and regular part of classes and rehearsals. Frequency is a critical component and consideration for each step in the process.

Transition requires frequent opportunities for students to practice skills and knowledge in context. Although several school experiences appear similar to adult experiences (e.g., performing in a small ensemble; attending concerts of classical music), these types of activities are infrequent occurrences in the lives of students (e.g., performances may occur only in school concerts, and field trips to concerts may occur once every few years). Although they may be valued school experiences, they cannot substitute for frequent, regular instruction and practice. Competent instruction and frequent opportunities for contextual practice will increase the probability that students will learn the skills, knowledge, and attitudes to choose from, and participate successfully in, a wide range of music activities.

The following is a summary of steps useful for transition planning for school music programs:

Step 1. Decide what music experiences are meaningful for adulthood and the general contexts in which these experiences could occur.

Redesigning music classrooms and rehearsals does not require abandonment or revision or current district or state curricula, or the National Standards. It does, however, require teachers to begin by identifying music experiences for students that will be valued in adulthood and by giving priority to these experiences in their classrooms and rehearsals. This step is difficult for everyone because it requires making hard choices. It is a critical first step, however, in order for teachers to have the time to teach fewer things more thoroughly and deeply. All current school activities must be evaluated, and some activities will have to be eliminated or at the least reduced to less instructional time (effort, money).

One way to approach this decision is to choose music experiences that include skills and knowledge that will occur in many other music experiences, now and in the future. The experiences can be alone or with others; they may be in the home or in the community (including public schools); and they may range across many dimensions of music performance, listening, composing, thinking and talking about music, and music advocacy.

Individuals can also generate ideas by thinking about a young child they care about and then thinking about the kinds of music activities they would like this child to experience as an adult. What do music teachers value for the future adulthood of someone they really care about? I have found that some music teachers want this young child as an adult to sing songs to children, to sing or play holiday songs with family and friends, to initiate the singing of "Happy Birthday." They may want this adult to play an instrument or sing in a community organization, to read music well enough to select and play new music for his or her own pleasure at home, to attend school board meetings when music is discussed, to encourage his or her own children to study music, to contribute to music organizations or do volunteer work, and to attend concerts in the community and in public schools, even when the adult's own children are not performing.

It is important to recognize that long-term adult goals and many of the related school experiences that are defined as meaningful should be those that are valued for *all* students. The competent, sensitive teacher will know when and how to make appropriate changes or adaptations that will enable each student to participate successfully in an enjoyable and meaningful way.

Since the music experiences of attending concerts of classical music and performing music with and for others in a small ensemble have been discussed in this paper, and both appear to be valued by music educators, I have chosen these two experiences to illustrate the next two steps. The process of transition planning, however, can be applied to any long-term goal.

Step 2. Identify and analyze the adult music experience in context and identify related activities and their component tasks, contexts, and functional prerequisites.

Attending a concert of classical music is not a single activity—it is multi-dimensional in that it consists of many related activities. Some of the activities could fall within the scope and sequence of traditional music curricula (listening to, analyzing, and describing music; evaluating music and music performances; concert etiquette). Transition planning, however, goes beyond goals and objectives and includes a thorough analysis of the adult experience, including the identification of related activities, tasks, and contexts. For example, attending a concert most often involves watching the performers while listening to live performances, reading concert programs and notes and relating descriptions of music to the performance, and describing and evaluating the music and performance when talking to companions during intermission and after the concert. In order to talk intelligently about a music performance, an individual may need to identify groups of instruments by sight and sound, read descriptions of music and identify events when they occur, and use conventional terminology to describe and analyze music and discuss preferences with companions.

The music experience of performing with and for others in a small ensemble also consists of many related activities, some of which are part of traditional sequenced music curricula (sing or perform on an instrument a varied repertoire of music; demonstrate ensemble skills; read instrumental or vocal scores) Again, transition planning requires attention to tasks in contexts: various learning settings such as homes, classrooms, concert stage and the social/cultural dimensions of those settings that involve individuals such as peers, parents, teachers, and others. Performing in large ensembles under the leadership of a conductor who chooses the music is a different experience than performing as a member of a small ensemble. Small ensembles often do not have traditional conductors, and members are the ones who are engaged in the related activities of selecting appropriate music and programming, rehearsing, and performing for different audiences (adults in concert venues, family concerts in the park, friends in informal settings, or groups of elementary age students). Again, related activities and prerequisite knowledge and skills for the related activities should involve tasks that would traditionally be associated with the activity (e.g., singing and playing with technical accuracy and with a good tone in small ensembles, sightreading ensemble music with several peers, demonstrating good practice skills when working on ensemble music, maintaining a steady tempo while performing with others).

Step 3. Develop a hierarchy of appropriate experiences for students at each grade level that are similar to the adult experience, related activities, and tasks. Choose, develop, and structure experiences that will provide frequent opportunities to practice and apply the same skills and knowledge using numerous and varied examples in multiple contexts throughout the school year at each grade level.

In order to keep the school experiences as close to the adult experience as possible, it is useful to develop experiences for the "exit" grade level first. Ideally, twelfth grade should be the exit grade for music, although the exit grade may be the last grade level taught by the same teacher (e.g., fifth for elementary) or the last time music will be a required subject for students. Activities for each grade level, with age-appropriate modifications in task complexity and contexts, can then be developed from the exit grade level to the lowest grade level in a kind of top-down process.

Although school experiences will vary somewhat from the adult experience of attending concerts of classical music, it is important to keep the related activities, contexts, and tasks as similar as possible to those that occur in the adult experience and also to choose those that provide frequent opportunities for practice. Occasional field trips to concerts in the community may have some benefits for students since they involve real concert venues; however, these experiences are usually infrequent and lack opportunities for students to practice skills and use knowledge that are important and valued components of the concert experience.

Compared to field trips, opportunities for practice and transfer of knowledge and skills are increased when teachers structure experiences that focus on short performances that are given in the classroom or rehearsals. Live "concerts" can be given by the teacher, peers, parents, or other members of the community. Professional videos of performances of great artists and ensembles also provide excellent opportunities for students to practice related activities that are associated with concert contexts. Although the venue is not identical, teachers now have flexibility to structure age-appropriate experiences and frequent opportunities for students to practice skills and tasks, and apply knowledge using numerous and varied examples in multiple contexts (e.g., choice of music, length of music, type of ensemble, performers, topics and music terminology for discussion). For example, consider the related experience of adults talking intelligently about music with companions during intermission or after the concert. For a primary level experience, after students listen to the teacher perform (on any instrument) several short musical excerpts or watch and listen to a short performance on video, they select at least two words from a list of familiar music terminology and use those words to describe the music to a partner (teacher monitors discussions and expands discussion in class). Upper elementary students may use appropriate music terminology in small-group discussions to explain their personal preferences after listening to different short videos or live musical excerpts, and older students may verbally identify and explain the stylistic features of the musical selection and explain some of the compositional devices that were used to evoke feelings or emotions.

The complexity of the tasks and contexts for school experiences involving small-group performances will also vary for students at different grade levels. Again, the experiences that are developed for transition should provide frequent opportunities for practice and be as similar as possible to those that occur in the adult experience. Year-end concerts, holiday concerts, and performances of small ensembles at contest may have benefits for students but, similar to the field trips to concerts, these experiences usually occur infrequently and may lack opportunities for students to participate in important related activities and learn valued skills and knowledge (e.g., understanding the technical requirements of music and making appropriate selections for performance; working cooperatively with other musicians in making independent decisions regarding the music, interpretations, programming for particular audiences, rehearsal schedules, and rehearsal strategies; evaluating individual and group performances).

Teachers can structure numerous age appropriate experiences and provide frequent opportunities for all students to learn and practice performing in small ensembles in various informal contexts with friendly audiences. Some students will also perform in more formal concert venues. For a primary level experience, teachers can, on a regular basis, choose several students to sing (and/or play) familiar songs with or without accompaniments in class. Throughout the month, perhaps several students who are demonstrating good progress in singing and playing in class ("improving during rehearsal") can be selected to evaluate music as ready for performance, select a few short pieces, and perform them at the principal's office or for peers and teachers in other classrooms. Similar experiences can be structured for students in upper elementary, middle, and high school by simply varying the music, audiences, and the complexity of tasks that involve independent and small-group decisions regarding selecting and programming music. Teachers who rehearse large ensembles can structure experiences for older students where students select group members for a small ensemble (with some supervision from the teacher) and perform current repertoire for students in lower grade levels. This type of experience provides students with additional opportunities for decision making in the selection of members who will perform critical voice (instrument) parts and perhaps in creating appropriate arrangements.

Creative teachers will find many ways to extend the experiences of attending a concert of classical music and playing with and for others to other meaningful music activities performed by adults. It is important, however, that principles of transfer (e.g., learning something well, frequent opportunities for practice) are applied to any new experience. The key components of school experiences (in these examples of attending concerts of classical music and performing with and for others) must be age appropriate and yet remain as similar as possible to adult experiences. Principles of transfer must be applied in situations in order to increase the probability for transfer and for successful transition across grade levels into adulthood.

CLOSING

Inspiring, beautiful words have been written (many of them in this book) about music and its value in the world. Music and music making are valued by a large majority of individuals in our society, many of whom have experienced only a few years of formal music education. Music and music making were integral to the lives of individuals in societies before the discipline of music education, and no doubt will remain in future societies should the profession of music education vanish. How will the quality of life of future generations change, and for the better, as a result of children's attending required or elective music classes with competent music educators today? How will music education change so that all people will continue to be involved in meaningful music participation? What good can music education do?

The idea of deciding what is important and meaningful for others is difficult. Many people may want educators to "expose" children to different music experiences (all valued and good) and let children decide for themselves. Competent music educators understand the importance of time for practice and study, key ideas supported by transfer research and applications in all disciplines. The success of education is based on deciding what is important to learn and structuring frequent opportunities for practice and learning to occur over time. Who better to decide what music experiences are important and meaningful for students and adults than music teachers?

Many music teachers across this country every day provide pleasurable, enjoyable, creative music experiences for their students. Yet, it appears that many children and adults do not choose to continue many of these music experiences outside of school. Perhaps we need to plan more directly for the future musical lives of students. Curricular and instructional decisions must be based on the reality that students leave school and that the frequency of their successes in school will greatly influence their opportunities for choice outside of school.

Transition planning begins with thinking about the future and the music experiences of generations of future adults. Decisions focus on how to bring adult music experiences that are most valued into school music programs and how to structure and implement a sequence of age-appropriate experiences for children at each grade level, beginning at the earliest possible age. All of the principles for competent instruction remain as students become more skilled, knowledgeable, independent, and confident within enjoyable learning contexts that are age appropriate and similar to those valued for adulthood.

As children and adults we experience many transitions in life. Whether transitions are seen as planned, capricious, or just an inevitable part of time and growing older, many transitions bring different responsibilities, decisions, and choices requiring different skills and knowledge. In order to make these transitions smoother, many forward-thinking adults engage in transition planning for retirement, medical and health care for their families, college for their children, vacations, and "rainy" days. We should do no less when planning for the musical lives of future generations of children and adults.

What good can music education do? Much good, if good means preparing students for transition and successful participation in the kinds of music experiences valued by professionals in the discipline of music education. And much good, if good means designing meaningful school experiences that will increase opportunities for individuals to make real choices in their musical lives and participate in experiences that would not be available to them otherwise. How will the quality of life of future generations change for the better as a result of children's attending required or elective music classes with competent music educators today? We'll begin to answer that question by observing the adult musical lives of each graduating class. We'll need to ask the class of 2020.

NOTES

1. Ideas related to adults as artifacts of education past and several other ideas developed in this paper first appeared in previous publications of invited presentations Judith A. Jellison, "Beyond the Jingle Stick: Real Music in a Real World," *Update: Applications of Research in Music Education* 17, no. 2 (1999): 13–19; and "History, Bias, and Living Artifacts," *Bulletin of the Council for Research in Music Education* 1, no. 17 (1993): 66–70.

2. Robert A. Choate, ed., *Documentary Report of the Tanglewood Symposium* (Washington, DC: Music Educators National Conference, 1981), iii.

3. Ibid., 139.

4. Music Educators National Conference, *Opportunity-to-Learn Standards for Music Instruction: Grades PreK–12* (Reston, VA: Music Educators National Conference, 1994), v.

5. Music Educators National Conference, *The School Music Program: A New Vision* (Reston, VA: Music Educators National Conference, 1994), 3.

6. Ibid., 2.

7. American Music Conference, "American Attitudes towards Music 1997," available from NAMM: The International Music Products Association.

8. John Maher, ed., *Music USA* (Carlsbad, CA: NAMM: The International Music Products Association, 1998).

9. Introductory remarks by Gerson Rosenbloom, NAMM chairman, and Larry R. Linkin, NAMM president/CEO, published in *Music USA*, 5.

10. Maher, ed., *Music USA*.

11. Ibid., 11.

12. Ibid., 33–34.

13. Richard A. Peterson and Darren E. Sherkat, "Effects of Age on Arts Participation," in *Age and Arts Participation with a Focus on the Baby Boom Cohort*, National Endowment for the Arts Research Report #34, ed. Ervin V. Lehman (Santa Ana, CA: Seven Locks Press, 1996), 13–67.

14. Judith H. Balfe and Rolf Meyersohn "Arts Participation of the Baby Boomers," in *Age and Arts Participation with a Focus on the Baby Boom Cohort*, 68–116.

15. Ibid., 104, 114.

16. Alan R. Andreasen, *Expanding the Audience for the Performing Arts*, National Endowment for the Arts Research Report #24 (Santa Ana, CA: Seven Locks Press, 1996), 36.

17. Hilary R. Persky, Brent A. Sandene, and Janice M. Askew, *The NAEP 1997 Arts Report Card* (Washington, DC: National Center for Education Statistics, 1998).

18. The assessment for dance was not implemented because a statistically suitable sample could not be located.

19. For a stimulating discussion of issues related to music assessment and particularly the NAEP, see *Arts Education Policy Review* 100, no. 6 (July/August, 1999).

20. Persky, Sandene, and Askew, 38–39.

21. This requirement was included with several new 1990 amendments, which expanded *the Education for All Handicapped Children Act*, P.L. 94–142, and renamed the law the *Individuals with Disabilities Education Act* (referred to as IDEA). Essentially, individuals involved with the student's education must anticipate the student's transition into three elements of life: work, residential living, and recreation/ leisure time activities. A thorough description and analysis of the transition amendment is given in H. Rutherford Turnbull, *Free Appropriate Education: The Law and Children with Disabilities* (Denver, CO: Love Publishing Company, 1993). Turnbull states that the law's provisions for the specific means of instruction, the identification of functional daily living and vocational skills, and the emphasis on community-referenced, community-based, and community-delivered instruction "acknowledges the principles of generalization and durability (that students learn best when they must actually use their skills), and it acknowledges that skill development should take place in the least restrictive, most normal settings" (p. 126).

Chapter Nine

Response to Judith A. Jellison's "How Can All People Continue to Be Involved in Meaningful Music Participation?"

Warrick L. Carter

Warrick L. Carter is former director of Disney Entertainment Arts for Walt Disney Entertainment in Lake Buena Vista, Florida.

INTRODUCTION

Our topic addressing "How can *all* people continue to be involved?" presupposes that at one time "all people" have been involved in some form of meaningful music participation. I would suggest that, although it has been an historic goal of music education, we have failed to successfully provide meaningful music participation for all people. Our question rather should be, "How can we provide meaningful musical experiences so that all people will seek to continue music participation in later life?"

As indicated in the introduction of the paper, the main issue is about "learning" and what knowledge is needed to function in adult life. My response will address this aspect of learning to identify current trends in adult music activities; describe how to positively impact adult choices of music activity; and describe what may be or should be our curriculum challenges in the future. As Judith Jellison has stated, "Education is intended to improve the quality in life." Therefore, all that is learned should have some direct implication for the quality of one's activities in later life. As it places the emphasis on the development of skills needed to function effectively as an adult, I like very much Jellison's use of the language "adults and future adults."

When one looks at the study of other disciplines, it is apparent that there is a direct correlation between what is learned as a future adult and its implication and application for adult life. For example, the study of languages provides the foundation and tools needed to negotiate the languages; the study of math gives one the tools that will be used in day-to-day function for adding, subtracting, multiplying, and dividing. The study of health and physical education gives students the information and exercise skills needed to function as healthy adults. There is no separation between adult discipline needs and in-school preparation; nor is there a separate terminology that differentiates between in-school subjects and out-of-school application. Use of the terms "school athletics," "school English," "school math," or "school dance," are avoided, but rather dance, art, English, math, athletics, and so on, are used. It is only in the study of music that specific kinds of music are known as "school music," separate from other music with which students may participate as adults. The line drawn between what we define as school and nonschool music may be fundamental to the difficulty that adults have in connecting "school music experiences" with music activities in later life. In other words, school music experiences have frequently neglected large areas of music making and music expression and have consistently not only failed to validate these but have in many cases relegated them to areas that seem to be less desirable and unimportant. Hence, when many adults have the opportunity to participate in music, they do not relate school music activities to adult music involvement, opportunities, and activities.

SCHOOL TO ADULT LIFE

The MENC document *Opportunity-to-Learn Standards for Music Instruction. Grades PreK–12* appropriately identifies the participation of music in adult life as the ultimate goal for music education experiences: "[I]t is important to note that the ultimate objective of all standards, all music curriculums, and all school personnel is to help all students gain the broad skills and knowledge that will enable them to function effectively as adults and to contribute to society in today's world and tomorrow's."[1] As the ultimate goal of music education, the all-important and encompassing concept is, therefore, to identify those skills and experiences that are important building blocks on which to structure adult music experiences. We must look at the kind of music involvement of adults today; interview adults who either participate or do not participate in music and identify reasons for their choices; and study the industry data that reflects present and future adult music involvement experiences. We must be cautious in validating any present or projected adult music experience and speedily work to join the concept of school music experiences with all music experiences.

Jellison writes eloquently and forcibly in presenting a philosophy regarding the focus of music instruction as means for preparing future adults for adult music making. Inherent in this philosophy are a number of questions that I think should be raised:

1. What are the present music-making activities of adults?
2. Is there a projection that these activities will significantly change in the future?
3. If not, what can music education professionals do to make those music activities more meaningful?
4. If so, what are the new activities in which adults will be involved, and what instruction can be provided to make instruction more meaningful?

I would argue that presently, most adults' music activities do not include performing music; attending concerts; creating music (composing, arranging, improvising); analyzing music; conducting music; not even listening to music. Rather, I think the major music activity of most adults is the "hearing of music." Because we in music education have identified very specific skills that we feel should be exhibited when one is engaged in meaningful listening activity, I use the word "hearing" to differentiate this activity from listening. We, as music educators, list the following as appropriate skills that demonstrate meaningful listening:

- Listen to, *analyze*, and *describe* music
- *Demonstrate perceptual skills* by moving and by answering questions
- Use *appropriate terminology*
- Identify the *sounds of a variety of instruments*
- Respond through purposeful movement to selected prominent music characteristics or to specific music events while listening to music
- Describe specific music events
- Analyze the *uses of elements*
- Demonstrate knowledge of the basic principles
- *Analyze aural examples*
- Demonstrate extensive knowledge of the technical vocabulary
- Identify and *explain compositional* devices and techniques
- Demonstrate the *ability to perceive and remember music* events by describing in detail significant events occurring in a given aural example
- *Compare ways* in which musical materials are used in a given example
- Analyze and describe uses of the elements of music
- *Identify* simple *music forms*

- Use *appropriate terminology* in explaining music
- Describe specific music events in a given aural example
- Analyze elements of music in aural examples representing diverse genres and cultures

Hearing, on the other hand, can be described as the first or second level of the Affective Domain: Receiving and Responding, which is defined by Bloom & Associates as follows:

- "At a minimum level we are here describing the behavior of being willing to tolerate a given stimulus, not to avoid it."
- "It involves a neutrality or suspended judgment toward the stimulus."
- "Given the opportunity to attend in a field with relatively few competing stimuli, the learner is not actively seeking to avoid it. At best, he is willing to take notice of the phenomenon and give it his attention."
- "Concerned with responses which go beyond merely attending to the phenomenon."
- "Sufficiently motivated that he is not just willing to attend, but perhaps it is correct to say that he is actively attending."
- "Committing in some small measure to the phenomenon involved. This is a very low level of commitment."
- "In doing something with or about the phenomenon besides merely perceiving it."[2]

Hearing, at this level, requires minimal personal emotional involvement, and seldom does the individual have to demonstrate any personal responses. Now, granted there are various levels of hearing, some of which can be extremely meaningful and can be described at the Bloom areas of Valuing. However, one does not have to operate at the higher level to participate in enjoyable hearing experiences. Therefore, in order for us to help all future adults have more meaningful experiences, we must help them develop better hearing skills, which we *hope* will lead to listening.

Using the Bloom Affective Domain taxonomy as our guidepost, the listening standards to which we would hope to bring our pre-adults would be in the higher levels of Responding and the category of Valuing. However, we seldom teach value for all music listening, hearing, or participating experiences, but rather for specifically prescribed "school music" activities. If our music instruction is to lead to enjoyable adult musical activities, and a "satisfaction in response" is a desired musical behavior, we should be less concerned with the musical genre that produces that satisfaction and more concerned with enabling students in gaining the requisite skills to function and react musically, regardless of music genre.

THE DATA

As we are well aware, the pre-adult and adult worlds are bombarded with various musics, which present many hearing and listening opportunities. The plethora of music that is programmed for pre-adults and adults is too numerous to mention here. However, I do believe that these two or three examples may conservatively serve our purpose.

1. The radio industry has created many hearing experiences for individuals as they are involved in a variety of activities. We have such terms as "drive time radio," "work time radio," all of which include specific types of music to attract specific types of audiences and responses.
2. The term "easy listening music" moves directly to the concept of hearing as opposed to listening. It lets the prospective audience know that few listening skills are needed to participate in this music activity; the mind can therefore concentrate on other "more important" activities. This is not all bad. Many of us, present company included, frequently use a variety of musics as background to other activities. Personally, I have classical music playing in my office (probably a surprise to those of you who know of my jazz involvement). This creates an ambiance for me that makes it an extremely pleasant and productive working environment.
3. The popularity of TV channels dedicated to specific music genres is further evidence of the great "needs" for and interest in music of pre-adults and adults alike. MTV, VH1, BET, and CMTV are each developed to meet the hearing needs of specific publics. Where are the like channels for other music, or should these outlets reformat their offerings to be more inclusive?

Data reported in "American Attitudes towards Music 1997," an executive summary of a survey conducted by the Gallup Organization for NAMM, show that 84% of those surveyed felt that music is a very important part of their life; that music is a good hobby (95%); and that music brings the family together (82%). A number of those surveyed agreed that playing a musical instrument (84%) is fun and playing a musical instrument provides lifetime enjoyment (96%).[3] These attitudes are reinforced when one looks at the product retail sales from 1990 to 1998 as reported by NAMM. With the exception of fretted products (guitars, etc.), where there was a slight decline in the amount of revenue between 1997 and 1998, all categories of product sales, from drum machines to sound reinforcement, showed significant increases over the previous year.[4] Comparing that to historic data, over the past ten years, we see a great increase (sometimes fourfold) in the expenditures for products used for making and participating in music. The 1998 figures reported by the National Association of Recording Arts & Sciences and the consumer products associations mirror those of NAMM and show consistent increases in revenues for the sales of records, CDs, and tapes (12.2 billion) and of equipment (10 billion). All of these studies show an increasing interest in music participation and a demand for music-related products and activities. *More and more adults are seeking more and more experiences in music.*

The most telling numbers are reflected in the NAMM report, which indicates that of the 6.5 billion dollars in manufacturing shipping for the 1997–1998 year, 804 million dollars were spent on fretted products (electric guitars, acoustic guitars, banjos, etc.) and 833 million dollars were spent on sound reinforcement equipment. For acoustic instruments (wind, percussion, and stringed instruments), as well as printed music—all of the stronghold of music education—the numbers reported were much smaller.[5] I feel that the implications are clear; if we plan to more effectively meet the demands, interests, and needs of adults, we need to change/expand instructional opportunities and offerings for pre-adults. The following findings in the report "American Attitudes towards Music 1997" bear special notice:

- Of the total number of former players, 55% stopped playing before the age of 18 and 24% stopped before the age of 35. Of the total number who currently play, 33% are aged 15 to 17, 24% are aged 35 to 49, and 19% are aged 50 and older. Piano and guitar are played by larger portions of children age 5 to 17 (and adults) than any other type of instrument.
- A large majority (84%) of people who played instruments or who were former players, first learned to play between the ages of 5 and 14; a smaller proportion began the studying of instrumentals after the age of 14 (23%), and over the age of 16 (6%).[6]

Although the NAMM report shows continuous growth in the instrumental market, it does not show that growth in what is indicated as the school music market (brass, woodwind, and stringed instruments). I concur with Jellison that it appears adults often discontinued what they studied as students in school and they are not listening to the classical music they may have heard in their music classrooms. They are also not attending classical concerts and opera but are increasing their attendance and appreciation for other music experiences; that is, CDs and videotapes, television, and nonclassical concerts.

In a 1993 article, "Personal Observations on Integration and Music Programs," I investigated the lack of participation of African American students in post-integration music programs. I looked, historically, at the number of black students who participated in instrumental programs in pre and post-segregated environments in the South. Although, most of the content of the article may be irrelevant to this discussion, some specifics have credence for this topic.

> Black students are quite active in music outside of the school's music programs; there are no indicators that Blacks have lost interest in making and learning music, in fact, the numbers reflect the opposite. . . . Black students have found a variety of non-school related activities to which they can receive music instruction, such as community music schools, churches, music stores, local private teachers, and self-instruction. These "in parallel schools" provide teaching and learning outside the formal education setting. Maybe this is an example of how music education can remain attractive to students and how music education should be undertaken. Two well known our of school programs that have had great results are those offered through Jazz Mobile in New York City and the Association for the Advancement of Creative Musicians (AACM) in Chicago. These programs retain many of the qualities that made many pre-integration black music programs so successful:
>
> • Needs and accessibility
> • Effective, sensitive, culturally aware and broadly trained music teachers
> • Relevant, open and rigorous curriculum and
> • Strong black community identity and or support[7]

The point made in that article was that many music programs failed to meet the needs of their constituency, who had been actively involved in school music programs during pre-integration but found the offerings wanting in post-integration settings. A similar parallel can be drawn for some current music education programs that fail to connect with students in any meaningful ways, causing students to seek their music training and activities external to the schools.

I don't foresee (with my crystal ball) that there will be a significant change in the kinds of activities in which adults will be involved in the future. I feel that recorded musics will be the *number one* activity for adults for the future. So then, the most important question is therefore: "What kind of music experiences are needed for pre-adults to positively enhance the projected dominant music experience for adults?"

TRANSITION

Jellison has defined transition as "the movement of individuals across a variety of school and nonschool environments throughout life" (p. 108). Hence, if this is to be used as a valued principal and foundation for the instruction of music, all students must participate in realistic school music experiences that are grounded in the principals of transition. "Planning for transition requires music experiences in school that are directly referenced to contexts for music experiences valued for adulthood" (p. 114). Jellison cites examples describing the need and the uses of transition and how instruction based upon this concept would change to prepare for later life participation.

Of particular interest is the following:

> If students, as a part of most classes, reviewed program guides for their local classical radio station and selected dates and times for listening, would they, as adults, be more likely to listen to that station and lend financial support? . . . If students left elementary school and middle school having had a choir (band/ orchestra) "big brother" or "big sister" for several years and had, on several occasions each year, performed with the older students, would they be more likely to join and stay in their ensemble? (p. 115)

These questions lead me to think of four possible scenarios for different individuals and the manner in which transition, if used as the foundation for an approach for music to education, could have an important impact and effect on their participation and involvement in music. I feel that *any* involvement in music, not just classical music and other forms of the European tradition, can be meaningful and valuable, and that it is incumbent upon us in music education to find ways to help students, and then later, adults, find value in the many varied music experiences that are available.

1. Individual #1 studied piano from the age of 5 through high school. She served as a pianist for the local church and served to accompany fellow students from the school as they participated in solo contests. In high school she also performed with a "garage band," performing at weddings and various other kinds of events in the community. As an adult this individual has chosen to continue her participation in music, serving as a church organist and still finding the opportunity to serve as an accompanist for various community groups. Although very active in music throughout her life as a student, she did not benefit from the music instructional programs in the school system, other than her participation in mandatory general music instruction in the elementary grades. She sees no connection to her present music activities and the school music program in which she participated.

2. Individual #2 was a band student. This individual began participating in band in the fourth grade, started first with mellophone and graduated to performing on baritone horn. He continued this activity throughout high school by switching to mellophone again in the marching band program in college. Since graduating from college, he has not participated in any music activities, nor has he attended any band concerts in the local community. Now he is the parent of two children who are actively involved in sports, and the activities of this individual are aimed at supporting the sports activities of his children. When

interviewed, he indicated he valued music and enjoyed performing, but failed to see a relationship between school activities and the present. With limited opportunities for mellophone players as adults, he is an active music listener and has a large collection of rock and pop CDs.

3. Individual #3 is a vocalist who began participating in vocal music ensembles in elementary school. Frequently singled out as an individual with good range and pitch and with strong musical qualities, he was a highly sought feature soloist and performer. As a student, he participated in elementary and high school choirs and in musicals and continued those activities into his adult life, seeking out community choral and church groups. Actively involved in music all his life, he has excellent musical memory and is able to "catch on" very quickly; however, he is unable to read music. He feels that music has been a very valuable part of his life and continues to seek out a variety of music opportunities and activities. He attends choral concerts and has a growing classical (vocal) CD collection.

4. Individual #4 is a self-taught musician. Having developed interests in rock music, he was drawn to the guitar. As guitar instruction was not available in the school setting, he taught himself and sought some evening instruction from music stores, private teachers, etc. He has developed strong skills in a specific genre and is felt to be a rather strong player in that area. Although never having learned to read music, he has wonderful improvisational skills and a very "good ear" for music. Throughout high school and after, he participated in various "garage bands" and has continued this activity as an adult. He frequents rock concerts, buys CDs of rock music, and listens to rock radio. Now a successful attorney, he has participated in adult rock-and-roll camps. He feels that music is a valuable component in his life, but sees no direct relationship to the instruction he received in school and the activities in which he is presently engaged.

How would transition have been helpful and meaningful to any of the above individuals? How could their schools' music programs have better served them as adults? Did those programs serve any of them properly?

According to Jellison, the support of transition "comes from educational research on transfer of learning and from the application of this research to models that have been used successfully in education" (p. 116). In order to increase the possibility for transfer from in-school music experiences to "useable" out-of-school music skill, the author suggests that students must:

1. "participate in music experiences and learn skills and knowledge that are similar to music experiences, skills, and knowledge that are valued for adults";
2. "have frequent opportunities to practice the same skills and tasks, and apply the same knowledge using numerous and varied examples in multiple contexts";
3. "learn fewer things more deeply and thoroughly"; and
4. "learn meaningful principles rather than isolated facts and skills" (p. 116).

Further, she identifies four transfer-of-learning principles, derived from the research literature, that can and should be used in a transition approach to pre-adult music education that should lead to meaningful activities and involvement for adults. Let's examine the four principles in relation to the four adult cases above and see how the transition approach for transfer of learning might have been of help to their adult music activities.

"Principle #1. The more similar two situations are, the more likely that learning in one situation will transfer to the other situation" (p. 117).

For all practical purposes, it appears that Individual #1 was well served by her pre-adult music education. The music with which she was involved as a child is, by and large, the music with which she is participating as an adult. She has continued to seek out performing experiences on piano and feels very strongly that the foundation laid in her piano study has led to her success as an adult pianist. However, the piano experiences she had as a pre-adult were external to the school music program. She has indicated very affirmatively that she sees no relationship between what she learned in school music (i.e., general music programs) and her present involvement in music. In order for the school music program to have had any impact on her present activities, piano instruction should have been included in her school music program. Ways of including the study of piano, in a meaningful way for large number of students, need to be investigated so that these students (who presently get their instruction outside the school) can participate in the school's music program. Granted there are opportunities for accomplished pianists to serve as members of jazz ensembles, accompany the school choirs, and accompany the solo ensemble festivals; however, ongoing activities like those available for instrumentalists and vocalists are not available for pianists in the school's music program. Individual #2 appears to have been served well by his pre-adult experiences. That they were valued is seen in his continued participation through college. It appears, however, that he feels there is no place for adult baritone horn or mellophone players. This is indicative of the belief, held by many adults, that the music and instruments associated with school band programs exist only for pre-adults, as one sees very few professional role models performing on many of the school band instruments. The lack of pop and rock music as part of his high school and college band performance serves as an additional indicator of the lack of similarities between the music experiences and activities of pre-adults and those to which this individual was drawn as an adult. Part of the reason for reduction in pre-adults playing brass instruments is the absence of popular role models performing on these instruments. At the same time, because of the large number of saxophonists in popular music, there has been a consistent growth of the popularity of this instrument. Another example can be drawn from my own teaching. As a music teacher during the '60s, I found it very difficult to convince students to play bass clarinet. It was very fortunate when Benny Mauphin, a rising jazz star, made bass clarinet one of the instruments of his arsenal. His recording with Miles Davis on the historic "bitches brew," and the use of bass clarinet on this and subsequent recordings, through the late '60s and early '70s, was helpful in attracting students to play the bass clarinet.

Individual #3 gives music education a homerun. The music experiences and activities he experienced as a pre-adult continue to be those musical activities to which he is drawn as an adult. His great interest in choral and classical music is a direct reflection of the experiences and exposures that he had as a pre-adult. The only concern I would have is whether or not the music program was broad-based enough to have provided exposure to a variety of choral performing activities, including mandrigals, swing choir, jazz choir, pop, quartet singing, and so on, so that, as an adult, he would have more choices from which to select his ongoing music activities.

Individual #4 appears to be one of the great failures of our educational system. As a pre-adult, this individual was drawn to music, sought out opportunities in which to perform, and made music a priority. There were no experiences or specific instruction within our school's system to accommodate him. Hence, he developed his skills on his own and through the help of out-of-school instructional opportunities. He has continued to seek out these experiences and has developed rather strong skills independent of the school music program.

"Principle #2. The more frequent the opportunities to practice a skill or demonstrate knowledge using numerous and varied examples, the more likely it is that learning will transfer to new situations" (p. 118).

All four individuals needed many opportunities to demonstrate their skills in a variety of music styles. Individual #1 could have benefited greatly from performing with school choirs, piano ensembles, and jazz and pop ensembles and the accompanying of groups to develop other skills and to be exposed to a plethora of musics. Individual #2 would possibly have continued as a performing musician had he had varied musical offerings in his music education. Individual #3 benefited greatly through being afforded the opportunity to demonstrate his knowledge with varied examples. I would, however, suggest that a wider music offering should have been available. Individual #4 sought out and created his own opportunities to demonstrate his knowledge with varying performance opportunities and venues independent of the school music program.

"Principle #3. The more deeply and thoroughly something is learned, the more likely it is that learning will transfer to new situations" (p. 118).

As Jellison has indicated, "Learning to perform, discuss or analyze only a few pieces of music well is not the same as learning a skill or knowledge. In some situations, students practice and learn a limited repertoire throughout the school year or can discuss and analyze only a few pieces heard in class. Learning to perform particular pieces well can be important at times, but skills and knowledge will be acquired only when students have frequent opportunities to practice, when practice is efficient, and when practice involves numerous and varied examples in a motivating environment" (p. 119). Of our four individuals, it appears that only Individuals #1 and #3 were placed into environments that enhanced their musical development according to the concepts of Principle #3.

Outside of the school community, Individual #1 spent a sufficient amount of time in developing her skills within a variety of settings and was exposed to a vast amount of different literature so that she could function in a variety of musical settings both as a pre-adult and adult. Individual #3, although performing in a very narrow scope, was exposed to a wide array of literature within that scope and consequently developed rather significant skills that led to meaningful adult music experiences. Individuals #2 and #4, on the other hand, appear to have not had experiences that were deep and thorough in their preparation. For Individual #2, the steady diet of band music, although enjoyable as a pre-adult, was limited and did not carry over to adult life. Individual #4, self-taught and self-directed, did not have the benefit of meaningful exposure to a wide array of musical examples; therefore, his scope of music activities was limited.

"Principle #4 Meaningful principles will more easily transfer to new situations than rote learning of isolated facts and skills" (p. 119).

Again, it appears that Individuals #1 and #3 are the "winners"; while Individuals #2 and #4 are not necessarily losers, they could have had more meaningful experiences as adults if the precepts of Principle #4 had been followed when they were pre-adults. We are well aware that in too many cases, specifically in choral music, a large amount of note learning takes place. Although this may expedite the rehearsal, this does not give the preadult the kind of universal skills that can be used in later adult life for lifelong music making. Although they lack music reading skills, Individuals #3 and #4 still appear to have high-quality adult music experiences. Granted these experiences could have been even higher had music reading been a part of the learning process as pre-adults.

CONCLUSION

I feel that the concept of transition, within the principles of transfer learning, has important implications for music learning for future adults to create meaningful experiences as adults. I am concerned that some of the aims we describe in music education are much too narrow. They do not relate to the whole spectrum of music. If we as music educators are interested in elevating the quality of musical life in America, then our concerns should be with the quality and inclusion of all music making as opposed to a very narrowly defined "school music" genre.

In a recent *Jazz Times* article on the "Yellow Jackets," Bob Mintzer, the woodwindist of the group, stated the following:

> I'm not a purist. I never have been. I'm highly impure. I've always liked playing all kinds of music. When I used to do a lot of freelance work in New York, on a given week, I might play with the New York Philharmonic on Sunday, with the Vanguard Orchestra on Monday, and a punk band on Tuesday, and free jazz on Wednesday. I tell young players that "You're crazy not to take a broad approach to this business, because it just means you'll be working a lot more." The players who seem to work a lot, who are in demand, are guys who have a large vocabulary. That comes from being fairly open-minded about music. [8]

Back to our original question, "How can all people continue to be involved in meaningful music participation," and how can we make all music education experiences meaningful for later life? I feel, we start first by ensuring that all people receive some form of music instruction in school; that we base this instruction upon the concept of transition and use the principles of transfer of learning for transition; that we provide learning experiences that help develop better "hearing skills" regardless of genre; that we expose our future adults to varied and diverse musical styles; and last, that we embrace all forms of music making and set as our goal the rise in the quality of the music in America. This includes embracing and valuing rap, rock, funk, jazz, classical, gospel, country, bluegrass, and so on. As Libby Larsen has stated in her keynote speech to this symposium, "Music is very generous, as it allows us to do anything with it."[9] However, we in music education can be very stingy, as we put limits on what we let students do with and experience in it!

Again from Larsen, "It is okay for all roads not to lead to Mozart" as long as the roads lead to good-quality musical experiences for lifelong music exploration.[10]

There should be no separation between music and school music. Perhaps by the year 2020, we'll all get there.

NOTES

1. Music Educators National Conference, *Opportunity-to-Learn Standards for Music Instruction: Grades PreK–12* (Reston, VA: MENC, 1994), v.

2. Benjamin Bloom et al., "Affective Domain," *Taxonomy of Educational Objectives* (New York: David McKay, 1964).

3. American Music Conference, "American Attitudes towards Music 1997," available from NAMM: The International Music Products Association.

4. John Maher, ed., *Music USA* (Carlsbad, CA: NAMM: The International Music Products Association, 1998).

5. Ibid.

6. American Music Conference.

7. Warrick Carter, "Personal Observations on Integration and School Music Programs," *Quarterly Journal of Music Teaching and Learning* 4, no. 2 (Summer 1993): 5–11.

8. Josef Woodard, "Yellow Jackets: Educating the Ear," *Jazz Times* (October 1999): 22–32.

9. Libby Larsen, "Music Instruction for 2020," speech presented at Vision 2020: The Housewright Symposium on the Future of Music Education, The Florida State University, 23–26 September 1999.

10. Ibid.

Chapter Ten

How Will Societal and Technological Changes Affect the Teaching of Music?

Commission Author: Carlesta Elliott Spearman

Carlesta Elliott Spearman is professor emerita of music at Keene State College, University System of New Hampshire.

Commission Members:
Hal Abeles
Donna Brink Fox
Alexandria Holloway
Gerald Kember
Brian Moore

Response: Sandy Feldstein

INTRODUCTION

Today, two of the most influential phenomena of life in the United States and the world are the societal and technological forces at work in our human existence. Even more important to this reality is how much one is affected by the other. Indeed, innovations in technology provide a useful backdrop for viewing the milestones of social changes, while at the same time, developments in sociological actions and thoughts are propelling technology forward. It is important, therefore, that MENC—The National Association for Music Education, in keeping with its mission to provide musical knowledge, skills, and understanding to people of all ages, take a very hard look at developments in those two phenomena as we approach the next millennium and beyond. This overview is necessary in order for MENC to prepare for the new century and make wise decisions regarding the appropriate path toward achieving its mission most effectively. This is no small task, but it is one that would not be possible at all without such proactive steps.

Societal forces are many-faceted and far-reaching. Culture, environment, geography, economics, politics, medicine and health, religion, and education are all major societal forces that interact in very complex ways. In the past, we in the United States focused our attention on these important events as they concerned only our nation's social institutions. However, as the farthest reaches of the earth have become more accessible through technological advances in mass communication and transportation technology, a study of the larger world and our society's place in it is required.

Moreover the dominant position of our country in the larger world system demands that focus. John Macionis, a noted social scientist states,

> Human lives do not unfold according to sheer chance, nor do people live in isolation relying on what philosophers call "free will" in all our choices and actions. On the contrary, while individuals make important decisions every-day, we do so within a larger arena called "society"—a family, a campus, a nation, an entire world. The essential wisdom of sociology is that the surrounding society guides our actions just as surely as the seasons influence how we dress and the kinds of activities we engage in. And, because sociologists know a great deal about how society works, they can predict with a good measure of accuracy how we all behave. [1]

Sociology, then, is the scientific study of human social activity. Music teaching is both an art and a social activity. A classroom is a social structure. Therefore, an effective teacher of music must combine knowledge of each student's sociological context with knowledge of music in order to develop successful teaching strategies within that social structure. Indeed, for teachers, the practice of "thinking sociologically" opens the way for appropriate academic and social interaction in any and every classroom circumstance. This treatise takes a diagnostic and prescriptive exploration into the future in an effort to provide a background regarding the cultural factors and sociological changes that will affect the teaching of music beyond the year 2000.

SOCIETAL CHANGES THAT WILL AFFECT THE TEACHING OF MUSIC

Recently, many within the United States have attempted to face the challenges of multiculturalism and promote an educational program that recognizes the cultural diversity by advancing the equality of all cultural traditions. Yet *what does multiculturalism really mean?* Social scientists (contrary to many others within our society) use the term "culture" to refer to all elements of a society's way of life, realizing that cultural patterns vary throughout a population. It would seem that this understanding is critical to the teaching profession. Our nation contains striking cultural diversity. Heavy immigration over the centuries has turned the United States into the most multicultural of all industrial countries. Between 1820 (when our government began keeping track of immigration) and 1990, more than fifty-five million people came to our shores from other nations. A century ago, most immigrants arrived from Europe; today, a majority of newcomers arrive from Latin America and Asia.

The Census Bureau's most recent population profile indicates that children born in the 1990s may well live to see people of Asian, Hispanic, and African ancestry as a majority of this country's population. The United States is truly becoming a microcosm of the world's people. With that reality in mind, proponents see multiculturalism as needed preparation for living in a world in which nations are increasingly interdependent. Our national economy is certainly reflecting this condition. Teaching global connectedness will probably be easier through education that includes music of the world's people. The National Standards for Arts Education address this reality emphatically in the following statement:

> The cultural diversity of America is a vast resource for arts education and should be used to help students understand themselves and others. The visual, traditional, and performing arts provide a variety of lenses for examining the cultures and artistic contributions of our nation and others around the world. Students should learn that each art form has its own characteristics and makes its distinctive contributions, that each has its own history and heroes. . . . Subject matter from diverse historical periods, styles, forms, and cultures should be used to develop basic knowledge and skills in the various art disciplines.[2]

The 1997 Population Profile of the United States, published by the U.S. Department of Economics and Statistics Administration, contains data that have significant implications for education in general, and for music education in particular. According to that report, the U.S. population is projected to increase to 394 million by 2050; this is about 50% larger than today's population. This growth will be concentrated among the school-age population, people in their thirties and forties, and the elderly. It is predicted that the average age of the population will be older than it is now. During 1996, growth rates were highest for the Hispanic (of any race) and for the Asian and Pacific Islander populations. The African-American population is projected to reach 40 million by 2010, and 61 million by 2050.

In October 1995, 69.6 million people were enrolled in school. Among 3- and 4-year-olds, 44.9% were enrolled in nursery school. The number of elementary and high school students was lower in 1995 than in the peak years of the early 1970s but higher than in the mid-1980s. At the college level, there were 14.7 million students in 1995, 41% of whom were aged 25 and over. About 5.4% of all students in the tenth, eleventh, and twelfth grades dropped out of school in the one-year period from October 1994 to October 1995. Among people aged 25 and over in 1996, 81.7% had completed high school and 23.6% had completed four or more years of college. High school completion for people aged 25 and over stood at 82.8% for Whites, 74.3% for Blacks, and 53.1% for Hispanics. Racial differences in educational attainment continued to narrow noticeably between Blacks and Whites. Since 1980, African Americans have made remarkable educational progress, with the proportion of Black adults completing high school rising from half to almost three-fourths, nearly closing the historical gap between the two. Between 1980 and 1995, moreover, the share of African American adults with at least a college degree rose from 8% to 13%. But, at the college level, there remains striking racial disparity. African Americans have attained little better than half the national standard when it comes to completing four years of college. These data will have an impact on the faculty make-up of the next century, which will be discussed later in this paper.

Among the states, California had both the largest number and percentage of foreign born; that is, eight million people or one-fourth of California's total population. Most of the rapid population growth states were located in the West and South. Some states, such as California and New York, were gaining many new residents from international migration while losing even larger numbers through net out-migration to other states. By 2025, nearly one billion people are projected to move interstate. The most populous states in the South will continue to grow fairly rapidly. During 1994, Texas replaced New York as the third most populous state, and it is expected to remain in that position throughout the projected period. Florida is projected to become much larger by 2020. Demographic changes typically transform some parts of the country more than others.

Between 1995 and 2025, California, Texas, and Florida expect the greatest state population gains, more than six million people to each state. Each year from now to 2050, the race/ethnic group adding the largest number of people to the population will be the Hispanic-origin population. After 2020, the Hispanic population is projected to add more people to the U.S. every year than will all other race/ethnic groups combined. By 2010, the Hispanic origin population may become the second largest race/ethnic group. Thus, the already-apparent problem of high Hispanic school-aged dropouts may be the most critical issue in the educational system in the next millennium. Also, by 2025, young people are expected to make up less than 25% of the population of most metropolitan areas. In more than one-third of the states, the elderly are projected to double their share of those states' total population, with metropolitan areas showing the greatest rate of growth.

Considering these changing demographics, other issues need clarification. Our nation is officially committed to the credo that all men are created equal, yet race and ethnicity will continue to permeate the lives of men, women, and children in many ways. We might develop a better understanding of these two categories by considering how social scientists define them. *Ethnicity* is a shared cultural heritage. Common ancestors, language, and religion confer a distinctive social identity. *Race* is a category composed of men and women who share biologically transmitted traits. While some people classify each other socially based upon physical characteristics such as skin color, hair texture, facial features, and body shape, racial features have nothing to do with being human. As human beings we are all members of a single biological species. Over the course of history, human migration spread genetic characteristics throughout much of the world. No society lacks genetic mixture, and increasing contact among the world's people ensures that racial blending will accelerate in the future.[3]

Interracial births have doubled since 1980. Moreover, when completing the 1990 census forms, almost ten million people omitted checking a racial category. The Census Bureau is likely to respond to the growing racial complexity of our society by adding a new "multicultural" option in the near future.[4] The term "minority" has usually connoted a category of people who are socially disadvantaged, who have a disability, and/or who are underrepresented in the economic and professional arenas. With the demographic numbers forecast herein, that connotation will have to change as well. In the next millennium, because of the blurring of lines of racial and ethnic identities, we in music education will have to adhere to a more egalitarian posture that urges us to refrain from being judgmental or guilty of racist behaviors and unfounded assumptions.

Although there are several controversial issues that cause divided opinions among educators regarding cultural diversity (i.e., ethnocentrism vs. eurocentrism; divisiveness vs. unity; separatism vs. universalism), our demographic forecast for the next millennium mandates that our nation's schools, teachers, and administrators find a workable solution to these problems. Indeed, our students are not the problem, and they deserve that we "work it out." We must provide solutions that give them a chance for a better life in which music literacy matters and is an integral part of who they are. It is central to our vision that we remember that culture is ever changing, and while these changes sometimes function as a constraint, they also serve as a continual source of human opportunity, enrichment, and growth.

TECHNOLOGICAL CHANGES THAT WILL AFFECT THE TEACHING OF MUSIC

Technology has produced new objects, ideas, and social patterns, as well as new ways of thinking about them. We are reminded that Max Weber traced roots of social change to the world of ideas.[5] Social change happens everywhere. The rate of change, however, varies from place to place. What is social change? Sociologists define it as the transformation of culture and social institutions over time. Social changes are sometimes intentional but are often unplanned. As we observe the effects of technological advances, cultural changes have dynamics that continually show gains and losses. For example, diffusion of information has created change in trade, migration, and mass communication that has spread cultural elements from one society to another. Technology is accelerating social change worldwide so fast that it has become difficult to identify the change in definitive ways. Time is an important factor in that recognition.

Since the Industrial Revolution more than two centuries ago, the latter half of this century has witnessed the unfolding of another technological transformation—the Information Revolution. Just as industrialization increased society's capacity to produce "things," this new information technology is vastly expanding our ability to create ideas and new forms of communication. The Information Revolution is changing virtually every dimension of our lives altering the workplace by recasting the meaning and location of work, revising the curricular content and teaching methods of all disciplines in education including music instruction, and even altering the nature of human relationships.

The computer has become central to our way of life. The development of the Internet places more than one hundred million people in 90 percent of the world countries in instant communication with one another.[6] As stated in the opening paragraph, because society comprises countless interdependent elements, the development of new information technology is likely to cause changes in all aspects of our lives by rewriting the rules for those living in the next century. People will probably work either at home or often at some place far from the "central office." As people pay less attention to their neighbors and spend more time communicating with others "on line," human communities will be reshaped as a result. Personal isolation may also be a significant byproduct in music teaching as well. That same ability to participate online with other students will allow for team projects, group-oriented research, interchange of musical ideas in composition and arranging, and countless other creative endeavors for the musical development of students, some of whom may live on another continent and be of another culture; hence "the classroom without walls."

Education is likely to be the common denominator that will separate and stratify our society, causing greater inequality. As we know, there is a high correlation between education and affluence; in other words, between education and the use of technology and ideas. Indeed, it is noted that more affluent people are acquiring new information technology while poor people are not. The Information Age is literally dividing our society into two distinct groups: those with sophisticated symbolic skills (who are likely to prosper) and others without these abilities (destined for low-income jobs), thus producing another dimension of the "haves and have nots." This circumstance will present a formidable obstacle to educators regardless of their subject or specialty. With more than 97 percent of schools reporting the use of computers for instruction, making sure that computer use is equally shared by ad students must be the rule. Computer Assisted Instruction (CAI) as a technology advance continues to support the teaching and learning of music. More sophisticated CAI software will enhance the development of aural skills, theoretical and historical understanding, and actual performance, as well as programs that seek to stimulate music experiences associated with composition and improvisation.[7]

One of the most significant technological changes on the horizon within the next ten years, according to Christine Hermanson, is the development and commercialization of interactive TV as the next wave of technology that will affect the way music is taught in the schools and in the home/studio.[8]

Another trend on the horizon is that more and more of the cultural symbols that frame our lives will be created via animation. A continuous flow of Disney characters (Pocahontas, Tarzan, Mulan), as well as Power Rangers, Ninja Turtles, and Ronald McDonald, are cultural icons that help shape our values. Today, young children are becoming preoccupied with virtual culture, elements that spring from the minds of contemporary culture makers for commercial gains. New technology is virtually changing reality and will compete with traditional cultural symbols, values, historical events, and even music makers (composers and performers).

Technology has grown and will continue to grow in its power, complexity, and prevalence. The fantastic depth and breadth of music today creates a sense that music surrounds us and is simply a part of life. Music education will need to instill the realization that such diversity and quantity of music has various levels of sophistication. Quantity is not synonymous with high quality. Having the computer resources to make it possible to create original music does not mean the user will become an expert composer. Furthermore, an intelligent consumer of this musical information requires a high level of music literacy and maturity. Technology has spawned numerous institutional changes. The following are examples:

1. Technology is affecting our economy and changing the way our commerce is conducted. Individuals can purchase CDs, tapes, music scores, and new manuscripts directly from composers and performers, thus eliminating the middleman . . . the music distributor.
2. Technology is defining the skills needed to find employment. Working with one's head has replaced the need to work with one's hands. Musicians with computer skills are able to search out available positions more expeditiously and cover a wider geographic area within less time. International job searches are more common.
3. By digital imagery, photographers can combine and manipulate pictures and combine animation with people and animals. Although few music teachers have such skills, for those who do, teaching aids can create a delightful learning environment with untold possibilities.
4. In colleges, universities, and the public schools, students now have a proliferation of images on tape, film, and computer disk. Texts are available on CD-ROM and can be downloaded directly from across the Internet. Exploring the use of the computer and technology in the many aspects of the music experience in undergraduate and graduate courses of study is perhaps one of the most beneficial avenues for the future of music teacher education. While the technology exists to deliver practically any musical concept, the question of curricular integrity and instructional efficiency still needs to be addressed. Music education must be able to continue its traditions of the music academy and conservatory, while at the same time provide "cutting edge" curricula and instructional strategies that will facilitate distance education opportunities.
5. Interactive computer-based instruction is fast eliminating the need to travel to classrooms to learn, receive, and complete assignments. Students can be graded through the same process. Distance learning will present an alternative to attending college in person. A growing collaboration between college campuses and the Internet—called "on line education" or "distance learning"—lets one take courses and earn entire degrees via computer without ever setting foot on a campus. A distance-learning course might incorporate one or more of these techniques: videotaped courses, e-mail, interactive video, computer conferencing, and courses where information is distributed on the Web. Advanced systems provide embedded video film, whereby a student can see and hear lectures, and online chat, which lets a "virtual" classroom of students interact "in real time" at home. Matriculation costs are expensive for these programs. Yet in some cases travel and hotel expenses for face-to-face meetings are included in the program costs. Cyber-degrees should improve as traditional universities offer more of their curricula online.[9]

6. Performance classes, ensemble rehearsals, recitals and concerts, and private lessons will still require the physical presence of students and audiences, but practice formats will be altered by CAI software that can provide instrumental accompaniments.
7. E-mail, fax, online discussion groups, "chat rooms," and the ability to search out libraries around the world are merely a sampling of cyberspace capabilities for communication and dissemination of information.
8. Technological developments are affecting gender stratification. They promise to propel the trend toward gender equality by centering on manipulating ideas that are gender neutral. The elimination of face-to-face communication will also eliminate the need to know a person's sex, race, or age.
9. Cyber-work fits easily into flexible schedules and does not hinge on punching a time clock. One can care for a loved one or "baby-sit" for example, and still work and/or complete homework assignments.

These trends in technology are exciting and thought provoking. However, computers cannot supplant or substitute for the imagination or the motivation of a human teacher; nor can a machine solve many of the social and academic problems we live with on a daily basis. The problems in our public schools are rooted in the larger society. [10]

As we approach the next century, we should understand that the schools alone cannot raise the quality of education but will improve only to the extent that teachers, parents, communities at large, and students themselves are committed to the pursuit of educational excellence. Social problems have no "quick fixes." If we are to even approach the effective implementation of our National Standards and the goal of "music for every person and every person for music" we must first seek a broad plan for social change and educational equality that reaffirms our country's early ambition to embrace quality universal schooling. Excellent music teachers who care about their subject and are committed to the students they teach are even more critical to those goals as we move into the next millennium.

MUSIC TEACHING IN THE TWENTY-FIRST CENTURY

For several years, music educators, scholars, and researchers have been using the phrase "in the next millennium" in their discourses. At this writing, it is disquieting to suddenly realize that that historic event is now only a few months away. Indeed, "ready or not, we *shall* be caught."

Given the demographics discussed herein, one does not have to stretch the imagination too far or be too perceptive to realize that music educators in

America have a tremendous responsibility to develop a wider pool of culturally diverse students, including minorities, who will be both talented in music performance and exhibit music literacy, understanding, skills, and knowledge that qualify them to enter college and university programs as music majors for the purpose of joining the music profession as teachers and administrators. Unfortunately, our track record in this area has been abysmal. The music teaching profession in the United States is in dire need of well-trained individuals who will serve the diverse multicultural school-age students they will confront in our nation's public-school classrooms for years to come.

Why should the ethnic and cultural demographics of the music teaching force reflect the diversity of the students it serves? Why recruit minority music teachers? First we should consider the issue of the importance to minority children of having various models among their teachers. For example, a cadre of all-white music teaching staff will not give African-American, Latino, or Asian-American students the perspective that they might become professional music educators. James Fraser suggests that in schools where the majority of students are from disempowered groups, having a teaching force that includes few representatives of the community creates power relationships that reinforce disempowerment. [11]

Willis Hawley has argued: "The most effective way to combat racism is to undermine the assumptions upon which it rests and to arm persons with the skills to overcome its consequences. These objectives can be achieved by placing persons of different races or ethnic backgrounds in situations where they have the opportunity for recurrent interaction involving cooperative and rewarding activities." [12] This statement suggests that it is only after teachers of different races have the experience of working together that they will learn to treat each other as equals. A more diverse teaching force would provide the experiences that many music teachers may need to relate well to parents, community leaders, and their own students.

A second and important reason for recruiting minority music teachers is the role teachers play in defining the music curriculum. It continues to be important for the United States to build a culture that represents the diversity of its population. Having representatives of different cultures and races on the music teaching staff in a community is an important step toward building that more diverse culture and developing a representative music curriculum.

STRATEGIES FOR MINORITY RECRUITMENT

While there are good reasons for recruiting minorities into the music teacher profession, increasing the number of minority music teachers will not be easy. There are many social and school factors that contribute to making the pool of minority college students and music education graduates small. Thus longer-term strategies must be implemented to help resolve larger issues such as institutional racism. While short-term things can be done to improve minority teacher representation, unless the larger more culturally based issues are addressed, little progress will be made.

Areas on which the music education profession can focus to begin to initiate change include:

- simplifying certification requirements
- avoiding the development of new barriers
- early recruitment of minority teachers
- providing support in undergraduate programs
- mentoring during the first years of teaching

Simplifying certification requirements. State music education certification requirements are based on the model of a four-or-more-year educational experience. For minority musicians with undergraduate degrees and an interest in teaching, a traditional route to certification typically would include a year or more of study, including student teaching. For experienced adults, these traditional paths to certification can constitute a difficult hurdle, having a negative impact on families and limiting financial resources.

Innovative certification routes, which require some additional study, possibly over a summer with immediate entry into a teaching position in the fall, with close supervision and mentoring may help limit the expense and disruption to families that such a transition into teaching might cause. In some states where the bar to provisional certification has been lowered, the requirements for permanent certification have been raised; thus the combination of coursework and teaching experience required for permanent certification has not changed dramatically. Alternative certification requirements that insure quality should be vigorously pursued.

Avoiding the development of new barriers. One new barrier some states have initiated is the expectation that prospective music teachers will have a five-year college experience (awarding both a bachelor's and master's degree) prior to entry into the profession. Five years of study does not necessarily make better music teachers, and it places additional burdens on minority candidates for music teaching as it requires an additional year of financial expenditure before income can be realized. While the profession should continue to advocate additional professional study culminating in a master's degree, an approach that integrates teaching experience with graduate study can be more beneficial to the development of the music teacher, allowing the teacher to mature and integrate the knowledge and skills from courses with the experience of the classroom.

Another new barrier many states are placing in the paths of prospective teachers is competency testing. Fraser states, "There is virtually no correlation between success in tests and success in the classroom."[13] In addition, he states that it is a "clearly documented fact that any test available today has considerable race, class, and gender bias in it,"[14] thus making such testing inappropriate and contributing to the difficulty in finding minority teachers. While it is important to advocate for high standards, the challenge is to produce enough minority candidates who can meet high standards that meaningfully measure a prospective music teacher's fitness for the job.

Early recruitment of minority teachers. Rather than placing barriers, the music education profession must seek innovative ways of attracting minorities to music teaching. One approach may be to identify and recruit prospective music teachers at an early age. This might be as early as middle or high school. By identifying minority students with potential at that age and providing support and mentoring, one may begin to limit the dramatic dropout rates that plague the high schools with large enrollments of students, consequently limiting the pool of potential minority applicants for undergraduate programs. Such efforts have been undertaken in Boston by the teacher's union, which has proposed a program in which area colleges, in cooperation with public school teachers, would work with middle school students to help them complete high school, find college placement and scholarship support, and ultimately find jobs as teachers in the Boston Public Schools. New York City is also supporting this notion with the establishment of a High School for Teaching, which gives its students early experiences in tutoring younger students.

Providing support in undergraduate programs. Undergraduate music teacher programs are often organized with a series of "hurdles" instituted with the notion of insuring the quality of graduates. The first clearly identifiable hurdle is the admissions process. Many undergraduate music programs look for prospective students in traditional sites and with traditional backgrounds (e.g., played in the high school concert band). If undergraduate programs are going to increase the presence of minority students, they need to institute affirmative action programs that pursue prospective minority musicians in nontraditional venues. Some potential minority students may have extensive music backgrounds comprising primarily informal music experiences, such as playing in a "rock band." While these atypical experiences may not provide prospective music teachers with the skills and understanding, such as reading music, that undergraduate music programs often expect of their entering students, they may still provide the students opportunities to develop very high levels of musicianship.

In addition to the admissions process, music teacher education programs often include other hurdles, such as a second admissions process into a specific education major at the end of the sophomore year. For a music education program, this screening may require a particular grade-point average, an audition, an interview, and additional recommendations. Faculty must monitor such hurdles to make sure they do not constitute a special barrier to minority students. Other affirmative actions can be taken to help students succeed in preservice music education programs. These include the presence of minority faculty in music teacher education programs and the mentoring of younger minority undergraduates by more senior minority teacher education students.

Mentoring during the first years of teaching. As many educators involved in teacher education realize, the development of career professional music educators does not end with undergraduate education. The first several years of teaching are often difficult and may be especially challenging for some teachers, particularly if they find themselves isolated within teaching environments that do not include models with whom they can identify. Several strategies can be employed to help the novice minority music teacher.

College teacher education programs can provide support and mentoring for their graduates, efforts that include both on-site visits to new teachers and on-campus seminars to help minority teachers with the transition to the professional world. Teachers' unions and professional groups such as the National Association for the Study and Performance of African American Music (NASPAAM) can also provide support for new teachers. School systems should also make efforts to hire a core of minority teachers so that isolation will be less of a problem.

Conclusions. Increasing the number of minority music teachers requires multiple efforts at different stages in the development of career professional music educators. With the profession's best efforts, it will still likely take a generation before significant numbers of minority music educators will be present in the nation's schools. Therefore, a continuing effort needs to be made to improve prospective music educators' understanding of diversity issues. A token course in music from other cultures is not sufficient to develop the depth of understanding required.

Music teacher education programs in colleges and universities must provide a well-structured and culturally inclusive core-curriculum representative of (a) traditional areas of music study that have undergirded the competencies and standards required to complete high-quality degree programs, and (b) ethnomusicological perspectives and competencies in order to prepare well-trained graduates for the teaching profession. If music education is to survive and progress in the future, these two components must work in close partnership with one another. The significant rise in the minority population indicates a marked transformation of the workforce, with women showing the greatest increase by 2005. Institutions that begin to plan now for this growing social diversity will tap the largest talent pool and enjoy a competitive advantage throughout the next century.

Music education needs the best and brightest as much as any other profession. That must be one of our priority efforts beginning now. Music occupies a very important place in the cultural lives of most minorities outside of the school setting. Our challenge is to capitalize on that inherent interest as a conduit into the serious pursuit of musicianship and skills requisite to entry into higher education music programs. That effort will call for support systems that assure that all students will receive unbiased instruction, sincere counseling, and role model mentors, as well as cultural representation included within the teaching materials.

Transforming the classroom environment to develop the potential of all students, regardless of their ethnicity, will require music teachers with highly developed crosscultural sensitivities and social skills. Music teachers should realize that the social needs and concerns of minorities are often not the same as those of majority students. For example, the competitive mode of the teaching/learning environment so favored in our American style of instruction does not receive positive responses from minority students who react more favorably to a cooperative mode.[15] Hispanics tend to be more concerned with the quality of relationships over time, rather than with simply getting the job done. They have a strong sense of family loyalties. They tend to maintain closer physical contact in their personal space than many nonHispanics.[16] Asian students value education and have a high regard for teachers and their role in the instructional process. They have been reared by their parents to show obedience and respect in the school setting. Their studiousness and strong work ethic often translate into high academic accomplishment. However, lack of communication skills may sometimes pose a language barrier that will be a challenge to overcome for both students and teachers. Communication skills are also a problem for Hispanic students. As for the new Asian students, each is striving to balance two cultures; the culture of their homelands and that of mainstream American societies.[17] Argyle suggests the presence of seven skills for engaging in social transactions such as those of instruction: perceptive skills, expressive skills, conversational skills, assertiveness, emotional expression, anxiety management, and affiliative skills.[18]

Effective music teachers will have to devise appropriate classroom strategies for defusing tensions that normally arise from social differences. Teachers will have to work harder at treating all students equally and respectfully, bearing in mind the vital importance of consistent verbal and nonverbal behaviors in the acculturation process. Moreover, before academic behaviors can be effective, these social behaviors must be firmly established.[19] Research in classroom discipline and subject-matter presentation, as well as in establishing music behavior within applied settings, offers music educators, regardless of specialty, a wealth of data addressing the teacher-training process for future music educators.[20] The issues involved in improving undergraduates' skills are of vital interest to all music educators throughout the profession. Madsen wrote: "Besides the obvious role of college professors, most music teachers who have even a few years of experience serve as models for observations, supervisors of student teachers, and members of peer-review committees. Just as we care deeply about teaching children music, we are all concerned with teaching those who will themselves teach children."[21]

MINORITIES IN HIGHER EDUCATION

The "Sixteenth Annual Status Report on Minorities in Higher Education"[22] summarizes the most recent data available on key indicators of progress in American higher education. The report analyzes high school completion and dropout rates and trends in college participation, educational attainment, college enrollment, degrees conferred, and higher education employment by race and ethnicity. Although the report does not indicate specific subject areas and disciplines in which minorities major or are employed, it does offer national data beneficial as indicators of access to and progress within higher education for African Americans, Hispanics, Asian Americans, and American Indians.

Recent legal challenges to affirmative action in higher education have already resulted in reduced enrollment of minority students in both California and Texas. Efforts to promote a diverse student body are under attack in other states, including Washington, Georgia, and Michigan. "Lessening degree attainment among underrepresented groups in America also undermines the nation's ability to remain a globally competitive democracy in the twenty-first century," writes Stanley O. Ikenberry, president of the American Council on Education. He further states, "The challenge for higher education to expand access to opportunity must remain high on our collective agenda. The very future of our nation—the health of our economy, the strength of our democracy, our quality of life as a people—depends on broad access to high quality higher education."[23]

College Enrollment

The Status Report shows that more African Americans and Hispanics are enrolling in the nation's colleges and universities and that, as a group, these students (including Asian Americans and American Indians) are earning more undergraduate and graduate degrees. Although the enrollment and graduation rates of these students continue to rise, the rate of growth has slowed compared to previous years. Minority students continue to lag behind Whites in educational attainment at all levels, and on too many of our campuses the make-up of the faculty and staff members does not yet reflect the diverse society we serve now or that is projected in the very near future.

The report presents a vast amount of data. What follows are samples from that report:[24]

College participation rates among all high school graduates aged 18 to 24 continued increasing to 43.5% in 1996. From 1995 to 1996, Hispanics achieved the greatest progress of the four major ethnic minority groups with an increase of 5%. All of those groups posted enrollment increases at two-year and four-year institutions from 1995 to 1996. Minority students achieved their greatest gains in enrollment at the graduate level, where enrollment rose by 5.7% from 1995 to 199G. They recorded the smallest gains at the professional school level, where enrollment increased by only 2.9%.

African Americans' total enrollment has increased each year during the 1990s, with a cumulative gain of 12.3% from 1991 to 1996. Hispanic enrollment in higher education increased by 33% from 1991 to 1996, the largest gain among the four major ethnic minority groups. College enrollment among Asian Americans increased by 3.4% from 1991 to 1996, continuing an upward trend. From 1991 to 1996, African American college enrollment increased by 29.3%. American Indian and Alaska Natives recorded some gains in higher education in enrollment in 1996, particularly at four-year institutions and graduate schools. However, their numbers remain small. In 1996, only 133,972 American Indians were enrolled in higher education.

Graduation Rates/Degrees Conferred

Minorities achieved progress in all four major degree categories from 1994 to 1995, led by a 9.3% increase at the master's degree level. Women were awarded more bachelor's and master's degrees than men, and they also out-gained men in their rate of increase from 1994 to 1995. Minorities earned 18% of all bachelor's degrees in 1995, up by about 1% from 1994 and by nearly 5% since 1990. Nonetheless, minority students were underrepresented in degrees awarded compared to their enrollment levels. American Indians in 1996 had the lowest graduation rate of the four major ethnic groups at Division I colleges and universities. Hispanics lost ground as well. Asian Americans had the highest Division I graduation rates of the four ethnic minority groups; their 1996 rate of 64% was 5% higher when compared to all others, including Whites.

The number of doctoral degrees earned by these minority students remained steady from 1995 to 1996 following moderate growth during the past decade. Overall, minority students have achieved gains of 74.1% in the number of doctoral degrees earned during the most recent decade.

Employment in Higher Education

The number of full-time minority faculty increased by 6.9% from 1993 to 1995. Among full professors, the number of faculty rose by 6.7%, while the rate of Whites remained largely unchanged. All four major ethnic minority groups achieved moderate gains in terms of the number of full professors from 1993 to 1995, although minority faculty made the greatest progress at the associate and assistant professor levels. Tenure rates of minority faculty did not change from 1993 to 1995, while the rate of Whites increased slightly. In 1995, 74% of White faculty and 62% of minority faculty held tenured positions. A 9.1% increase in the number of Asian-American full-time faculty was the largest 1993 to 1995 gain among the four ethnic minority groups. A 15.2% gain by Asian-American women accounted for much of this progress. African Americans continue to have the lowest tenure rate among the four major ethnic minority groups. In 1995, African Americans trailed Whites in tenure rate by 5%. The tenure rates for American Indians, though small, was unchanged. Faculty rank data for Hispanics showed wide differences by gender. The number of Hispanic fulltime faculty increased by 7.2% from 1993 to 1995, with women achieving a 10% gain compared to men at 5.4%. Nationwide in 1997, African Americans, Hispanics, Asian Americans, and American Indians accounted for 11.3% of all college and university chief executive officers where racial and ethnic identity was verified.

AT-RISK STUDENTS: A CRISIS IN EDUCATION

Despite the encouraging data reported herein, there is another underlying problem that must be addressed by educators if all students are to be served adequately. That problem is the increasingly high rate of our at-risk students regardless of ethnicity.

At the high school level, 12% of youth aged 16 to 24 had dropped out of school in 1995, a slight increase from 1993, but a decline from levels during the 1980s. Gender was not a factor. The 12.1% dropout rate of African Americans in 1995 was higher than the 8.6% dropout rate among Whites aged 16 to 24. Hispanics had the highest dropout rate—30%—among the three groups in 1995. Foreign-born Hispanics and Hispanics who spoke little or no English at home were more likely to have dropped out of school.

Two model university programs that have distinguished themselves as successfully attacking the problem of children-at-risk are the University of Wisconsin System's Institute on Race and Ethnicity and Yale University's Child Study Center. The University of Wisconsin System has led the nation in its pursuit of educational excellence and diversity through expanded opportunity. In 1988, it was the first university system to adopt a long-range plan for racial/ethnic diversity. That plan, *Design for Diversity*, was based on the belief that a public university must serve all the people of the state and must lead the way in increasing educational opportunity for targeted racial/ethnic groups. *Design for Diversity* is concluding this year, and *Plan 2008*, its successor, has just been completed and builds on collaboratively developed plans that offer a vision of a better, diverse University of Wisconsin (UW) System for the decade ahead. *Plan 2008* statewide contributors included students, faculty, staff, community members, regents, administrators, legislators, representatives of the Department of Public Instruction and Wisconsin Technical College System, and others. The UW System recognizes "the need to provide educational experiences in and out of the classroom, that respect cultivate and build upon the diversity that all groups bring (i.e., gender, religion, nationality, sexual orientation, and differently-abled)."[25] Concept #5 of that plan states, "African American, Hispanic/Latino, Southeast Asian, American Indian, and economically disadvantaged students in grades K-12 have often been stereotyped as 'children-at-risk.' The UW System views all students as 'children-of-promise.' They are valuable assets to society, their communities and the University."[26]

The problem of Hispanic school dropouts is currently one of the UW System's foremost areas of academic concentrations and research efforts.[27] U.S. Secretary of Education Richard Riley, at the urging of New Mexico Senator Jeff Bingaman, appointed a group of research scholars, policy analysts, and practitioners to study issues surrounding Hispanic school dropouts and to report back to him with a set of relevant policy recommendations. From 1995 through 1997 the Hispanic Dropout Project (HDP)[28] held open hearings and took public testimony in locations around the nation whose schools enrolled large numbers of Hispanic students. The HDP held press conferences at those sites to publicize the problem of Hispanic dropout. The project reviewed the extant research on at-risk students and school dropouts. "No More Excuses," the commission's final report,[29] reemphasized the need for the collective will of parents and families, teachers, school districts, state and national policymakers and stakeholders, and communities to work together to solve a very important but, until now, largely invisible national problem. The report concluded that while some Hispanic students behave in an antisocial manner and there does exist some dysfunctional behavior within their family structures, their problems are not unlike many other ethnic students, and the crisis of Hispanic dropout is neither acceptable nor does it reside within the Hispanic community alone.

The School Development Program (SDP), in Yale Child Study Center, has for three decades worked to serve the needs of children by fostering schools that nurture them through a collaboration of teachers, administrators, families, and others in the community.[30] Inspired by universal wisdom of the African proverb "it takes a whole village to raise a child," and backed by extensive child-development research, SDP brings caring adults together to work for the children of each school or "village." The program (which began in two New Haven, Connecticut, public schools) has been adopted by six hundred schools in twenty states, the District of Columbia, Trinidad, Tobago, and England. The program originally addressed the needs of urban students and schools, but experience has shown that it benefits all children in a broad array of diverse communities. High student retention is but one of its outstanding accomplishments.

A report sponsored by the Council of Arts Accrediting Associations (CAAA), entitled *Minority Students and Access to Arts Study*[31] addresses the question of building minds through access to study by briefing the reader on a large number of facts that have connecting issues derived from those facts. The report verifies the data that have been presented in this paper. It acknowledges and supports the premise that involvement of qualified minority students in higher education depends, to a large degree, on the availability of quality instruction and the development of competencies in the precollegiate years. The premise refers both to formal school-based arts education and to specialized training in the arts. The report further points to a glaring need: assessment of the readiness of minority students to do college-level work in the arts. It further asserts that research on the issue of precollegiate arts education for minority students has not to date been a priority for researchers in arts education, the arts, or education.

By not conducting studies in classrooms populated by minorities, researchers are ignoring a veritable cornucopia of data that are sorely needed by music educators. How do minorities learn specific skills and knowledge in the teaching/learning process most effectively? What are their music preferences and aptitudes? Are there specific teacher behaviors by which to achieve desired student academic and social behaviors? Music teachers need that kind of information more than ever. That area of research will more than likely take on a new urgency as we move into the next millennium. Ultimately, all students regardless of ethnicity will benefit from such research efforts. The following studies are examples of empirical work needed for our future success in music teaching.

Nancy Barry found that students who had participated in music ensembles in schools and churches did not agree strongly with a questionnaire statement: "Elementary classroom music should include experiences with ethnic music of different cultures."[32] She concluded that this result reflects the eurocentricity prevalent in the repertoire of many performing groups. It appears that participation in an ensemble that limits its repertoire to specific types of literature (usually from the Western European tradition) may serve to bias students against those of other forms and styles that are excluded.[33]

Jan McCrary examined *the effects of listeners' and performers' race on music preferences.* Her findings acknowledge the importance of the "cultural legacy" of diverse racial and ethnic groups and offer data to recommend the use of specific teaching strategies and curricular materials that should not be limited to familiar and easily accessible popular styles that tend to stereotype, but should be extended to Black performers of art music as well. [34]

E. Victor Fung investigated undergraduate nonmusic majors' world music performance and multicultural attitudes. His study explored two other variables: (1) world music preferences as a function of age, and (2) knowledge of a foreign language. A significant correlation between world music preferences and multicultural attitudes supports the view that social/cultural attitudes play a role in world music preference. Knowledge of foreign language(s) also has an impact on world music preference. [35] Several implications were advanced: (1) Music may be a means for students' cultural experiences that could help to foster multicultural education for the general education of students, (2) instrumental world music may be a good medium to begin with when teaching world musical styles that involve listening, [36] and (3) among the eight style categories included in the study, music from China, Indonesia, Japan, Africa, and India may be used in the early stages of teaching world music most effectively. Vocal styles received lower preference ratings, probably due to unfamiliar vocal tone production, language barriers, unusual tessitura and gender of singer. Younger students had more positive multicultural attitudes.

The Status of Arts Education in American Public Schools [37] was summarized in the CAAA report. The report states, "It has been found, however tentatively, that many minority students are undoubtedly affected, perhaps disproportionately so, by program inconsistency. Finally, compensatory education programs of the federal government aimed, in large part, at minority students, seem to stress instruction in the arts as a means to other educational and social goals and not in the art forms themselves. Such an emphasis is not conducive to future specialization in the arts." [38] The report discusses two possible avenues to access of minorities to higher education programs that are germane to the focus of this paper:

1. *The future collaboration of arts high schools and arts magnet schools, arts organizations, community schools of the arts, private instruction, and parental influences.* Community music schools of the arts especially, would seem to be fertile territory for the preparation of minority students qualified for admission to post-secondary arts programs, especially if those experiences serve to supplement the skills and knowledge students gain through quality school-based arts education programs. [39] A briefing paper by the National Association of Schools of Music suggests that the success of community schools of music can enable music units in higher education to be more effective for all students.

Historically this impact has been felt more in regions where community education movement continues to expand. Its influence will be increasingly felt by all postsecondary music programs. This prospect places special responsibilities on the shoulders of those involved with music in higher education who seek to begin or expand community education programs in their institutions. A primary goal must be to extend the potential for accomplishment already evident in the community education movement to serve a broader and more varied constituency in communities throughout the nation. The potentials are enormous.[40]

2. *School-college partnerships in the arts.* The report cites programs that vary in purpose from enrichment to skill development to college preparation and recruitment. A number of these partnership programs evidence features that may point to successful minority preparation for and involvement in higher education. These include:

- a early identification of minority students with high academic potential
- a provision of a sequential set of learning experiences that progressively build upon each other
- comprehensive approaches that address the breadth of skills needed for college admission
- attention to preparing students for the precollege work necessary for admission to higher education
- evaluation of program effectiveness in terms of minority recruitment and, in some cases, retention
- explicit objectives to encourage students toward specific career paths[41]

THE ROLE OF THE COMMUNITY COLLEGE IN VISION 2020

In the 1960s, expansion of the community college system at a rate of nearly one per week provided greater access to higher education. This new educational revolution was designed to more adequately provide educational opportunities for the typically underserved individuals. The community college heralded its new image as the "open door." This concept presupposed that any individual, regardless of level of academic preparedness or college readiness, would be allowed to pursue a college degree. Further, the community college would provide an affordable, accessible education with adequate assessments and remedial and college-level instruction that would effectively ensure a seamless transition into either university transfer programs or directly into the workplace.

The community college has successfully adapted to the changing sociological trends as demonstrated by its significant growth in population, academic programs, and physical size. In fact, enrollment has doubled since 1970.[42] In many states such as California, Florida, New York, Texas, and Illinois, the community college system has evolved so rapidly that systems have distinguished themselves by campuses. A campus may have been created to attract a particular professional program or a certain population, or may simply have been positioned as a comprehensive institution in a new and growing community. As it has attempted to become more responsive to the needs of its constituents, the community college is widely recognized as the community's college.

While the community college has prided itself on its access, or rather its "open door," it has actually been "a door" itself. In 2020, this door will be more restrictive or may become a physical barrier for the new student. By virtue of their work responsibilities, home obligations, constraints of time and urgency to complete specialized job training and retraining needs, students will seek short-term opportunities and distance learning methods to accommodate their educational needs.

Data from a large community college system show the steady changes reflected in the demographics of the new community college students.[43] Diversity is the most apparent demographic icon. Diversity in ethnicity, age, gender, academic readiness, culture, and expectations is a major reality. The influx of immigrants into major cities has changed the face of the "majority" population generally and the community college student population in particular. Students are older, returning to college to retrain for a different career after having entered the workplace or wanting to rectify the failed first attempt at college. More women are starting college for the first time after having raised a family or finding themselves as a single parent with great responsibilities.

The following list summarizes a few demographics of the new student:

- 69% of credit students are enrolled part time (number tripled since 1970)
- 63% of credit students are Hispanics; 21% are Black non-Hispanics
- 42% of credit students are not U.S. citizens
- more than 41% of credit students are aged 26 or older
- only 25% are the traditional college age of 18 to 20 years old
- 33% of credit students are resident aliens
- 8% of credit students are refugee or asylum categories
- while 58% are U.S. citizens, many of these are naturalized citizens
- only 45% report a native language of Spanish
- nearly 3,000 Haitian students report Creole or French as their native language
- only 21% of incoming students test as college-ready

- 10% of all students and 14% of Hispanics test into ESL coursework
- 69% of all students need help in reading, writing, algebra, or all three

In addition to the existing demographics, societal trends reflected in the place or physical-setting needs of the client will require special attention to instructional delivery. Technology will be even more important. The home setting will be different as determined by the client's parental situation. Bicoastal marriages, multiple homes in multiple locations, and shared custodians are new trends in our society. The thirty-year mortgaged home in the same neighborhood and with the same family structure will be sparse. Further, educators will be forced to pay special attention to a variety of instructional delivery options. The demands of individual needs, as influenced by a requirement for employment mobility in the workplace, especially in telecommuting, and the application of extended twenty-four-hour workdays and of cross training and retraining mandates suggest that independent learning will be a driving force.

Distance education is the viable resource. Offered today by most colleges and universities, it enables clients to access some courses for personal development, as well as a few limited programs for professional growth. More and more, the availability and utilization of RealVideo, Web-based support with shared resources, virtual lessons, America Online Messenger for interaction, digital media, visual imaging, and the incorporation of the telephone, cable, and Internet will facilitate use of site, content, and traffic for effective instructional delivery. [44]

In 2020, school as we know it will be more than a facility. It will by necessity become a service, accommodating and facilitating the learning process as mandated by the client. The community college has begun to address the needs for individualized instruction through programs such as independent studies, life labs, or open college. The construction of the open courtyard was thought to have provided students the opportunity to work on their own time and on any subject in a single location. Unfortunately, students were required to go to the community college campus in order to access the equipment. There will be a need to provide access to technology for students outside the structured facility. Many institutions have begun to establish a technology fee, payable along with course registration (and therefore, eligible for financial aid), that allows the student access to a portable or laptop computer.

There will be a greater need for providing opportunities for students to complete an entire program by attending classes on weekends and evenings. Students will want to know how long it will take them to complete a particular training. For example, given the number of credits and hours as required by the appropriate agency, state, or accrediting body, a student may earn an associate in science degree in twenty-one weeks by attending classes on

Friday evenings, Saturdays, and Sundays. Or the student may earn an associate in arts degree in one hundred weeks by attending evening classes, Mondays through Fridays. To respond to the demands of this new student population, community colleges will need to rethink their scheduling format from the horizontal twelve-to-sixteen week schedule to a more vertical or intensive format (a four-week, six-week, two-week, etc., format), which will allow students to complete training in short periods of time.

Serious attention through a variety of distance learning approaches will better equip educational institutions to address the new concepts of time and place; in other words, same time-same place, same time-different place, different time-same place, and different time-different place.

The greatest challenges before the community college in the year 2020 will be to move much more swiftly and creatively to accommodate the rapid changes in demographics and the individual needs of its students.

Additionally, employees who came aboard in the rise of the community college system are now leaving the system to retire, change careers, and so on. A new crop of faculty, staff, and administrators will need to understand the concept of the "open door" and demonstrate a commitment to serve the under-prepared student. The new employees will need to mirror the image of the new students in ethnic diversity. They will be required to "wear several hats" to accommodate the needs of students and be directed to work multiple shifts, a phenomenon new to education.

SUMMARY AND CONCLUSION

In the twenty-first century, society will be marked by change, complexity, creative innovation, and continental interdependence. Demographic shifts and the move from the Industrial Age to the Information Age have triggered trends and issues of places and people. The traditional physical settings of home, school, community, and workplace have become varied and are identified differently. Home, literally where "one hangs his or her hat," is characterized by more mobility and multiple locations, especially in the case of bicoastal marriages, and is a circumstance that is increasingly more prevalent. On the more adverse side are the "homeless" people, recognized by transience and rootlessness. Today there are public, private, home, charter, and magnet schools with the time of school varying according to the settings in which they occur. The workday has become a twenty-four-hour, seven-day-a-week situation aided by technological advances. Families and communities have also undergone changes and new definitions. Besides the traditional family structure, family units now consist of multiple adults, single parents (either gender), and extended families. In many ways, the traditional family is now the nontraditional family.

With all of these relationships at work in our society, a causal effect of interdependence is developing, and yet there is a great need for self-actualization and individualization—a desire for personal choices and space, learning styles, and preferences. More and more, institutional structures are embracing collaborations and partnerships. Business and industry, government, education, community organization and agencies, and professional service organizations (health and medical) are developing programs designed to benefit one another collectively and at the same time to have greater impact in the communities of which they are a part.

As a consequence of all of these changing environments and relationships, the music teaching profession must give a new meaning to a place called school and view it as a process called education. We need to expand the focus of music education to include all ages (from early childhood through adulthood) and all settings. At the same time, we need to increase access to quality music instruction for all members of society and celebrate cultural differences and similarities. How do we create programs that draw teachers from broader backgrounds, representing the students of diverse cultures—welcoming them into the profession? How do we maintain high standards and excellence in teaching? As the world community shrinks, music education will need to broaden its perspective and revitalize and restructure its teaching methods, curricula, and teacher-training procedures.

In view of demographic indicators discussed herein, which forecast a huge minority population explosion and its numerical dominance in the next millennium, the greatest challenge to America is not in the arts; the greatest challenge to America is to provide a superior education and equal access to it, as well as equal job opportunities with fair employment and housing practices, so that economic prosperity is also, on balance, spread among all of its hard-working and deserving citizens, regardless of race or ethnicity, age, or gender. If America were to live up to the principles written in the Constitution, that actualization would provide a society more complete and sophisticated than the world has ever seen. To do this our collective efforts must be directed: Will we learn from the lessons of the past (i.e., slavery and the civil rights movement, the Holocaust, ethnic uprisings in Bosnia and Kosovo, the apartheid in South Africa)? How will we use the wonderful advances in technology to achieve our goals? The basic question remains paramount: In the next millennium, what can music education do to enhance its place in our educational system and in the lives of America's vast and varied population? How can we make certain that our long-established goals to educate every person, regardless of age, gender, or race, will be realized?

It is becoming abundantly clear that the time is past for more pronouncements, speeches, and expository and exploratory scholarship centered on cultural diversity and multicultural issues as they have an impact upon the American people and the social institutions that influence our lives. Certainly, there has been more than enough said and written about these issues in music education, in our accreditation agencies, in arts funding organizations, in our national associations, and in the conferences and publications they provide.

The supporting businesses (the music industry) that supply materials and equipment that we use in our profession have made a wealth of related teaching tools available. As we learn more about world music, we discover a wide array of instruments to be used as tools for music making. We will need to include knowledge and experiences with these in our music classrooms. Technology is helping us redefine these tools, as well. Wind controllers, samplers, synthesizers, and sequencers are examples of how this is being done. Students who participate in computer-based music instruction are making more choices about what they use to invent for musical examples. When they make those choices, there is ownership in the curriculum and they discover through experiences that there is more to learn and know about the subject in which they are already interested. Music educators will need to become more knowledgeable about what music students are choosing to listen to and use the information to make their teaching and curriculum more relevant. "Westernization" of the music of other cultures robs them of their true character. With this understanding, creative movement and improvisation therefore take on a new meaning and will be elevated in importance in the curriculum of the future. Now is the time to implement new strategies for restructuring our curricular designs (infusing the National Standards), to reform policies and practices, to improve and increase human resources, and redefine/reorganize schedules to allow for a more accommodating use of teaching time in the school day.

In order for the National Standards to enjoy widespread use in our nation's schools, not only will curricula require careful revision but music teaching schedules will need skillful redesigning with realistic time allotments to allow for the quality instruction required to aid the development of music skills and understandings specified in the Standards. Music literacy can never be achieved on a once-a-week (45–60 minutes) class schedule, which is so often the case in our schools. The school year and the school day will have to be redefined. Many districts are experimenting with varied instructional formats (i.e., "early bird" classes, evening sessions, summer opportunities, and year- round schools).

Today a "one size fits all" mentality does not work in designing school schedules. While a seven-or-eight-period schedule is ineffective for some subjects, a four-period- only schedule creates new problems for others. Flexibility in scheduling seems to be the key, for it may be in the best interest for the students and learning. We need to explore new forms of scheduling as an opportunity to improve the school music program. For example, without a common planning time, integrating music with other subjects or classroom activities will occur sporadically and in all likelihood be superfluous.

Early childhood and adult music education will factor into that schedule. A recent issue of the *Music Educators Journal* included a special focus titled Music and Early Childhood.[45] That issue provides timely information regarding training to prepare music educators to use music with young children; offers a list of characteristics MENC recommends that early childhood music teachers have; and lists model programs established in university and community settings around the country. Emerging research suggesting that children's early years are a key time for musical growth, and considering that this population will constitute a large segment of our society in the next millennium, indicates a growing concern for how music teaching will be impacted in the future. Harriet Hair states that research procedures with young children will be greatly influenced by the rapidly changing computer technology.[46] Therefore centers for research on the musical characteristics of children should be established to provide electronic databases that would be available to educators and researchers.

Community partnerships with music education to provide for people of all ages may cause a relocation of "where music teaching happens" and the forms it will take. Venues may include churches, community music schools, after-school programs in child- or day-care centers, and other social agencies such as Boys and Girls Clubs and retirement centers.

> In the United States, current and ongoing demographics that affect the nation's cultural, social, religious and political conditions mandate that curricular revisions across disciplines in education are necessary in our nation's public and private schools, colleges and universities. At the same time, sophisticated telecommunications technology (including expanded global use of cyberspace), rapid aerospace travel, geopolitical dynamics, increasing transcontinental corporate presence, and universal changes in ethical and moral values are all forms drawing the cultures of the world together.[47]

The next millennium will be an exciting opportunity for innovations and creative adaptation of teaching methodologies and materials in music education. Indeed, the traditional cycle by which music education achieves its leadership must be redefined. It must begin with the training of teachers representative of diverse cultures who will instruct our youth (also of diverse cultures) and extend into music major programs in colleges and universities. In this manner we will be presented with increased opportunities to learn about music of the world's cultures even as we teach the people of those cultures. Crosscultural fertilization of musical ideas and traditions will surely take place in the academy. Music education has the opportunity, indeed the responsibility, to lead our nation in becoming a true democracy, where every person learns to sing and play in harmony, dance with rhythmic grace, and truly become an instrument of peace for the world's people. Music really is a universal language . . . of, for, and by the people.

NOTES

1. John J. Macionis, *Society: The Basics*, 4th ed. (New Jersey: Prentice Hall, 1998), 1.

2. Consortium of National Arts Education Associations, *National Standards for Arts Education* (Reston, VA: Music Educators National Conference, 1994), 13–14.

3. Stephen Molnar, *Human Variation: Race, Types and Groups*, 2nd ed. (New Jersey: Prentice Hall, 1983).

4. Gabrielle Sandor, "The Other Americans: American Demographics," *Population Today* 16, no. 6 June 1944): 36–41; Susan Kalish, "Interracial Births Increase as US Ponders Racial Definitions," *Population Today* 23, no. 4 (April 1995): 1–2.

5. Max Weber, *Economy and Society*, ed. G. Roth and C. Wittich (Berkeley, CA: Berkeley of California Press, 1978).

6. Macionis, 17.

7. David Brian Williams and Peter Richard Webster, *Experiencing Music Technology* (New York: Schirmer Books, 1996), 79.

8. Christine Hermanson, "Music Wares, Piano," in *Experiencing Music Technology* (see note above), 83.

9. Sally Johnstone, ed., *The Distant Learners Guide* (New Jersey: Prentice Hall, 1998).

10. Macionis, 346.

11. James W. Fraser, "Preparing Teachers for Democratic Schools: The Holmes and Carnegie Reports Five Years Later—A Critical Reflection," *Teachers College Record* 94, 1 (Fall 1992): 22.

12. Willis D. Hawley, "The Importance of Minority Teachers to the Racial and Ethnic Integration of American Society," *Equity and Choice* 5 (March 1989).

13. Fraser, 23.

14. Ibid.

15. Lawrence Lyman and Harvey C. Foyle, *Cooperative Grouping for Interactive Learning: Students, Teachers and Administrators* (Washington, DC: NEA Professional Library, 1990).

16. Gerardo Marin and Barbara Van Oss Marin, *Research with Hispanic Populations* (Newbury Park, CA: Sage, 1991).

17. Patricia Shehan Campbell, "Cultural Issues and School Music Participation: The New Asians in American Schools," *Journal of Music Teaching and Learning* (Summer 1993): 55.

18. M. Argyle, "New Developments in the Analysis of Social Skills," in *Non-Verbal Behavior*, ed. Aaron Wolfgang (London: Academic Press, 1979).

19. Carlesta Henderson, "The Effect of In-Service Training of Music Teachers in Contingent Verbal and Non-Verbal Behavior" (Ed. D. diss., Columbia University, 1972).

20. Charles H. Madsen and Clifford K. Madsen, *Teaching/Discipline* (Boston: Allyn and Bacon, Inc., 1970); Clifford K. Madsen, Douglas R. Greer, and Charles H. Madsen, Jr., *Research in Music Behavior* (New York: Columbia University Teachers College Press, 1977); Clifford K. Madsen and Terry Lee Kuhn, *Contemporary Music Education* (Arlington Heights, IL: AHM Publishing, 1978); Clifford K. Madsen and Carol A. Prickett, *Applications of Research in Music Behavior* (Tuscaloosa, AL: University of Alabama Press, 1997).

21. Madsen and Kuhn, see note above, 71.

22. American Council on Education, "Sixteenth Annual Status Report on Minorities in Higher Education" (Washington, DC: American Council on Education, 1998).

23. Ibid, iv.

24. Ibid.

25. University of Wisconsin System, *Plan 2008* (Madison, WI: University of Wisconsin System, 1998), 2.

26. Ibid, concept #5.

27. Walter G. Secada, "The Problem of Hispanic School Dropout," *Kaleidoscope II* (Milwaukee, WI: University of Wisconsin System Institute on Race and Ethnicity, 1998), 4–9.

28. Hispanic Dropout Prevention, http://www.senate.gov/-bingarnan/bingaman/hispanic_dropout_prevention.html.

29. Walter G. Secada et al., February 1998, "No More Excuses," http://www.senate.gov/-bingaman/bingaman/hispanic_dropout_prevention.html.

30. James P. Comer et al., "Rallying the Whole Village," *The Comer Process for Reforming Education* (New York: Columbia University Teachers College Press, 1996).

31. Council of Arts Accrediting Associations, "Minority Students and Access to Arts Study" (Reston, VA: Council of Arts Accrediting Associations, 1994).

32. Nancy H. Barry, "Music and Education in the Elementary Music Methods Class," *Journal of Music Teacher Education* 2, no. 1 (Fall 1992): 16–23.

33. Ibid.

34. Jan H. McCrary, "Effect of Listener's and Performer's Race on Music Preference," *Journal of Research in Music Education* 41, no. 3 (Fall 1993): 200–211.

35. C. Victor Fung, "Undergraduate Nonmusic Majors World Music Preference and Multicultural Attitudes," *Journal of Research in Music Education* 42, no.1 (1994): 45–57.

36. Patricia Shehan Campbell, "World Music: Windows to Cross-Cultural Understanding," *Music Educators Journal* 75, no. 3 (1988): 22–26.

37. Charles Leonhard, *The Status of Arts Education in American Public Schools* (Urbana, IL: National Arts Education Research Center, University of Illinois, 1991).

38. Council of Arts Accrediting Associations, 5.

39. Michael Yaffe and Scott Shuler, "Will We Train Fiddlers While Rome Burns? Community Arts Schools and the Public Schools," *Design for Arts in Education* 93 (July/August 1992).

40. National Association of Schools of Music, "Community Education and Music Programs in Higher Education" (Reston, VA: National Association of Schools of Music, 1991).

41. Council of Arts Accrediting Associations, 25.

42. C. Morris, ed., "Overview of Institutional Research," in *Miami-Dade Community College Fact Book* (Miami, FL: Office of Institutional Research, 1999).

43. Ibid.

44. Peter Webster and David Williams, "Through the 2020 Looking Glass: Music Education and Technology," teleconference presented to the Housewright Commission on Music Education, The Florida State University, 9 April 1999, http://pubweb.nwu.edu/~webster/.

45. Lili M. Levinowitz, guest ed., "Music and Early Childhood, Special Focus," *Music Educators Journal* 86, no. 1 (July 1999).

46. Harriet L. Hair, "Children's Responses to Music Stimuli: Verbal/NonVerbal, Aural/Visual Modes," *Applications of Research in Music Behavior* (1997): 59–70.

47. Carlesta E. Spearman, "Editor's Introduction," *Black Music Research Journal* 16, no. 2 (Fall 1996): 217–18.

Chapter Eleven

Response to Carlesta Spearman's "How Will Societal and Technological Changes Affect the Teaching of Music?"

Sandy Feldstein

Sandy Feldstein is president of Carl Fischer LLC.

It is a pleasure to be able to respond to Carlesta Spearman's paper. It was not until this morning that I realized her connection with Rawn Spearman with whom I had the pleasure of working when we were both getting our doctorates and performing recitals in New York.

I think Dr. Spearman's paper states facts that we can all agree upon. There are changes in society that are going to affect all of us. The average age of our society is increasing and lifelong learning is going to be essential. More of our society is going to be made up of people of Asian, African-American, and Hispanic descent, where in the past our population was made up of more people of European descent. All of this is going to affect what we have to do in education. On the technology side the paper points out the importance of the working environment and the learning environment becoming more decentralized. Moving the workplace away from the central office and moving education away from the traditional school setting, as we know it, also is going to have a great impact on us.

The Internet is obviously having an impact, as are interactive television and all of the other technologies. The implications of all these things on music teacher training are immense. Teachers must know technology, both how it works and how to use it effectively in their teaching. Today's teachers and teachers who will be teaching in the future must also know the music of other cultures. And the teaching population needs to reflect the cultural diversity of the student body, which means we have to recruit. But teacher recruitment in general is at a crisis stage for us. The crisis is not only in music, but it definitely is in music. We have been working very hard to keep music programs alive, and now that we have made some progress in keeping programs, we do not have the teachers to supply them. We are going to lose those programs if we do not create a pool of talented creative educators.

This need is going to mean changes in certification. Indeed, we must have alternative types of certification. I implore you to look at enlisting the help of professional musicians, many of whom, besides being talented performers, are educators as well. We must come up with ways of getting them certified so they can help in alternative learning situations. This will include developing programs that can have short residencies so that people can continue "with their day gig" while they start to learn more about education.

In my comments, I would like to present various random ideas for you to consider that I believe can help open other avenues for discussion.

We must learn to understand the music that children like. You heard it in the first statement from Libby Larsen (Housewright Symposium keynote speaker) and you have heard it since. I am not saying you have to embrace it and go home and put it on your CD player. I do not expect you to refit your cars with big bass amplifiers, but you must at least show your students that you care about what they listen to. You must know the names of the artists. If we do that, we will have more opportunities to transfer learning.

Current teachers need this same training; so the implications for in-service are tremendous. Someone mentioned the other day, "Just what I really want to do after a full day is go home, put on the television and take a course." Well, you know, we are going to have to. No one said that devoting your life to music education was going to be easy. And we are at a crisis situation where we are going to have to put in the time and the effort to do what is necessary to bring our profession to the year 2020.

All of this will have a great impact on the curriculum. I would like to propose the idea that music must help make kids want to stay in school. There are tremendous numbers of dropouts in certain communities, and music can be a terrific tool in having kids turned on about school in general. This will not happen with the programs we now are providing for them, but future programs should address this. We should teach not only skills and concepts but obviously how they relate to life.

We must treat all of the students equally. Our goal should not be to get a grade A in level 6 band. That should be an outcome of a strong overall music program for all students, and if we do not change our mind-set as educators, we are not going to get there.

I am sorry that at the last moment, Remo Belli was not able to be here. He has a great analogy when he talks about physical education. In school every student takes physical education, everyone is exposed to it, and then they may make a choice. "I'd like to be on the girl's volleyball team." "I'd like to be on the basketball team." "I'd like to be in the football program." But before that, everyone is involved in physical education. This model is one we might want to look at more deeply as a concept for music education.

Our fear of teaching music for any reason other than its intrinsic value is unfounded. We must get away from that. We should teach music but not be afraid when is it "used" in other areas of education.

After reading all of the papers, I basically said, "Why am I here, Why was I asked to speak?"

I assumed I was asked to be here to give an industry perspective, and that is what I am going to do. In his paper, Paul Lehman said, "Implementing this program will require the cooperation and support of all who value the arts." Industry and education must work together. But except for a brief moment in time, when MENC, the National Academy of Recording Arts & Sciences, Inc. (NARAS), and NAMM joined forces for the National Coalition for Music Education, we have not been very good at working together.

The opening paper emphasized what we have accomplished since Tanglewood. It included positive concepts about the inclusion of music and the other arts in the Goals 2000 legislation. The implication was that MENC did that. Well, in fact, MENC did not do that alone. The National Coalition did that. And that showed the best of how a coalition works.

If you remember those years (and they were not that long ago), Michael Greene from NARAS took one minute on national television during the Grammy Awards and accomplished what we were not able to accomplish for ten years by ourselves. He brought to the table what he did well, having a minute to talk to a billion people about music education. NAMM came to the table and brought funding and coordination to try to bring these elements together, and MENC did the rest: supplying the content, the excitement, and the concept of working as a group. The Coalition was terrific. I would like to see it happening every day.

I was very excited speaking with Joe Lamond, who is here representing NAMM, over the past two days. There is a new advocacy kit coming out from the Coalition, the *Music Education Advocates Toolkit*, and the Coalition actually has been expanded. Besides the original three, VH-I, the American Music Conference, the National School Boards Association, the Iowa Alliance, and the Music Publishers Association are all now involved in this new program.

Most of you have already started to hear the buzz about the new Miramax movie, *Music of the Heart.* The Coalition is supporting it, and hopefully we will have the same kind of responses we did with *Mr. Holland's Opus.* This is another positive thing that one group could not do on its own.

But all too often, each of us is there only for the glory of our own group. The industry is at fault just as well as education. We have too many organizations. We have too many egos. But luckily most of them fall under the umbrella of NAMM, which is a real umbrella (not just a verbal one containing listings under a name). NAMM represents an effective interaction of groups working together to reach goals that are important for everyone.

In education we have a profession with more splinter groups than any profession I have ever seen. It is mind-boggling. Just think about instrumental music, or forget that, just think about band. We have NBA, CBDNA, and ABA. Then you start going into the states and we have TBA, OBA, and on and on. Every state has an individual band organization, besides the three major band organizations. And if that is not enough, the people who play any one of the band instruments think that those organizations are not doing anything. So we have a flute organization and a double-reed organization. We do not even have a woodwind group—evidently that is too broad. I have a theory that in music education there are as many organizations as there are people who want to be the president of something.

Imagine what we could accomplish if we took the time, energy, and money spent in these splinter organizations and put those resources behind one single mission. And what *are* we trying to accomplish? I was taken aback when reading in one of the papers presented at this forum that, "goals of industry and education are sometimes at odds." That is ludicrous.

We all want people to experience the joy of music making. We all want to develop more music makers. That is part of MENC's mission statement. That is part of NAMM's mission statement. We agree that our goal is to develop more music makers. And if we develop more music makers, will it be good for the industry? Obviously it will. We will sell more instruments and we will sell more publications. There will become more music-making opportunities and the business will be kept alive. But it also will be good for the music education business—excuse me, profession. It will provide an opportunity for the employment of those people involved in the profession of music education. There is a major difference, though. The industry cannot fail and stay in business. If we do not do a good job our employees do not have a job—our employees do not have tenure.

If music education in the traditional setting is not meeting the challenge of making more music makers who will love music for a lifetime, then we are going to have to do it alone. We cannot wait. But doing it alone is wrong. The challenge is to do it together, and the Coalition proves that working together works.

I believe that most music educators do not realize the depth of resources that are available in the industry. Of course, we are always asked for money; we are asked for money to fund anything and everything. But we are rarely asked to input our expertise. You should realize that industry people are highly trained musicians. Many are past music educators. We can add a lot if you give us the opportunity.

I also believe most music educators are not aware of what the music industry does. One of the papers being presented at this symposium talks about technology. It states you can go on the Internet, put in music, and look at all of these lesser-known sites. Among them were *Banjo in the Hollow, Off Wall Street Jam,* and a lot of esoteric sites. But in the middle of this listing was AMC, the American Music Conference. If you do not know what the American Music Conference is, and you feel it is a lesser-known site, then you have not done your homework.

Last year the American Music Conference was responsible for 1.2 billion impressions on advocacy in music education—1.2 billion impressions to the general public. This is not preaching to the choir, and it is listed in one of our papers as a lesser-known organization. It should not be. We in the industry have not done our job in letting you know what we do.

Why does a local music store give lessons? To make money? Maybe. But I say that more likely it is to fill the need of the community that is not being serviced by traditional music education.

Why do papers at this forum ask for a source of reference for music education research? Don't they know about the Foundation for Music Research, where NAMM has invested over one and a half million dollars in the last few years and is scheduled to go up to five million dollars for music education research? And speaking of research, why do we always rain on our own parade when something is happening that is valuable to us?

It may be that some people have been a little overzealous in stating what the research findings imply. But in reality it is the first time we have had a volume of material (and an ever-growing volume of material) that looks at the positive aspects of music from a research standpoint. And instead of embracing it, we, even at this forum, say, "But it doesn't really make you smarter . . . ?" Why are we looking at the negatives? Every time there is one research finding that says something positive, there are ten other researchers who are going to prove it wrong. That's human nature.

We cannot embrace that type of activity. We have to be positive about the good aspects of the research. Of course, we must be careful not to exaggerate. We should not say that because of one little piece of research every child is going to get smarter, or that every baby that listens to Mozart is going to be an asset to the community. But we do have a volume of positive research material. We as an industry and we as educators must support the positive and not jump on the negative bandwagon.

The New Horizons Band has been mentioned a few times and I think that is wonderful. No one mentioned the fact that the financial support that made the Horizons Band possible (and helped Roy Ernst expand the wonderful job he's doing) came from the industry.

Nothing was said about the Weekend Warrior program, which is a big industry initiative similar to what Roy's doing, but geared for people who want to be in garage bands and who played in the '50s and now want to play again. So, we are doing the same thing for "pop music" as we are for concert band music.

And what about the Music Making and Wellness research at the University of Miami? It is showing a tremendous relationship between music and wellness for senior citizens. You know, we are all going to be one of those—hopefully.

Why did the music industry start TI:ME, to train teachers in technology? They did not want to do it, but they believed that it was not being adequately addressed by traditional music education. It should not be that way; it should be done together. I think the challenge for all of you is not only to look into your profession but also to look to the industry that serves you. Do what you do best but encourage us to do what we do best.

If you remember the *We Are the World* recording, Quincy Jones had a major problem in that he had a room full of the biggest pop personalities in one room. And I will never forget the sign he had hanging on the door, going into the studio. It was a big sign that said, Leave your egos at the door." I think we have to do that. We have to leave our egos at the door and work together for the benefit of the kids. And speaking of kids, in a day and a half I have heard kids mentioned only in Paul Lehman's paper. I mean isn't that what we're here for? If we do what's right for the kids, we'll be doing what's right for your profession and our industry.

Wynton Marsalis has a great way of teaching collective improvisation to young children. He speaks about it as the clearest form of democracy. How's that for interdisciplinary transfer of learning? He says, first you have to listen to each other, then you interact with each other, and then you use elements that are around you and you add your own personality to it. And you end up with something complete that is the creative work of all of us.

We are here to begin that process in music education, and if ever there was an opportunity to guarantee the role of music in our present and future society, the time is now.

Chapter Twelve

What Should Be the Relationship between Schools and Other Sources of Music Learning?

Commission Author: Cornelia Yarbrough

Cornelia Yarbrough is the Derryl and Helen Haymon Professor of Music and Coordinator of Music Education at Louisiana State University Baton Rouge.

Commission Members:
Wilma Benson
Robert A. Cutietta
Randall DeWitt
Jeffrey Kimpton
Michael L. Mark
Richard Zellner

Response: Richard Bell

THE SCHOOLS AND MUSIC EDUCATION

The twenty-first century will usher in many changes and challenges for every individual and institution in the United States. To answer the question "What should be the relationship between schools and other sources of music learning?" we must first consider the issues that will affect the schools and music education. Secondly, we must explore other sources of music learning that will exist in the future. Finally, relationships among these various sources can be contemplated.

It has been said that perhaps the best way to predict the future is to examine what is happening in the present. The discussion that follows contains many examples of events and trends that are already well under way. We, as a profession, have not found ways yet to adjust to these current events and trends. Thus, we will need to catch up while at the same time we will need to make ever-more-radical adjustments to new developments that will confront us in the future.

The issues of most importance for music education and the schools in the twenty-first century are: wider choices for schooling, ethnic and music diversity, the impact of technology and the digital revolution, and new approaches to teaching and learning. The following discussion describes what is happening now while hinting at what might occur in the future.

Choice and Diversity

The public schools will still exist, but they will be only one facet of a wide diversity of systems for enhancing education, many of which will be privately operated. Public and private school choices will include schools affiliated with a religious denomination, home schools, magnet schools, charter schools, and contracted schools. Some public schools will become confederations of subschools that cater to students' special interests, from physics to the performing arts. Many corporations now operate what amount to employee universities. These will be joined by profit-making chains and special schools catering to special students.

These trends toward more options and greater choice have created a great philosophical debate that will continue well into the twenty-first century. On one side, education is seen as a private or personal good, with parents as consumers of whatever public, private, or parochial education best suits their needs. On the other side is the argument that public education is provided for the common good, and that all children should share some common experiences in common settings. Because both sides of the argument have strength and passion, we will continue to see greater diversity in learning scenarios.

Arthur C. Clarke describes several learning scenarios for the twenty-first century:

> On the evening of July 20, 2019, John Stanton is taking yet another teleclass. His classroom is actually a room in his own home that is outfitted for teleconferencing. At the moment, he is posing a question to his teacher [who] appears in the room as a life-sized three-dimensional holographic image.
> Meanwhile, in a nearby public school, an early-education specialist is teaching a four-year-old how to read. . . .
> Across town, at a McSchool franchise, a grandmother is taking a course on small business management. . . .

Nearby, at the university operated by a major corporation for its employees, students are taking classes in new technological developments in their fields. [1]

These scenarios suggest a wide variety of learning environments. Some futurists predict dramatic shifts away from the place-specific learning buildings we call schools to a "placeless society" where everything can be accessed via technology. For example, William Knoke, founder and president of the Harvard Capital Group and author of *Bold New World: The Essential Road Map to the 21st Century* describes a twenty-first century placeless society as

> the awakening omnipresence that will allow everything—people, goods, resources, knowledge—to be available anywhere, often instantaneously, with little regard for distance or place. We already see it in many forms. CNN broadcasts bring an Ethiopian drought into lush living rooms. Multinational appliance companies subcontract manufacturing to wherever it is cheapest. Capital ebbs and flows freely around the girth of the globe defying government controls. Mass immigration into Western Europe and North America continues. Everywhere, people, money, goods, and knowledge flow so effortlessly from point to point that place becomes an irrelevant concept. The world is becoming placeless. [2]

While recognizing the ease of communication provided by the Internet and other mass communication media, music educators also realize the great societal need for socialization. There may indeed be no need for a physical place for educational activity, but people will continue to seek out opportunities for live interaction with others. For example, when VCRs became widely used, the motion picture industry feared the demise of movie theatres. This has not occurred; instead there has been an expansion of movie theatres into large multi-theatre complexes.

In a similar way, participation in music learning activities will become an important way to fulfill the need to interact with one another in a social and educational setting. The challenge for music educators will be one of blending the social and academic aspects of music learning toward the goals of both enjoyment and education. Additionally, music educators will need to become increasingly involved in developing, monitoring, and facilitating the private music experiences being produced via advances in technology.

Impact of Technology and the Digital Revolution

The purposes of schooling are changing now and will change more dramatically as we progress into the twenty-first century. In societies characterized by hunting and agrarian economies, children learned from observing and imitating adults; in industrial societies, children learned how to fit into the bureaucratic, hierarchical, factory system, with everyone in one place from the beginning to the end of the shift; but in an information-based society increasingly dominated by technology, massive amounts of information will be created, often without regard for quality or accuracy. Both teacher and learner will need skills in accessing, evaluating, and interpreting information from worldwide sources.

The impact of the digital revolution will be profound and complex. In addition, changes in how we go about everything we do will occur with breathtaking speed. The Commerce Department's April 1998 report *The Emerging Digital Economy* states that radio existed for thirty-eight years before fifty million people tuned in, while television required thirteen years to reach the same benchmark. Yet once the Internet was opened to the general public, it crossed the fifty-million-user threshold in a mere-four years. By the end of 1997, the report revealed, more than one hundred million people were using the Internet, and traffic on it was doubling every hundred days.[3]

There will be ever-widening choices of pedagogical and curricular approaches, most of which will involve technology. The rise of computer technology, distance education, telecommunications and television will impact the speed and accuracy of the delivery of information to everyone involved in the educational process. Computers will increase the ability of musicians and nonmusicians to self-educate in virtually every aspect of music.

In some ways, demands for greater speed and accuracy of information will improve everyday life. In other ways, these demands will only increase the distance between the "haves" and the "have nots." Those individuals who are at-risk because of poverty or illiteracy will continue to be of great concern to societal institutions like the public schools. As those who have the means to do so choose options for schooling outside of the public sector, the support for those at-risk may diminish.

Traditional textbooks will in many cases be replaced by interactive multimedia systems approaches (combined with heightened sensory stimulation such as 3-D sound and wrap-around vision), with computer and satellite technology serving as deliverer of information.[4]

The question arises, "How virtual can music education become?" The technology is now available to teach private lessons in piano and other instruments via the Internet. Soon it will be possible to play with others in an ensemble through Internet connections in real time. Indeed it may be possible in the next century to attend a concert, conduct, and rehearse a major ensemble without leaving one's home.

New Approaches to Teaching and Learning

While it would be foolish to put all our eggs in the computer basket, this technology can be used as a magnificent tool in allowing individual creativity and pacing during the teaching/learning process and in providing experiences with music of cultures where context is so important; for example, where music is wedded to some rite of passage or traditional ceremony.[5] Thus, technology will provide more opportunities for music education to be inclusive of every style and genre of music rather than exclusive in exposing children only to music of the Western European tradition.

It is a fact that students in today's public schools are of many different ethnic origins with diverse learning styles, that our American society today is exposed to a wide variety of musics, and that many music teachers are unprepared but willing to deal with both ethnic and musical diversities. The question music educators are asking is, "Can the musical preparation of future teachers include not only the acquisitions of skills to work with a comprehensive repertoire of music from the current popular and concert hall musics of our own time, but also include the contemporary music practices of the entire global village, and the music that comprises the heritage of each community represented in our schools?" The answer to this question may lie in a different approach to teacher training, an approach relying on the development of research and acquisition of information rather than one relying on the mastery of specific content.

As more people enjoy increased leisure time, schools will become round-the-clock and open-to-all-ages institutions, replacing "age specific compulsory learning institutions (called schools)." A learning society will emerge, which means that most people will spend a great deal of every day of their lives in some kind of learning environment. There will be nothing that cannot be formally or informally studied if the students are interested.[6]

Community centers will evolve where people of all ages can gather to participate in music ensembles. These centers may be at the current school buildings, which will be open and functioning from dawn until late night. The intergenerational involvement in music ensembles may begin during the normal school day. For example, in Eugene, Oregon, a retired 76-year-old pipe fitter is in his third year with a middle school band. The eighth-graders he plays with no longer see him as an oddity, but as an inspiration who plays the French horn with a passion for music and thick fingers gnarled by a lifetime of hard work. In addition, he is studying opera, the piano, and the harmonica.[7]

Wilma Benson shared the following description of the involvement of senior citizens at Pleasure Ridge High School in Louisville, Kentucky:

> Senior citizens are invited from the community to come into the school, attend classes, participate in classes, and generally join the students throughout their day. Some come for the social aspects and can often be found playing cards or working out on the exercise equipment in the senior center. Several would come to ensemble rehearsals and listen; one of them played in the ensemble from time to time. With this group around, it was never a problem to find chaperones for field trips. They were always eager to go along and were especially excited to go along on the music related trips.[8]

The proliferation of knowledge and the ease of accessibility to it will result in more interdisciplinary approaches to learning and will require earlier starts to a lifetime of learning. Educators will devote many hours of every day organizing massive amounts of information into meaningful content and providing ways for students to study this content in some authentic context. As a result, music will be taught across the curriculum from the beginning of schooling in early childhood throughout the formal enrollment period. It will be understood that music is and has been a vital and ubiquitous part of society throughout history and no subject area will be taught without its inclusion. This interdisciplinary approach may even replace that of separate classes for music appreciation, fine arts, music history, and so forth. Yet formal instruction in music performance, both individual and ensemble, will continue to be a means for self-expression and enjoyment as well as a discipline requiring a team approach to obtain an artistic product.

New theories of learning that hold that the mind constructs knowledge within constraints of prior belief, experience, and understanding will result in new ways to deliver information and assess learning. The "mind-boggling" amount of accessible information may confirm the notion that children "cannot simply accept new knowledge as a bank accepts a deposit."[9] As a result, learning in formal settings will be more individualized and will involve more team approaches. Collaborations among music teachers, their students, and experts worldwide will form to explore music of all cultures.

Fewer classroom teachers may be needed, but there also might be an increase in the number of people engaged in teaching and learning. In fact the tension between formal and informal instruction may represent our greatest challenge: Will there be fewer teachers in those subjects not considered "essential?"

A major alternative to the traditional structure of education could be an intellectual apprentice system. Under such a system, any member of society—a manual laborer, a journalism, a musician, an academic historian, a shop clerk, or a mechanic—could become a teacher. These people would simply choose to devote part of their time to the teaching of the young. Students wishing to eschew the classroom for this kind of apprentice system would have their portion of the publically [sic] funded school budget returned to them as credits (a kind of educational scrip, perhaps) with which teaching "masters" could be paid.[10]

Behind the scenes, an industry of programmers, multimedia specialists, and educators will produce interactive scripts designed to stimulate and develop all minds to the maximum of their potentials.

Classroom teachers will still exist, since . . . there is no substitute for the human touch. But they will act more as facilitators, making sure the student is working on the right material, and that progress is being made. They will challenge, guide and bring students to their full potential as human beings, as individuals.[11]

These changes will require a dramatic alteration in the role of the teacher. Historically, the teacher has been viewed as an authority regarding subject matter, a developer of curricular materials, an evaluator of student performance, and a controller of classroom discipline. In the twenty-first century, the teacher must become a knowledgeable navigator through massive amounts of information, a task analyzer and organizer, a collaborator with students in the development of subject matter processes and products, and a creative evaluator of students' achievements and attitudes. These qualities are often not found in music experts who, although they have enormous reservoirs of knowledge, do not understand how to organize and present that information to students who have different backgrounds and learning styles.

Concern for the quality of education has stimulated the widespread demand for accountability in the education profession. Several states have issued "report cards" resulting in declarations that some schools have failed to educate. These failing schools will be closed and students attending them will be sent elsewhere.

Music education has fought long and hard for the inclusion of music as part of the curriculum. The creation and acceptance of the National Standards for Arts Education[12] are significant steps toward accountability. Yet society's concern for accountability traditionally goes through cycles, and efforts to accommodate any "correct" cycle may be a moot issue in the near future.

Regardless, we must go further. Music educators, like other professional educators, must help students and their parents understand and make the connection between music and life. We must help students transfer what they have learned in music to what they will do with it when they leave the school setting. Teaching must include not only musical concepts and skills, but also how those concepts and skills can function for us through our lifetime. This blend of information and application will be extremely important.

While we must continue our advocacy efforts, it is perhaps time to redirect them. Instead of fighting to save the same approaches and content (i.e., general music in the elementary schools and ensembles in middle and high schools), we must become accountable for making music an important part of every person's life. We should maximize efforts to involve all people in our communities in meaningful, functional music listening and performing. If the community has access to a symphony orchestra, then we should teach the repertoire that our students will hear at those concerts. In addition, if the community is an isolated, rural one where students will hear bluegrass or country or gospel or any other popular genre, then we should in our music ensembles and classes teach them how this music "works."

This approach to accountability will involve more than reading and studying the many music textbooks, music repertoire lists, and other available music materials. It will involve also studying the preferences, experiences, and needs of the communities we serve. Then we can effectively proceed to both acculturate and lead our students forward to a broader musical experience.

Michael Mark says:

> Music educators will need to expand their vision in the coming years to recognize that music learning embraces all age groups and takes place in many venues beyond the school walls. They will also need to recognize that participation in music activities is not always for the purpose of learning, but is often recreational as well. We will need to examine the musical lives of our communities to determine the most effective and appropriate role for music educators in the future. We should assume that the constantly changing patterns of community life will be reflected in the continually changing role of the music educator. Music educators should expect to work with a variety of age groups and new teaching/learning paradigms. They will need to define the ways that they can continue to serve the musical learning and recreational needs of a dynamic and increasingly diverse society.
> Music education of the future could well be more community-based than school-based. If so, it will require the leadership of people who are informed of the musical tastes of their own communities and who are familiar with the various developmental stages of life. They will be concerned with helping people be involved in music throughout their lifetime.
> Music educators might not be able to do all of these things by themselves, but if not, they might find support roles in maintaining the richness of the musical lives of their communities. In this way, they can broaden their views of music education and can strengthen the role of music education in communities. [13]

OTHER SOURCES OF MUSIC LEARNING IN THE TWENTY-FIRST CENTURY

We know that many informal ways of experiencing music exist. These include television channels such as VH1 and MTV, garage bands, and specialized music festivals through which jazz, blues, bluegrass, Latino, rock, women's music, barbershop quartets, and others are celebrated. Robert Cutietta reports that:

> The local Pizza Hut in Tucson, Arizona has started having bluegrass night on Sunday nights. The idea is that you bring your instrument and there is a big jam session of musicians. The event is so popular that it now takes over the entire dining area. Tables are moved aside and 50 or 60 musicians play together. I would estimate that the average age is about 40 years old. There are guitars, banjos, mandolins, fiddles, and dulcimers. It is literally impossible to order any food except through the drive-through but the event continues.
> Several things strike me about this scenario. First is the commitment of the musicians to come together for the sheer joy of making music together. It is

total vibrant, participation for the sake of music. Second is the commitment of the restaurant which totally disrupts everything about their procedures (including selling pizza!) to support the making of live music. Third is that fact that while an event like this should be the ultimate goal of music education programs, the only instrument in the group which could have been learned in a school music program is the string bass . . . and there are normally only two or three of those. [14]

Other evidence of widespread interest in an abundance of musical genres and styles may be seen by accessing the Internet search engine Yahoo.com and requesting a search for music organizations. The initial search yields 288 organizations with an additional twenty categories to explore. In addition to the traditional organizations such as MENC, the American Symphony Orchestra League, and ASCAP, the lists include a wide variety of others:

- *Accordion Teachers Guild, International*—nonprofit organization dedicated to the advancement of the accordion, through raising of teaching standards
- *Acoustic Performers Guild*—international organization dedicated to the performance and preservation of unamplified music
- *American Music Conference*— national nonprofit educational association dedicated to promoting the importance of music, musicmaking, and music education to the general public
- *Association for Record Sound Collections*—nonprofit organization whose purpose is to develop and disseminate information related to all fields of recording and sound media
- *Banjo in the Hollow*—nonprofit corporation dedicated to preserving and promoting bluegrass and oldtime music
- *Brooklyn Zoo*—nonprofit organization dedicated to Hip Hop
- *Chinese Music Society of North America*—international nonprofit organization dedicated to increasing and diffusing the knowledge of Chinese music and performing arts
- *Doo-Wop Society of Southern California*—organization dedicated to the preservation and exposure of the group-harmony sounds of the 1950s and early 1960s
- *Folk Alliance*—umbrella service organization for individuals and organizations who participate in and support folk music, dance, and storytelling in North America
- *Fretted Instrument Guild of America*—nonprofit organization for enthusiasts of banjos, mandolins, guitars, ukuleles, and related fretted instruments
- *Hungry for Music*—nonprofit music organization that helps disadvantaged people learn about music

- *JazzReach*—nonprofit organization bringing jazz to schools with multimedia performances
- *Kosmic Free Music Foundation*—organization dedicated to the proliferation of freely accessible original music on the Net; hours upon hours of music free for the listening
- *M.U.S.I.C. World HO*—nonprofit organization that uses computer music, video, and the Internet to attract disadvantaged youth to learning computer skills
- *Off Wall Street Jam*—membership organization offering a wide variety of services and musical opportunities for the recreational musician
- *World Music Institute*—organization presenting music and dance concerts from around the world, selling world music CDs, and arranging concert tours

Another example, perhaps more significant to the cause of music education, is the third Music Education Summit sponsored by MENC and held in Washington, DC, in September 1998. More than seventy organizations with specialized music education interests traveled to Washington to participate in extended discussions about the future of music education.

Recreational music learning will become even more popular as increasing technological efficiency creates more leisure and the population of retired workers becomes larger. While this has been said for many years and has never really occurred, it is beginning to happen now as the population of well elderly increases dramatically. It has been said that by 2020, those who retire at ages 65–70 will have fifteen to twenty years of active, healthy life ahead of them. These senior citizens will fill that time with volunteer work, education, and recreation.

There will continue to be a rise in the number of youth and adult symphonies, bands, and choruses. For example, there are now more than thirty New Horizons Bands for senior adults, with many more on the horizon. The first of these bands was started by Roy Ernst at the Eastman School of Music in 1991 and is currently supported by a grant from NAMM: The International Music Products Association and the National Association of Band Instrument Manufacturers.

Many ensembles will be formed that will include people of all ages. An example of intergenerational participation in music outside of the schools is given by Michael Mark:

> When the Baltimore Colts moved to Indianapolis in 1986, the Colts Band didn't break up. Instead, it incorporated as a 501 (c) (3) organization and continued practicing, growing, and playing at public functions like high school and college football games, parades, and at other places. They also played the halftime shows a. NFL games in other cities. The band continued to include players of all ages, from high school to healthy elderly. Three years ago, the

Cleveland Browns moved to Baltimore and became the Baltimore Ravens. The new team let the band play at games and promised to adopt it officially when the new stadium opened last year. That happened, and the team bought the band new instruments and uniforms. The band really has been the city's band for over a decade and now it has been rewarded by becoming an official part of the NFL team. Over the years, the local newspaper gave it occasional coverage, with stories and photos, and it appears that the band was never in danger of disappearing because it was a true community organization. [15]

There will be a significant increase in the number of Elderhostels that offer music learning experiences. Senior Citizens will travel worldwide learning about music in a wide variety of different cultures.

Corporations such as MARS the Musician's Planet, the music superstore based in Florida, will offer opportunities to learn to play all instruments, not just those taught in the public schools. Everything musical one could possibly imagine will be available to students of all ages through these corporations.

Private music schools will continue to flourish in large metropolitan areas. These schools will have resident, fulltime faculty who teach both individual and group music classes.

Music lessons will be available on the Internet as well. Students will be able to interact with a teacher. They will be able to play for the teacher and hear as well as see the teacher's feedback, all in real time.

Computers will make music learning available to everyone at any time. Those who cannot buy a home computer will have access to one at public libraries and community centers. A rapid increase in available music software will enable anyone to compose, perform, and listen to music of all styles and genres. The entire relationship between the formal/informal and private/public sectors will continue to blur as people choose what their music experiences will be. Indeed, what people do not get from formal education they will probably re-create somewhere else.

RELATIONSHIPS BETWEEN SCHOOLS AND OTHER SOURCES OF MUSIC LEARNING

Peter Webster, professor of music education at Northwestern University, presented five challenges to music education by the year 2020:

1. Global access to people, classroom, and information may mean that someone has to assume the role of information broker. Will MENC be the information broker for music education? Will textbook and music series publishers be the brokers?

2. Who will take music lessons from whom if virtual music lessons are technologically feasible from anyone, any place?
3. How do we prepare music teachers for the ultimate in diversity: global access to any culture and any musics? (Will cultural differences be threatened?)
4. New interests in electronic ensembles (real and virtual) that may erode the interest in bands, orchestras, and choruses.
5. There will be continued redefinition of the role of music teachers as mentors to anyone.[16]

Webster's five challenges give emphasis to the issues and concerns discussed in the first section of this paper. They underscore the fact that a multitude of choices will be available to students and teachers in the coming century. Given these challenges (combined with the increasing number of well-elderly), music educators in the schools will need to consider ways to make their curricula such that it and they, as teachers, provide a meaningful transition to music participation in adult life. In keeping with the trend toward collaboration and team teaching and learning in music, we might insure meaningful transition by having our students assume the role of the teacher. In doing so, they might develop a deep commitment to and investment in the subject matter of music that will continue into adulthood. Judith Jellison says,

> What would happen if, in order to teach for transition, we engaged students on a regular basis in activities that were either identical or parallel to those that we perform as adults? Imagine that, as an ongoing part of our music programs, we had our older students select and learn a repertoire of songs appropriate for younger students in our school. Imagine that the older students sang for the younger ones for short periods of time, on many occasions, in nonperforming settings, and either in small groups or one on one. Would our older students have more positive attitudes about singing, sing better, and serve as positive role models for the younger children? Why are most adults afraid to sing? Can't we fix that?
>
> Let's imagine some other hypothetical possibilities. What would happen if students in middle school and secondary school served as public liaisons and advocates for community performing groups and collaborated, interacted or performed with the adult members on a regular basis? Would this involvement serve to increase participation in community performing organizations or attendance at their concerns when these students became adults?[17]

In addition, music educators will need to reconsider certain barriers to music participation in the schools that they have erected. These include (1) requirements to participate in another ensemble in order to participate in the ensemble of choice; for example, requiring participation in marching band in order to participate in jazz ensemble; (2) providing only one entry level to participation in instrumental ensembles, that occurring in the fourth or fifth grade;

(3) providing only traditional ensemble (band, chorus, orchestra) experiences in music after elementary school; and (4) failing to teach for transfer of musical knowledge to adult life. In an age characterized by an abundance of choices, we, as music educators, must be mindful of the fact that our students will make those choices whether we provide them or not. We should open doors to music rather than shut them.

We need to examine and support ways and materials for music instruction that encourage widespread participation in music learning and that are easily adaptable to multiple times, places, and environments. Music educators must make the connection to "music in our lives." We can do this by beginning early to show the role of music in life through interdisciplinary approaches and by taking every opportunity to show students how music of every genre impacts daily living. This will require a thorough knowledge of the communities in which we teach and a desire to make the connections necessary between those communities and music.

Richard Zellner says it this way:

> Now that we have convincing research establishing that music is fundamental to the way we learn, the way we feel and the way we develop as human beings, why is music being systematically eliminated from the school curriculum? Music education has not successfully made the connection to "music in our lives." We must expand the definition of music education, looking beyond schools for music learning, and affirm that everyone is a musician. Until music educators validate the music in the lives of our opinion leaders and political leaders, music education will remain a fringe activity for a chosen few. [18]

The music heard by most nonprofessional musicians includes jazz, pop (Latino, rock, soul, rap), religious music representing all sects, folk music of all countries, Broadway, and Western European classical music. Perhaps our foremost question should be: How might a music educator help a student make the transition from music in the schools to music in life? First, the music that we study must be the music that we will be able to access now and throughout the rest of our lives. Randall DeWitt, educational director at MARS the Musician's Planet, says:

> A common message I hear from those who are taught by and/or associated with the music education community is that they want to make more music and to make their music. Often these are reasons given by students when they drop music classes. It is not until a music learner leaves "school" that he or she has the opportunity to make their music, and to make more music, more often. Our challenge must be to outline the structure of music learning beyond K-12 and, where possible, explore relationships that can exist between schools and other opportunities for music learning. [19]

While it is important to recognize that students value and want to play "their music," we must teach our students how to find out about unfamiliar music. For example, the teacher's preparation for a music appreciation course must include a thoughtful analysis of the students to be taught. What musics will they be able to access after they finish the course? If students live in a small town, they might not be able to hear a symphony or attend an opera. However, they will be able to listen to the radio, watch TV, and buy CDs. Therefore, teaching them where and how to find the music you have taught them is of primary importance. Teachers cannot neglect their most important role, that of opening doors to a musical heritage left to us by great musicians of the past, but they must assume a new role, that of a bridge connecting students to music of all genres.

Involving future teachers and children in the public schools in program development using educational technologies will teach them both the technologies and the subject matter of the programs they are developing. The success of such a venture must involve the cooperation and expertise of the university faculty, teachers in the public schools, children, parents, music merchants, and administrators. The ideas will come from those in the trenches (teachers and children) and those in the towers (professors and future teachers). Support for the production phase of the development procession must come from music merchants and national arts organizations. Evaluation of the software and other program products must come from consumers of them including teachers and children.[20] While it is recognized that the goals of the music industry and the goals of music educators are sometimes at odds with one another, both can make a commitment to the realization of the National Standards that may help us to unite for a greater cause, the music education of our children.

Professional music educators must realize that most of the students they teach will be future consumers of music. A very few of these will be professional musicians and teachers. A retired, highly successful choral director commented that in his thirty years of teaching, only one student had become a professional musician. However, he proudly stated that many, many of his former students were continuing to make music in their communities. Making music an integral part of the lives of our students when they leave us must be our first priority.

Jeffrey Kimpton says:

> While we all recognize the accomplishments of MENC over the past 30 years since the first Tanglewood document, the next 20 years represent change that will make the previous 30 seem insignificant. The problem is that it will challenge or change the institutional hierarchies that MENC, school systems, and all organizations have created to deal with issues and problems. The whole notion of place-based learning rather than "education" is the driving force for new kinds of development in human capacity, collaborations and the unlimited

ability of millions of great minds to be allowed to further new learning (knowledge). It changes the concept of place, requires us to think about how we shape content in new ways for new learners in radically different contexts.

Yes, music learning will probably take place in some schools. But we have to recognize that it will also take place—in a host of other places, by "teachers" who won't or can't be certified, by processes that are not researched or analyzed, in ways increasingly more individual, and challenging the notion of aesthetic experience. Even given the use of technology, there are major issues facing those without access to technology that further stratifies music learning. MENC's Vision 2020 should be about dreaming, not substantiating an institutional relationship between organizations and music makers, lovers and teachers. If we are to invent the future, we can respect the past but need to wake up our colleagues around the country that the future will be largely what they choose to make of it. Hopefully this document will make them think about that in bold, real ways. [21]

Thus, our goals as music educators should be to prepare students for a lifetime of music, to reach more people by expanding our music curricula, to encourage intergenerational music participation in the schools or in community centers, and to meet the musical needs and preferences of the communities that support us by celebrating the diversity of music making in America. In so doing, music educators must be concerned with music of the past (acculturation), music of the present (the transition period between acculturation and innovation), and music of the future (innovation).

The unifying tie that can bind music in the schools with other sources of music learning must be the National Standards for Arts Education. Somehow we must work together to make music learning both educational and entertaining. Teachers in the schools can learn from people in the music industry about how to make music learning fun. Those in the music industry can learn from teachers about how to insure that music learning occurs. We must unite with the common goal of lifelong learning in music.

NOTES

1. Arthur C. Clarke, *July 20, 2019: Life in the 21st Century* (New York: Macmillan Publishing, 1986), 75.

2. William Knoke, *Bold New World: The Essential Road Map to the Twenty-First Century* (New York: Kodansha International, 1996), 20–21.

3. U.S. Department of Commerce, *The Emerging Digital Economy*, April 1998, http://www.ecommerce.gov/emerging.html.

4. Knoke, 304.

5. Cornelia Yarbrough, "Multiculturalism: The Use of Technology," *Bulletin of the Council for Research in Music Education* 117 (Summer 1993): 71–75.

6. John D. Pulliam and James Van Patten, *History of Education in America*, 6th ed. (Englewood Cliffs, NJ: Prentice-Hall, 1995), 279–80.

7. Jeff Barnard, "Love of Music Take Man, 76, to School," *The Morning Advocate* (Baton Rouge, LA, 30 January 1999): 3A.

8. Wilma Benson, orchestra director, Louisville, Kentucky, e-mail communication to author, 4 May 1999, wbensonl@jefferson.kl2ky.us.

9. Joseph P. McDonald, *Redesigning School: Lessons for the 21st Century* (San Francisco: Jossey-Bass Publishers, 1996), 5–10.

10. Robert Weil, ed., *The Omni Future Almanac* (New York: Harmony Books, 1982), 214.

11. Knoke, 305.

12. Consortium of National Arts Education Associations, *National Standards for Arts Education* (Reston, VA: Music Educators National Conference, 1994).

13. Michael Mark, Towson University, statement written at meeting of the Housewright Commission on Music Education, The Florida State University, 8 April 1999.

14. Robert Cutietta, University of Arizona-Tucson, e-mail communication to author, 23 April 1999, cutietta@u.arizona.edu.

15. Michael Mark, Towson University, email communication to author, 12 April 1999, mmark@clark.net.

16. Peter Webster and David Williams, "Through the 2020 Looking Glass: Music Education and Technology," teleconference presented to the Housewright Commission on Music Education, The Florida State University, 9 April 1999, http://pubweb.nwu.edu/-webster/.

17. Judith Jellison, "Life Beyond the Jingle Stick: Real Music in a Real World," *Update: Applications of Research in Music Education* 17 (Spring–Summer 1999): 13–19.

18. Richard Zellner, The Arts Foundation, El Cajon, CA, statement written at meeting of the Housewright Commission on Music Education, The Florida State University, 8 April 1999.

19. Randall DeWitt, statement written at meeting of the Housewright Commission on Music Education, The Florida State University, 8 April 1999.

20. Yarbrough, 74.

21. Jeffrey Kimpton, University of Minnesota, statement written at meeting of the Housewright Commission on Music Education, The Florida State University, 8 April 1999.

Chapter Thirteen

Response to Cornelia Yarbrough's "What Should Be the Relationship between Schools and Other Sources of Music Learning?"

Richard Bell

Richard Bell is the national executive director of Young Audiences.

First, I want to thank MENC and June Hinckley for inviting me to join your deliberations this week. It has been a very stimulating time. One of the great advantages of speaking last is that you get to hear what everybody else has to say. It also turns out to be the greatest disadvantage since you may find that you do not have very much to say that has not already been said. Fortunately, I have Dr. Yarbrough's paper to address, which brings us an entirely new landscape to consider.

It is a truly visionary paper. This provocative, thought-provoking survey of music education's future fulfills its stated conviction, that "MENC's Vision 2020 should be about *dreaming*, not substantiating an institutional relationship between organizations and music makers, lovers and teachers" (p. 193).

This clarion call, we are told, is intended "to wake up our colleagues around the country"—to let them know that the future reality will be "a placeless society." (Do you remember when we used to talk about a paperless society? I don't think it ever happened, but the challenges and opportunities brought by technology have transformed our lives.)

But a *placeless* society. Imagine that! Increasingly driven and defined by technology, schools would be open round the clock to all ages, teaching would focus on not only "the acquisition of skills to work with a comprehensive repertoire of music from the current popular and concert hall musics of our own time, but also . . . the contemporary music practices of the entire global village" (p. 183). Music would be taught across the curriculum through "collaborations among music teachers, their students, and experts worldwide" (p. 184).

In this vision, the continually changing role of the music educator will call on you to access, evaluate, and interpret "massive amounts of information" that will be created, often "without regard for quality or accuracy." We are told that "the challenge for music educators will be one of blending the social and academic aspects of music learning toward the goals of both enjoyment and education," and one of "developing, monitoring, and facilitating the private music experiences being produced via advances in technology" (p. 181). Above all, music educators "must help students and their parents understand and make the connection between music and life," and become "accountable for making music an important part of every person's life" (p. 185).

Ladies and gentlemen, I come to you today to offer each and every one of you my congratulations—along with this bottle of aspirin, which you may need in abundance as you embark on this great adventure.

As I read Yarbrough's paper, I could not help but recall a character in Tennessee Williams' play, *Camino Real,* who set out across a vast, imponderable desert that Williams called the "terra incognito." Knowing that he would never return, he said, "Make voyages. Attempt them. There is nothing else."

But whether the scenario envisioned by the authors of this paper strikes you as prescient or preposterous or just plain scary, there can be little doubt that if we fail to anticipate the tidal wave of possibilities now bearing down upon us, our role in shaping the aspirations and expectations of our profession will surely be marginalized.

I want to reinforce and expand on two recurrent themes contained in Yarbrough's paper. But first, let me remind you that I am not a music educator. However, I have worked professionally in the musical, theatrical, and educational arenas for most of my life, beginning many years ago with Noah Greenberg's New York Pro Musica, then passing though several university stints and professional gigs. I finally settled down as the director of the nation's leading provider of arts and education in-school services, Young Audiences, which last year produced over 82,000 programs in music, dance, and theatre, and reached over seven million students. So I speak to you today from the perspective of the outsider looking in, albeit one whose nose has been pressed firmly to the glass for the better part of a generation.

I should also share with you that I am not a fence sitter regarding the philosophical debate referred to early on in this paper where on the one hand "education is seen as a *private* or *personal* good, with parents as consumers of whatever public, private, or parochial education best suits their needs. On the other side is the argument that public education is provided for the *common* good, and that all children should share some common experiences in common settings" (p. 180, emphasis added).

As a Queens, New York, boy in the 1950s and 1960s I was the beneficiary of an exceptionally fine public school education. My experience in public schools along with my parents' support is chiefly responsible for the professional life I enjoy today, and so I admit to a passionate bias and commitment to the egalitarian system of public education.

And in my view public education represents one of the singular achievements in American society. I believe its existence and success are worth striving and fighting for. Among the many characteristics that justify saving and strengthening the public education school system is its capacity to transform failure into success. American public education is the only system in the world that gives students multiple opportunities to succeed even after repeated failures. In *The Merchant of Venice*, William Shakespeare put it simply when he said, "the quality of mercy is not strained."

Who can say how many lives have been turned around, if not literally saved, because of this humane and pragmatic characteristic? This is in contrast to countries throughout the world where a single test or grade-point average can sometimes determine a child's professional options for life. The opportunities to succeed often turn on the efforts of a single teacher—one who is just stubborn and caring enough to keep students from falling between the cracks, which for many of our young people have become chasms in urban and rural areas today. So, with that as preamble, let me move on to the heart of the matter, which as I see it centers on addressing the assertion that music educators are teaching professionals whose command of the discipline of music may no longer be sufficient to justify their presence in schools.

Yarbrough and her colleagues quite rightly assert that in the future the role of music educators must be augmented to embrace the realities envisioned in this paper. In my view, two areas among the many cited here offer the greatest opportunities for ensuring a permanent and self-sustaining role for music educators in the schools of the future.

The first area involves teaching across disciplines, especially in elementary schools. The second involves using music as a means of engendering greater understanding and tolerance for the cultures that make up current and projected student populations. Now if this use of music as a means to an end appears overly pragmatic or causes concern about the intrinsic value of music let me recall how music first found its way into public education.

As many of you know, this occurred early in the last century in Boston, where it was the general consensus that the quality of singing in churches was so poor that only the regular systematic study of music in schools could remedy the situation. The evolution of the visual arts as a regular part of

public education fifty years later followed a similar pattern, in order to prepare students to work in the factories that designed and manufactured hats
and shoes throughout New England. Today, years after the hat and shoe
factories have closed, and choirs have long since supplanted the need for
singing congregations, music and art remain firmly ensconced in the public
schools.

As previous authors have noted so eloquently, music is a language that is
basic to the human condition, and once having gained entrance, by whatever
means and for whatever reasons, music will inevitably be established for its
intrinsic value. I love listening to Sam Hope. Only a composer could construct thoughts like that. One may not always understand or even agree with
his assertions, but I still love to listen and absorb them, as one might reflect
on a fine piece of music. His cautionary note about the importance of teaching the distinctive characteristics of Western European art music led me to
recall one of my earliest experiences in the theatre.

The first time I came to Florida, I was a young actor. I played the title role
in a play called *Cross and Sword* in St. Augustine. The play was about the
founding of St. Augustine. Does anybody know who founded St. Augustine,
the first settlement in the New World? It was Pedro Menendez de Alvilez. I
played Pedro and I was a dedicated Method actor at that time. For those of
you who do not know what the Method is, a simplistic definition is that as an
actor you work from the inside out, rather than from the outside in. In other
words, you have to find your motivation in order to say a line.

Well, as part of my research, I visited the local wax museum where they
actually had a statue of Pedro. And to my shock and dismay, and after
months of preparation, I found that Pedro Menendez was about five feet tall.
And I could not get that thought out of my mind. I had prepared for the past
two months, and in my mind, he was tall—probably very tall, just like me.

So on opening night in an outdoor amphitheater filled with two thousand
people, I entered my first scene of the play as Pedro Menendez having just
come ashore, and there waiting angrily are literally a hundred natives and
their leader, Chief Oriba, who has a long speech that goes on for two pages.
And any of you who know Paul Green's plays know that his work does go
on. I had an even longer speech in response that began, "I am Pedro Menendez de Avilez, king of the western seas" and so on, and so on, for another two
pages. And so, the Chief finished his part and he said, "Now, who are you?"
and I said, "I am . . ." and I thought of that *little* man in the museum and for
the life of me I could not think of my name. And you should have seen the
Chief's eyes. They bugged out! He couldn't help me. What could he do, tell
me my name?

So, in desperation after what to me seemed like hours but what I understand was only about fifteen seconds, but that's hours on stage, I stammered
"I am . . . I am . . ." And I turned to my right and there was my trusted

lieutenant, Lt. Alvarez, and so I said, "Lt. Alvarez." It was the only name I could think of. Now the fact that he was blonde and had just finished a scene with his lover and therefore was firmly planted in the audience's mind, meant nothing to me. I had to have a name.

Now, what could the audience have thought of Pedro? Either they were dealing with a schizophrenic who has lost all sense of reality or this is a very clever ploy by a general who is destined to rule all of Florida. The end of this story (and the point of it) is that after the performance, some friends came backstage and, of course, I was really despondent. And they said, "It was terrific. It was great." You know how people always do. And I said, "But what about the part when I couldn't come up with my own name?"

And, you know, they did not even notice. They had not even realized what had occurred. It was the first scene of the play. The audience was shuffling their programs, they were looking after the kids, eating popcorn. They were doing all the things that audiences do, so that excruciating moment just passed them by.

You see, the play is the thing, *music* is the thing. We will never lose that no matter what other subjects we focus on. Never be afraid of that. We will never forget our name.

Today and in the future, music specialists will be expected to use technology and hands-on professional development to connect students, classroom teachers, and the cultural community to the study of music, and to improve teaching and learning across the curriculum. Of course, this will create a conundrum of time and budgetary constraints, but these challenges can and will be addressed school by school, district by district, and teacher by teacher.

Unfortunately, the commitment of parents and communities in general to the study of music in schools is fragile. For the most part, the public perceives instruction as a necessary component of young people's education only if a student is talented and therefore potentially able to earn a living by pursuing music as a vocation. Yet music should be taught to all students for the same reason we teach math to all students. Not in the expectation that every student will become a mathematician, but rather because all students need basic math skills in their daily lives to balance their checkbooks.

The same case is now being made for the arts, but as Yarbrough notes, music educators will have to become researchers and facilitators in order to meet the needs of students and generalist teachers of the future. Classroom teachers, especially in elementary schools, have long been aware of the value of the arts, but they are often unsure how music can be used to improve student performance in other subjects. Through the use of new technologies and intensive professional development we now have the means to begin to address this challenge. We must provide generalist teachers with the skills and resources they need to create thematic units of study that connect the core subjects.

At this point, I am always asked, "Well, give us an example of what you're talking about." It is so hard to embrace interdisciplinary teaching, especially when we know what we are doing inside the discipline. But there are numerous examples.

Wynton Marsalis is an obvious choice. Every one of his music education programs is a model of interdisciplinary teaching. The last one I saw was about the life and music of Dizzy Gillespie. It was a lesson in music; it was a lesson in American history. It was a lesson in English, it was a lesson in the life of an individual and of a culture, and it all happened within about forty minutes.

Another example is a project called the Civil War Tapestry, developed by Kathleen Gaffney of Arts Genesis. Kathleen worked with a group of teachers and students in Wichita, Kansas. Each student assumed the character of a person who lived through the time of the Civil War, someone who was not famous, but a person for whom he or she felt a special affinity. The characters included farmers, slaves, and slave owners. And students learned about the context of each of those people's lives. And on the eve of the Battle of Gettysburg, each student wrote a letter home, in character. They could just as easily have written a song. Now that is interdisciplinary teaching and learning. But the truth is, we have very little experience in doing it, and it is very difficult to do well, and another truth is that most of us are not going to be very good at it, especially the first time.

I remember when I was in a production of *Julius Caesar,* and I played a little-known character. I do not think any of you would know this character. His name was Trebonius. Trebonius had one line in *Julius Caesar.* It was not a distinguished line. It was a line something like, "And so will I, thus and so." It was one of those lines. Not even, "Hark, the cannons roar."

Cassius had the lean and hungry look. Brutus, the noble Brutus. Casca was the first one to stab Caesar. Trebonius—nothing. But he was present, he was there. And so what did I do as the actor who was given the part of Trebonius? I made up a new play called *Trebonius Unbound.* And in this play, which ran parallel to *Julius Caesar*, Trebonius was the center of everything. And I constructed an entire life for him

Then, two weeks before the opening, the director came to me, obviously not in the best of spirits and said, "Richard, I'm sorry to let you know that you're no longer playing Trebonius." And of course, I was shattered, and asked "Why?" Because I had really worked on this role.

And he said, "You're too tall. You're getting in the way of Caesar and Brutus and Cassius in the stabbing scene. You're a little too tall for it." So instead, he gave me another part. Metellus Cimber. Now Metellus Cimber has no lines. He is an absolute zero. In fact, Hamlet is to Trebonius what Trebonius is to Metellus Cimber.

Now, I am sure some of you know that Shakespeare's theatre was an open stage with no curtains. So if you are on stage at the end of a scene, your job as an actor is to clear the bench or whatever scenery is on the stage so the next scene can begin, and whoever is the lowest actor gets this job. Needless to say, this task fell to me. Metellus Cimber is clearly the least-defined character in the play. And so out of that came the new play, "Metellus Cimber, Thief of Rome." And I can assure you, that at the end of that scene, I swooped down and took off that bench with a flourish of my cloak that would have put Count Dracula to shame.

The point is, we must not be afraid of what we do not know. We must simply make it up. If you don't know where you're going, every road will get you there. So be of good cheer, do not be afraid of these challenges. They are doable.

The key to achieving this goal of interdisciplinary teaching is to create peer-to-peer communication and resource networks using the interactive capacities of the Internet and the handson expertise of arts specialists. This approach offers a new role for music educators and may also help restore instruction in music because experience has taught us that interdisciplinary teaching and learning through the arts will not occur in the absence of serious arts study.

No other discipline lends itself to the use of technology and the concept of making connections across the curriculum so well as music and the arts. This is especially so in a multicultural context. The proliferation of musical genres and the explosion of languages and cultures in our schools are circumstances that even the most confident and experienced music teacher will find daunting. But high-speed transmission of video and audio via the Internet and CD-ROM provide access to a vast storehouse of musical experience that no one teacher or artist can provide alone.

Of course there is no substitute for the human touch, but technology and the live teaching experience are not antithetical. Quite the contrary, technology gives us the means to extend and transform teaching across cultures and the core curriculum. But we cannot accomplish this alone, and we will not succeed without the appropriate training or the necessary resources, which brings me to one of the few caveats I have with Yarbrough's paper. Although it provides many examples drawn from the nearly three hundred music organizations listed on the Internet search engine Yahoo.com, there is virtually no mention as to how these organizations might help meet the challenges and opportunities presented in this paper.

A cursory examination of programs offered by arts providers in most areas of the country reveals a mix of field trips to major museums and performing arts institutions; in-school programs by opera, dance, and theatre

companies; countless offerings by emerging arts organizations; and a wide
array of programs presented by individual artists. These include introductory
and career-centered programs, short- and long-term residencies, broad-based
curriculum integration, and comprehensive collaborations.

There are numerous examples of cities, including New York, Chicago
and Los Angeles, with robust arts-in-education services but few full-time arts
specialists. But there are also many examples of cities and districts that have
maintained and strengthened instructional programs in the arts while simultaneously building a value-added component with the cultural community.
Examples of these cities include Miami, Indianapolis, and Minneapolis
among large urban centers, and Columbus, Ohio, and Wichita, Kansas,
among mid-sized cities.

The role of artists and arts organizations in the schools has evolved over
the past fifty years. Today these service providers represent a major resource
to students and teachers in schools throughout the country. Although there
are no reliable statistics to confirm the overall growth of these programs, and
there is virtually no formal assessment of their value to student learning,
clearly these programs are increasing dramatically. Unfortunately, most of
the arts community is unaware of your deliberations concerning issues addressed in this paper. They often do not perceive the vital stake they have in
the realization of your aspirations, nor do they understand their own responsibility to support your efforts to strengthen arts instruction. And for some of
you I know the question arises regarding the possibility that these programs
may be perceived as an adequate substitute for instruction in the arts. In my
experience, this concern, though understandable, is groundless. It also represents the single greatest obstacle to developing more productive working
relationships among teachers and artists.

My second caveat also concerns an area of omission. We are all familiar
with the "chicken and egg" cycles that invariably accompany substantial
change in schools (i.e., if we are given the resources, the desired outcomes
can be accomplished, but in order to receive the necessary resources, we
must first meet these outcomes). The cadre of music educators teaching
today at first may not be willing or able to embrace the vision presented in
this paper. And our authors do not suggest how or where to begin. Quite
rightly, they focus their powers of prognostication on the *why* and *what* of the
matters at hand.

It would be tempting for this reviewer to sally forth at this point and call
for a thorough examination of the way in which we prepare prospective
teachers and artists. And clearly, there is much that could be said about the
need to establish closer working relationships among our preservice schools
of arts and schools of education where there is virtually no interaction at
present. But as our time is limited and since I believe that "discretion is the

better part of valor," I will simply note this area as one that sorely needs your further consideration.

In closing, let me say that the development of national standards in the arts, and the day-to-day efforts of music educators in schools has given new impetus to the need to define optimal working associations among educators and artists. The public-private sector partnerships that are a natural outgrowth of these collaborations may offer new opportunities to address many of the issues raised in Yarbrough's paper.

The arts community looks to the leadership of MENC and to music educators and your counterparts in the visual arts, dance, and theatre, to help us define ways in which we can support one another beyond advocacy for the value of arts education for all students. And so I invite each of you to work with your colleagues in the arts community, to help make your vision of the future as inclusive as possible. And as you proceed to the practical business of making these dreams a reality, I urge you to bring those who reside just outside your core constituency into the inner circle of your deliberations so that eventually we can harness these resources to help achieve a common vision of the future on behalf of the generations of students and teachers to come.

"Make voyages. . . . Attempt them. . . . There is nothing else."

Chapter Fourteen

The Housewright Declaration

Whenever and wherever humans have existed music has existed also. Since music occurs only when people choose to create and share it, and since they always have done so and no doubt always will, music clearly must have important value for people.

Music makes a difference in people's lives. It exalts the human spirit; it enhances the quality of life. Indeed, meaningful music activity should be experienced throughout one's life toward the goal of continuing involvement.

Music is a basic way of knowing and doing because of its own nature and because of the relationship of that nature to the human condition, including mind, body, and feeling. It is worth studying because it represents a basic mode of thought and action, and because in itself, it is one of the primary ways human beings create and share meanings. It must be studied fully to access this richness.

Societal and technological changes will have an enormous impact for the future of music education. Changing demographics and increased technological advancements are inexorable and will have profound influences on the ways that music is experienced for both students and teachers.

Music educators must build on the strengths of current practice to take responsibility for charting the future of music education to insure that the best of the Western art tradition and other musical traditions are transmitted to future generations.

We agree on the following:

1. All persons, regardless of age, cultural heritage, ability, venue, or financial circumstance deserve to participate fully in the best music experiences possible.

2. The integrity of music study must be preserved. Music educators must lead the development of meaningful music instruction and experience.

3. Time must be allotted for formal music study at all levels of instruction such that a comprehensive, sequential and standards-based program of music instruction is made available.

4. All music has a place in the curriculum. Not only does the Western art tradition need to be preserved and disseminated, music educators also need to be aware of other music that people experience and be able to integrate it into classroom music instruction.

5. Music educators need to be proficient and knowledgeable concerning technological changes and advancements and be prepared to use all appropriate tools in advancing music study while recognizing the importance of people coming together to make and share music.

6. Music educators should involve the music industry, other agencies, individuals, and music institutions in improving the quality and quantity of music instruction. This should start within each local community by defining the appropriate role of these resources in teaching and learning.

7. The currently defined role of the music educator will expand as settings for music instruction proliferate. Professional music educators must provide a leadership role in coordinating music activities beyond the school setting to insure formal and informal curricular integration.

8. Recruiting prospective music teachers is a responsibility of many, including music educators. Potential teachers need to be drawn from diverse backgrounds, identified early, led to develop both teaching and musical abilities, and sustained through ongoing professional development. Also, alternative licensing should be explored in order to expand the number and variety of teachers available to those seeking music instruction.

9. Continuing research addressing all aspects of music activity needs to be supported including intellectual, emotional, and physical responses to music. Ancillary social results of music study also need exploration as well as specific studies to increase meaningful music listening.

10. Music making is an essential way in which learners come to know and understand music and music traditions. Music making should be broadly interpreted to be performing, composing, improvising, listening, and interpreting music notation.

11. Music educators must join with others in providing opportunities for meaningful music instruction for all people beginning at the earliest possible age and continuing throughout life.

12. Music educators must identify the barriers that impede the full actualization of any of the above and work to overcome them.

THE TANGLEWOOD DECLARATION

by Allen Britton, Arnold Broido, and Charles Gary

The intensive evaluation of the role of music in American society and education provided by the Tanglewood Symposium of philosophers, educators, scientists, labor leaders, philanthropists, social scientists, theologians, industrialists, representatives of government and foundations, music educators and other musicians led to this declaration:

We believe that education must have as major goals the art of living, the building of personal identity, and nurturing creativity. Since the study of music can contribute much to these ends, *we now call for music to be placed in the core of the school curriculum.*

The arts afford a continuity with the aesthetic tradition in man's history. Music and other fine arts, largely nonverbal in nature, reach close to the social, psychological, and physiological roots of man in his search for identity and self-realization.

Educators must accept the responsibility for developing opportunities which meet man's individual needs and the needs of a society plagued by the consequences of changing values, alienation, hostility between generations, racial and international tensions, and the challenges of a new leisure.

Music educators at Tanglewood agreed that:

1. Music serves best when its integrity as an art is maintained.
2. Music of all periods, styles, forms, and cultures belongs in the curriculum. The musical repertory should be expanded to involve music of our time in its rich variety, including currently popular teenage music and avant-garde music, American folk music, and the music of other cultures.
3. Schools and colleges should provide adequate time for music in programs ranging from preschool through adult or continuing education.
4. Instruction in the arts should be a general and important part of education in the senior high school.
5. Developments in educational technology, educational television, programmed instruction, and computer-assisted instruction should be applied to music study and research.
6. Greater emphasis should be placed on helping the individual student to fulfill his needs, goals, and potentials.
7. The music education profession must contribute its skills, proficiencies, and insights toward assisting in the solution of urgent social problems as in the "inner city" or other areas with culturally deprived individuals.

8. Programs of teacher education must be expanded and improved to provide music teachers who are specially equipped to teach high school courses in the history and literature of music, courses in the humanities and related arts, as well as teachers equipped to work with the very young, with adults, with the disadvantaged, and with the emotionally disturbed.

From *Documentary Report of the Tanglewood Symposium*, Music Educators National Conference, Washington, DC, 1968, p. 139.

THE GOALS AND OBJECTIVES PROJECT

The purpose of the Goals and Objectives Project was to identify the responsibilities of MENC as they pertained to future needs. The Project, directed by Paul Lehman, began in 1969 with a steering committee and eighteen subcommittees, each of which related in some way to the Tanglewood Declaration.

1. Preparation for Music Educators
2. Musical Behaviors—Identification and Evaluation
3. Comprehensive Musicianship—Music Study in the Senior High School
4. Music for All Youth
5. Music Education in the Inner City
6. Research in Music Education
7. Logistics of Music Education
8. Fact Finding
9. Aesthetic Education
10. Information Science
11. Music for Early Childhood
12. Impact of Technology
13. Music in Higher Education
14. Learning Processes
15. Musical Enrichment of National Life
16. MENC Professional Activities
17. Professional Organization Relationships
18. Music of Non-Western Cultures

After the committee reports were condensed, Paul Lehman drafted the proposed MENC goals and objectives. This statement was submitted to the federated and associated organizations, and by the chairpersons of the national committees. In October, 1970, the MENC Executive Board adopted two goals for MENC, four for the profession in general, and thirty-five objectives.

The goals of MENC shall be to conduct programs and activities to build:

A vital music culture
An enlightened musical public

The goals of the profession are:

Comprehensive music programs in all schools
Involvement of people of all ages in learning music
Quality preparation of teachers
Use of the most effective techniques and resources in music instruction

The objectives:

1. *Lead in efforts to develop programs of music instruction challenging to all students, whatever their sociocultural condition, and directed toward the needs of citizens in a pluralistic society
2. *Lead in the development of programs of study that correlate performing, creating, and listening to music and encompass a diversity of musical behaviors
3. *Assist teachers in the identification of musical behaviors relevant to the needs of their students
4. *Advance the teaching of music of all periods, styles, forms, and cultures
5. Promote the development of instructional programs in aesthetic education
6. Advocate the expansion of music education to include preschool children
7. Lead in efforts to ensure that every school system requires music from kindergarten through grade six and for a minimum of two years beyond that level
8. Lead in efforts to ensure that every secondary school offers an array of music courses to meet the needs of all youth
9. Promote challenging courses in music for the general college student
10. Advocate the expansion of music education for adults both in at out of school
11. *Develop standards to ensure that all music instruction is provided by teachers well prepared in music
12. Encourage the improvement and continuous updating of preservice and inservice education program for all persons who teach music programs and in the certification of music teachers
13. *Expand its programs to secure greater involvement and commitment of student members

14. Assist graduate schools in developing curricula especially designed for the preparation of teachers

15. Develop and recommend accreditation criteria for the use of recognized agencies in the approval of school and college music

16. Support the expansion of teacher education programs to include specializations designed to meet current needs

17. *Assume leadership in the application of significant new developments in curriculum, teaching-learning techniques and technology, instructional and staffing patterns, evaluation, and related topics to every area and level of music teaching

18. Assume leadership in the development of resources for music teaching and learning

19. Cooperate in the development of exemplary models of desirable programs and practices in the teaching of music

20. Encourage maximum use of community music resources to enhance educational programs

21. *Lead in efforts to ensure that every school system allocates sufficient staff, time, and funds to support a comprehensive and excellent music program

22. Provide advisory assistance where music programs are threatened by legislative, administrative, or other action

23. Conduct public relations programs to build community support for music education

24. Promote the conduct of research and research-related activities in music education

25. Disseminate news of research in order that research findings may be applied promptly and effectively

26. Determine the most urgent needs for information in music education

27. Gather and disseminate information about music and education

28. Encourage other organizations, agencies, and communications media to gather and disseminate information about music and education

29. Initiate efforts to establish information retrieval systems in music and education, and to develop data bases for subsequent incorporation into such systems

30. Pursue effective working relationships with organizations and groups having mutual interests

31. Strengthen the relationships between the conference and its federated, associated, and auxiliary organizations

32. Establish procedures for its organizational program planning and policy

33. Seek to expand its membership to include all persons who, in any capacity, teach music

34. Periodically evaluate the effectiveness of its policies and programs

35. Ensure systematic interaction with its membership concerning the goals and objectives of the conference

*Priority objectives

Chapter Fifteen

The Housewright Declaration: Vision 2020

En español

Cuando quiera y como quiera que hayan existido los humanos, la música tambien ha existido. Debido a que la música ocurre solo cuando las personas deciden crearla y compartirla, y debido a que siempre lo han hecho y sin dudas, siempre lo haran, claramente la música debe tener un valor muy importante para las personas.

La música hace diferente la vida de las personas. Exalta el espiritu humano; mejora la calidad de vida. De hecho, actividad musical significativa, deberia ser experimentada en la vida de toda persona hacia la meta de intervencion continua.La música es una forma básica de saber y hacer debido a su propia naturaleza y por la reaccion de esa naturaleza con la condición humana, incluyendo mente, cuerpo,y sentimientos. Vale la pena estudiarla porque representa la forma básica de pensamiento y acción, y porque por sí mismo, es una de las formas que los seres humanos crean y comparten algo significativo. Debe ser estudiada al maximo para acceder a esta riqueza.

Los cambios sociológicos y tecnológicos tendrían un enorme impacto en el futuro de la educación musical. Los cambios demográficos y el aumento en el avance de la tecnologia son inexorables y tendrían una profunda influencia en la forma que la música es experimentada tanto en alumnos y profesores.

Los educadores musicales deberan construir las fortalezas de la practica actual para tomar la responsabilidad en el trazando al futuro de la educación musical para asegurar que lo mejor de las tradiciones del arte occidental y otras tradiciones musicales sean transmitidas a futuros generaciones.

Acordamos lo siguiente:

1. Todas las personas, no importa su edad, herencia cultural, habilidades, lugar de origen, o situación financiera, merece participar completamente en las mejores experiencias musicales posibles.
2. La integridad del estudio de la música debe ser preservada. Los educadores musicales deben guiar el desarrollo de instrucciones y experiencias musicalmente significativas.
3. Deberá ser asignado un tiempo formal para el estudio de la música en todos los niveles de instrucción tanto como comprensivo, secuencial y programas basado en estándares de instrucción musical donde sean disponibles.
4. Todo tipo de música tiene un lugar en el curriculum. No solo la tradición del arte occidental debe ser preservada y diseminada, los educadores musicales tambien necesitan estar pendientes de otros tipos de musica que la gente experimente y ser capaces de integrarla a un aula de instrucción musical.
5. Los educadores musicales necesitan ser competentes y estar concientes de los cambios y avances tecnológicos y estar preparados para usar todas las herramientas necesarias en el avance del estudio de la educación musical mientras se reconozca la importancia de que las personas se reunan para hacer y compartir música.
6. Los educadores musicales deberán involucrarse en la industria musical, otras agencias, individuos e instituciones musicales para mejorar la calidad y la cantidad de la instrucción musical. Esto deberia empezar en cada comunidad local, definiendo el rol apropiado de estos recursos en enseñanza y aprendizaje.
7. El rol definido actualmente de un educador musical expandirá como ajustes para que la instruccion musical prolifere. Los educadores profesionales de música deberan proveer un rol de liderzago en coordinación con actividades que vayan mas allá de las acomodaciones de la escuela para asegurar la integración curricular formal e informalmente.
8. Reclutar prospectos de profesores de música es responsabilidad de todos, incluyendo educadores musicales. Los potenciales maestros necesitan ser seleccionados con diferentes perfiles, identificación temprana, guiados a desarrollar ambas habilidades, enseñanza y musical, y mantenerla a traves de constante desarrollo profesional. Tambien, las licencias alternativas deberian ser exploradas en orden de expandir el numero y la variedad de profesores disponibles para esos que buscan instrucción musical.
9. Investigación contínua direccionando todos los aspectos que la educación musical necesita para ser apoyada, incluyendo aspectos em-

ocionales, intellectuales y respuestas físicas a la música. Resultados sociales adicionales del estudio de la música tambien necesita exploración asi como estudios específicos para aumentar significativamente la escucha musical.

10. Hacer música es una forma escencial en la que los aprendices saben como entender la música y las tradiciones musicales. Hacer música debería ser ampliamente interpretado para ser ejecutada, compuesta, improvisada, escuchada e interpretada notación musical.

11. Los educadores musicales deberian unirse con otros para proveer oportunidades para una instrucción musical significativa para todas las personas empezando a la edad mas temprana posible y continuar a traves de los años.

12. Los educadores musicales deben identificar las barreras que le impiden la completa actualización de muchos de los antes mencionados y el trabajo para superarlos.

THE TANGLEWOOD DECLARATION

Allen Britton, Arnold Broido, and Charles Gary

La evaluación intensiva del papel de la música en sociedad Americana y en la educación provista en el Tanglewood Symposium de filósofos, educadores, científicos, líderes, filántropos, científicos sociales, teólogos, industriales, representantes del gobierno y fundaciones, educadores musicales y otros músicos condujeron a esta declaración:

Creemos que la educación debe tener tantas metas como el arte de vivir, la edificación de la identidad personal, y creatividad nutrida. Debido a que el estudio de la música puede contribuir a estos fines, hacemos un llamado para que la música sea colocada en el núcleo del curriculum escolar.

Las artes permiten la continuidad de la tradición estética en la historia del hombre. La música y otras bellas artes, en gran parte no verbales por naturaleza, alcanzan acercarse a las raíces sociales, psicológicas, y fisiológicas del hombre en su búsqueda para la identidad y auto-realización.

Los educadores deben aceptar la responsabilidad de desarrollar oportunidades que alcancen las necesidades individuales del hombre y las necesidades de la sociedad plagada por las consecuencias en el cambio de valores, aislamiento, hostilidad entre generaciones, tensiones raciales e internacionales, y los desafíos de un nuevo ocio.

Los educadores musicales de Tanglewood acordaron lo siguiente:

1. La música da mejores resultados cuando su integridad como arte es mantenida.

2. La música de todos los tiempos, estilos, formas, y culturas, pertenece al curriculum. El repertorio musical debe ser expandida para involucrar la música de nuestro tiempo en su rica variedad, incluyendo la música popular entre los adolecentes y música experimental, música Americana, y música de otras culturas.

3. Las escuelas y las universidades deberían de proveer un tiempo adecuado para música en los programas que vaya desde preescolar hasta la adultez o educación contínua.

4. La instrucción en las artes debería ser en general y una parte importante de la educación en la secundaria.

5. El desarollo en tecnología educativa, la televisión educativa, instrucciones programadas e instrucciones asistidas por computadora, deberian ser aplicadas al estudio de la música y su investigación.

6. Deberia hacerse un gran énfasis en ayudar a cada estudiante a satisfacer sus necesidades, cumplir con sus metas y desarrollar su potencial.

7. La profesión de educación musical debe contribuir con sus habilidades, competencias, percepciones con el propósito de contribuir en la solución urgente de los problemas sociales como es en los sectores más pobres asi como en otras areas con individuos privados de cultura.

8. Los programas de la educación deben ser expandidos y mejorados para proveer a los profesores de música, quienes están especialmente equipados para enseñar cursos en secundaria de historia y literatura de música, cursos en humanidades y artes relacionadas, asi como profesores equipados para trabajar con niños, adultos, probres y con los emocionalmente perturbado.

———Del documental del Tanglewood Simposium (Washington, DC: Music Educators National Conference, 1968), p. 139.

THE GOALS AND OBJECTIVES PROJECT

El propósito del Proyecto Metas y Objetivos era identificar las responsabilidades de MENC pertenecientes a las necesidades futuras. El proyecto, dirigido por Paul Lehman, empezó en 1969 con la dirección de un comité y dieciocho sub-comités, cada uno a su modo relataron The Tanglewood Declaration.

1. Preparación de educadores musicales
2. Comportamiento musical—Identification y Evaluación
3. Maestria musical comprensiva—Estudio de Música en la escuela secundaria
4. Música para toda la juventud

5. Educación musical para la clase humilde/barrios
6. Investigación en educación musical
7. Logística de la Educación Musical
8. Investigación de los hechos
9. Educación Estética
10. Información Cientifica
11. Educación Musical para niños pequeños
12. Impacto de la tecnología
13. Educación Musical en Secundaria
14. Procesos de Aprendizaje
15. Enriquecimiento musical en la vida nacional
16. Actividades Profesionales en MENC
17. Organización de relaciones profesionales
18. Educación Musical para culturas no occidentales

Luego de que los reportes del comité fueran condensados, Paul Lehman redactó una propuesta con las metas y objetivos de MENC. Esta declaración fue sometida a las organizaciones federadas y asociadas, y por los presidentes de los comités nacionales. En octubre de 1970, la junta directiva de MENC adoptó dos metas para MENC, cuatro para la profesión en general, y treinta y cinco objetivos.

Las metas para MENC deberán conducir programas y actividades para construir:

Una cultura musical vital
Un público musical ilustrado

Las metas para la profesión son:

Programas comprensivos de música en todas las escuelas
Involucramiento de personas de todas las edades en el aprendizaje musical
Preparación de la calidad de los maestros
Uso de las técnicas y de recursos más efectivos la instrucción musical

Los objetivos:

1. *Dirigir esfuerzos para desarrollar programas de instrucción musical que desafien a todos los estudiantes, cualquiera que sea su condición socio-cultural, y dirigido hacia las necesidades de los ciudadanos de una sociedad del pluralista
2. *Dirigir en el desarrollo de los programas de estudios que se corelacionen ejecutando, creando, y escuchando música y que abarque una diversidad de comportamientos musicales

3. *Asistir a los maestros en la identificación de comportamientos musicales relevantes para las necesidades de los estudiantes

4. *Avanzar la enseñanza de música de todos los períodos, estilos, formas y culturas

5. Promover el desarrollo de de instrucción en la Educación Estética

6. Abogar para que la expansión de la Educación Musical incluya niños preescolar

7. Dirigir esfuerzos de asegurar que cada sistema escolar requiera música desde Kindergarten hasta sexto grado y por lo menos dos años después de este nivel

8. Dirigir esfuerzos de asegurar que cada escuela secundaria ofrezca una formación de cursos musicales que cumpla con las necesidades de toda la juventud

9. Promover cursos de música desafiantes para los estudiantes universitarios en general

10. Abogar por la expansión de la Educación Musical para los adultos dentro y fuera de las escuelas

11. *Desarrollar estándares que aseguren que toda instrucción musical es dada por profesores bien preparados en música

12. Alentar la mejora y continúa actualización de la Educación Musical en servicio para todos las personas que enseñan programas musicales y en la certificación de los profesores de la música

13. *Expandir programas que aseguren un mayor involucramiento y compromiso de los estudiantes que son miembros

14. Asistir a las escuelas de postgrado en desarrollar un curriculum especialmente diseñado para la preparación de profesores

15. Desarrollar y recomendar criterio de acreditación para el uso de agencias reconocidas en la aprobación de escuelas y universidades de música

16. Apoyar la expansión de los programas de educación de maestros que incluyan especializaciones designadas a satisfacer las necesidades actuales

17. * Asumir el liderazgo en la aplicación de nuevos desarrollos significativos en el curriculum, técnicas de enseñanza-aprendizaje y tecnologia instructivos y patrones de personal, evaluación y temas relacionados a cada área y nivel de la enseñanza musical.

18. Asumir el liderazgo en el desarrollo de recursos para la enseñanza y aprendizaje musical.

19. Cooperar en el desarrollo de modelos ejemplares de programas deseables y prácticos en la enseñanza musical

20. Alentar el uso máximo de los recursos musicales de la comunidad para mejorar los programas musicales

21. *Dirigir esfuerzos para asegurar que todos los sistemas escolares asignen suficiente personal, tiempo y fondos para apoyar un programa musical comprensivo y excelente

22. Proveer asistencia de consultas donde los programas musicales sean amenazados por legislativos, administrativos y otras acciones

23. Conducir programas de relaciones públicas para construir apoyo de la comunidad para la educación musical

24. Promover la conducta de investigación y actividades relacionadas a la educación musical

25. Diseminar noticias de investigaciones de manera que los resultados puedan ser aplicados de manera pronta y efectiva

26. Determinar las necesidades más urgentes de informa en educación musical

27. Recopilar y diseminar sobre música e información

28. Alentar otras organizaciones, agencias y medios de comunicación para recopilar y diseminar información sobre música y educación

29. Iniciar esfuerzos para establecer la recuperación de sistemas de información en música y educación y para desarrollar bases de datos y la subsecuente incorporación a dichos sistemas

30. Perseguir relaciones de trabajos efectivos con organizaciones y grupos que tienen intereses mutuos

31. Fortalecer las relaciones entre la conferencia y su federación, asociación y organizaciones auciliares

32. Establecer procedimientos para sus programas organizacionales de planeación y políticas

33. Buscar expandir su membresia para incluir todas las personas quienes, en cualquier capacidad, enseñen música

34. Evaluar periódicamente la efectividad de sus politicas y programas

35. Asegurar la interacción sistemática con su membresia concerniente a las metas y objetivos de la conferencia

*Objetivos prioritarios

Authors

Name	Association/Organization
Bell, Richard	Young Audiences International
Carter, Warrick L.	Disney Entertainment Arts
Feldstein, Sandy	Carl Fischer LLC
Gates, J. Terry	State University of New York at Buffalo
Glidden, Robert	Ohio University
Hinckley, June	MENC—The National Association for Music Education
Hope, Samuel	National Association of Schools of Music
Jellison, Judith A.	The University of Texas at Austin
Lehman, Paul R.	University of Michigan
Madsen, Clifford K.	The Florida State University
Mark, Michael L.	Towson University
Reimer, Bennett	Northwestern University
Spearman, Carlesta Elliott	Keene State College, New Hampshire
Walters, Jane	Partners in Public Education, Memphis
Yarbrough, Cornelia	Louisiana State University

Participants

Name	Association/Organization
Abeles, Hal	Columbia University
Adams, Bobby	Stetson University
Allen, Michael	The Florida State University
Anderson, Brian	Nebraska Music Educators Association
Anderson, William	Kent State University
Arrouet, Andre	Brevard County Schools, FL
Austin, Terry	Virginia Music Educators Association
Barbour, Ken	10th Street Elementary, Oakmont, PA
Barrett, Janet	University of Wisconsin–Whitewater
Barrows, Lorraine	Sweet Adelines International
Bauer, Margaret	Pennsylvania Music Educators Association
Bell, Josephine	University of Arkansas at Pine Bluff
Bell, Richard	Young Audiences International
Bennett, Peggy	Texas Christian University
Benson, Wilma	Jefferson Public Schools, KY

Beville, Jay	Virginia Music Educators Association
Blakeslee, Michael	MENC Staff
Blocher, Larry	Wichita State University
Bolton, Beth	Gordon Institute for Music Learning
Bowers, Judy	The Florida State University
Bowles, Chelcy	University of Wisconsin–Madison
Brandt, Ron	Retired Editor, *Educational Leadership*
Broido, Arnold	Theodore Presser Company
Brown, Sheila	Nebraska Department of Education
Bruhn, Karl	Bruhn & Associates
Buccheri, John	Northwestern University
Burns, Kimberly	Ball State University
Burton, Bryan	West Chester University
Byo, James L.	Louisiana State University
Calle, Ed	Freelance musician/composer
Carden, Joy	International Association of Electronic Keyboard Manufacturers
Carroll, Gwen	National Association of the Study and Performance of African American Music
Carter, Warrick L.	Disney Entertainment Arts
Carver, Hazel	Kentucky Music Educators Association
Cassidy, Jane	Louisiana State University
Chronister, Richard	National Keyboard Arts Association
Cohn, Mary Ellen	Maryland Music Educators Association
Connolly Potter, Anne	Massachusetts Music Educators Association
Cornell, Beth	Pennsylvania Department of Education
Croft, James	The Florida State University

Crowe, Don R.	South Dakota State University
Cutietta, Robert	University of Arizona
Davidson, Jennifer	Oakland Schools, MI
Day, Gloria	Arizona Music Educators Association
Deal, John	The Florida State University
DeGraffenreid, George	California State University, Fresno
Delp, Roy	National Association of Teachers of Singing
Demorest, Steven	University of Washington
DeWitt, Randall	MARS the Musician's Planet
Dingley, Bob	Warner Bros. Publications
Disharoon, Richard	Maryland Music Educators Association
Eckenrode, Jenny	Florida Elementary Music Educators Association
Eldridge, Terry	Maine Music Educators Association
Ernst, Roy E.	Eastman School of Music
Feldstein, Sandy	Carl Fischer LLC
Floyd, Suzanne	Sigma Alpha Iota
Fonder, Mark	Ithaca College
Fox, Donna Brink	Eastman School of Music
Fox-Miller, Linda	American School Bands Directors Association
Fraschillo, Tom	National Band Association
Gaddis, Bob	Campbellsville University
Gary, Charles	The Catholic University of America
Gates, J. Terry	State University of New York at Buffalo
Gazda, Doris	ASTA with NSOA
Geer, Barbara	North Carolina Music Educators Association
Glaze, Debbie	Oregon Music Educators Association

Glidden, Robert	Ohio University
Greene, Ben	New Hampshire Music Educators Association
Griffin, Margaret	Hillsborough County Schools, FL
Hair, Harriet	University of Georgia
Hanley, Darla	Shenandoah University
Hartenberger, Aurelia	Missouri Music Educators Association
Heller, Jack	University of South Florida
Hiatt, Michael	Minnesota Perpich Center for Arts Education
Hill, Willie	International Association of Jazz Educators
Hinckley, June	MENC
Holloway, Alexandria	Miami-Dade Community College
Holste, Benjamin	Pennsylvania Music Educators Association
Hope, Samuel	National Association of Schools of Music
Hopper, Kenn	Levine School of Music, Washington, DC
Housewright, Wiley	The Florida State University
Houtz, Randy	Utah Music Educators Association
Howes, Frank R.	Polk County Schools, FL
Jellison, Judith A.	The University of Texas at Austin
Johnson, Craig	Artistic Director, Chanticleer
Jordan, Joyce	University of Miami
Keenan-Takagi, Kathleen	Illinois State University
Kember, Gerald	La Crosse Schools, WI
Keroack, Marc	Massachusetts Music Educators Association
Kimpton, Jeffrey S.	University of Minnesota
Knapp, Ruth Ann	Michigan Music Educators Association

Koepfle, Rosemary	Ohio Music Education Association
Laird, Marcia	Georgia Music Educators Association
Lamond, Joe	NAMM: The International Music Products Associaton
Larsen, Libby	Composer
Laude, Isabella	National Federation of Music Clubs
Lehman, Paul R.	University of Michigan
Lehmberg, Lance	Morningside College, Iowa
Lindeman, Carolynn	San Francisco State University/ MENC
Lippert, Cindy	Sarasota County Schools, FL
Lippert-Coleman, Mary	Pennsylvania Music Educators Association
Lowery, Mary Ann	Virginia Music Educators Association
Madsen, Clifford K.	The Florida State University
Mahlmann, John J.	MENC Executive Director
Mark, Michael L.	Towson Unviersity
McAllister, Peter	Ball State University
McManus, Bill	Eastern Division MENC President
Miller, Anne Meeker	Olathe Schools, KS
Miller, Douglas	Minnesota Music Educators Association
Minear, Carolyn	Orlando Public Schools, FL
Misenhelter, Dale	The University of Alabama at Birmingham
Mollicone, Cheryl	NARAS Foundation
Moore, Brian	University of Nebraska–Lincoln
Moore, Janet	University of South Florida
Moore, Marvelene	The University of Tennessee
Moore, Randall	University of Oregon
Napoles, Jessica	Florida Vocal Association

Neilsen, Glenn	Wisconsin Music Educators Association
Nierman, Glenn	University of Nebraska–Lincoln
Olsen, Dale	College of Music Society
Ozeas, Natalie	Carnegie-Mellon University School of Music
Page, Fran	North Carolina Music Educators Association
Palmer, Mary	University of Central Florida
Patch, Joyce	Nebraska Music Educators Association
Parks, Mike	Florida Music Educators Association
Paul, Phyllis	Thomas College, GA
Paul, Tim	Leon High School, Tallahassee
Perry, James	Florida School Music Association
Persellin, Diane	Texas Music Educators Conference
Poe, Cheryl	Florida Elementary Music Educators Association
Potter, Barbara	Connecticut Music Educators Association
Power, Elizabeth	Florida West Coast Symphony
Quesada, Milagros	Kent State University, Tuscarawas Campus
Rabideau, Richard	New York State School Music Association
Reed, Larry	Escambia County Schools, FL
Reimer, Bennett	Northwestern University
Reist, Joan	Music Teachers National Association
Reynolds, Jeanne	Florida Music Supervision Association
Robinson, Charles	University of Missouri, Kansas City
Sanz-Griggs, Kathleen	Pasco County Schools, FL
Scheuerer, Daniel	Brevard County School Board, FL
Schmid, Will	University of Wisconsin–Milwaukee

Shafer, Ardene	MENC Staff
Sheldon, Deborah	University of Illinois
Shrader, David	University of North Texas
Sims, Wendy	University of Missouri, Columbia
Small, Ann	Stetson University
Small, Rosemary	Kaman Music Corporation
Smith, Brett	Minnesota Music Educators Association
Smith, David	American Music Therapy Association
Southall, John	Broward County Schools, FL
Southwick, Julie	North Carolina Music Educators Association
Spearman, Carlesta Elliott	Keene State College, New Hampshire
Spurgeon, Alan	Oklahoma Music Educators Association
Standley, Jayne	The Florida State University
Stein, Robin	Southwest Texas State University
Stone, Judy	Florida Music Educators Association
Swanson, Robyn	Western Kentucky University
Taylor, Frederick	National Association for the Study and Performance of African American Music
Taylor, John	Kansas Music Educators Association
Vincent, Phyllis	Kentucky Music Educators Association
Vita, David	United States Marine Corps
Volk, Terese M.	Buffalo Schools, NY
Waa, Loren	University of Louisville
Wagner, Michael	Florida International University
Waibel, Dianne	Delaware Music Educators Association
Walters, Jane	Partners in Public Education, Memphis

Webster, Peter	Northwestern University
Weigman, John	Florida Department of Education
Wharton, Phillip	Florida Music Educators Association
Wilder, Cecil	Georgia Music Educators Association
Williams, David	Illinois State University
Williams, Larry	Sioux City, Iowa Community Schools
Womble, Jeana	East Baton Rouge Parish Schools, LA
Yarbrough, Cornelia	Louisiana State University
Yob, Irish	Indiana University
Young, Jeff	American School Band Directors Association
Zakrajsek, Regina	Minnesota Music Educators Association
Zavislan, Tamara	American Music Therapy Association
Zellner, Richard	The Arts Center Foundation, El Cajon, CA